The Spread of Political Economy and the Professionalisation of Economists

This book presents the first systematic research and comparative analysis ever attempted on the rise and early developments of the Economic Associations founded in Europe, the USA and Japan during the nineteenth century.

Individual chapters reconstruct the events that led to the foundation of economic societies in Britain, France, Italy, Belgium, Spain, Portugal, the Netherlands, Sweden, Germany, Japan and the USA.

Contributors analyse the activities and debates promoted by these associations, evaluating their role in:

*   the dissemination of political economy
*   the institutionalisation of economics
*   the construction of professional self-consciousness among economists

With contributions from outstanding experts, this book will be of essential interest not only to historians of economic thought, but also to those working more generally in the fields of economics or the history of scientific thought.

Massimo M. Augello is Professor of History of Economic Thought and Head of the Department of Economics at the University of Pisa. He has published *Joseph Alois Schumpeter. A Reference Guide* (1990), and co-edited *Le cattedre di economia politica in Italia* (1988), *Le riviste di economia in Italia* (1996), and *Associazionismo e diffusione dell'economia politica nell'Italia dell'Ottocento* (2000). He is the managing editor of the journal *Il pensiero economico italiano* and a member of the Advisory Board of *History of Economic Ideas*.

Marco E.L. Guidi is Associate Professor of History of Economic Thought at the Department of Social Studies at the University of Brescia. He is the author of several works on Bentham and classical utilitarianism. He has co-edited *Le riviste di economia in Italia* (1996) and *Associazionismo e diffusione dell'economia politica nell'Italia dell'Ottocento* (2000). He is chief editor of the journal *Il pensiero economico italiano* and a member of the Advisory Board of *The European Journal of the History of Economic Thought*.

Routledge Studies in the History of Economics

The Spread of Political Economy and the Professionalisation of Economists

Economic societies in Europe, America and Japan in the nineteenth century

Edited by Massimo M. Augello and Marco E. L. Guidi

Routledge
Taylor & Francis Group

LONDON AND NEW YORK

In memory of Ernest Lluch

First Published 2001
by Routledge
4 Park Square, Milton Park, Abingdon, Oxon OX14 4RN
605 Third Avenue, New York, NY 10017

First issued in paperback 2013

*Routledge is an imprint of the Taylor & Francis Group,
an informa business*

Publisher's Note
The publisher has gone to great lengths to ensure the quality of this reprint but
points out that some imperfections in the original copies may be apparent.

Typeset in Garamond by Taylor & Francis Books Ltd

British Library Cataloguing in Publication Data
A catalogue record for this book is available from the British Library

Library of Congress Cataloging-in-Publication Data
The spread of political economy and the professionalisation of
  economists : economic societies in Europe, America and Japan
  in the nineteenth century / edited by Massimo M. Augello
  and Marco E.L. Guidi.
  Includes bibliographical references and index.
  1. Economics–Societies, etc.–History–19th century.
  2. Economics–History–19th century. I. Augello, Massimo M.,
1949– II. Guidi, Marco E.L., 1958–

HB85 .S63 2001
330.06–dc21   00–046018

ISBN 13: 978-0-415-23669-0 (hbk)
ISBN 13: 978-0-415-86817-4 (pbk)

Contents

Contributors

Salvador Almenar, born 1949, is Professor of History of Economic Thought at the University of Valencia, Spain. He has recently published several works on classical and Keynesian economics in Spain. He edited the *Curso de economía política* by Alvaro Flórez Estrada (Madrid: Ministerio de Hacienda, 1980). He is co-editor of the collection *Economía y economístas españoles* (1999–2000), and is a member of the Executive Committee of the European Society for the History of Economic Thought and of the Editorial Board of *The European Journal of the History of Economic Thought*.

António Almodovar, born 1953, is Associate Professor of History of Economic Thought at the University of Porto, Portugal. He is a specialist of the history of economic thought in Portugal. He has published *A Institucionalização da Economia Política Clássica em Portugal* (Porto: Edições Afrontamento, 1995), co-authored *A History of Portuguese Economic Thought* (London: Routledge, 1998) and edited *Estudos sobre o pensamento económico em Portugal* (Porto: Facultade de Economia, Universidade de Porto, 1990). He is a member of the Advisory Board of *The European Journal of the History of Economic Thought*.

Massimo M. Augello, born 1949, is Professor of History of Economic Thought at the University of Pisa, Italy. He has published books and articles on the French industrialist school and the Italian economic thought. He co-edited *Le cattedre di economia politica in Italia* (Milano: Angeli, 1988), *Le riviste di economia in Italia* (Milano: Angeli, 1996) and *Associazionismo e diffusione dell'economia politica nell'Italia dell'Ottocento* (Milano: Angeli, 2000). He is also the author of *Joseph Alois Schumpeter. A Reference Guide* (Berlin: Springer, 1990). He is the managing editor of *Il pensiero economico italiano* and a member of the Advisory Board of the *History of Economic Ideas*.

William J. Barber, born 1925, is Professor of Economics at Wesleyan University, Middletown, CT. He is the author of *A History of Economic Thought* (New York: Praeger, 1967). He edited *Breaking the Mould. The Development of Academic Economics in XIX Century America* (Middletown, CT: Wesleyan University Press, 1988). He also published, among others, *From New Era to New Deal. Herbert Hoover, the Economists, and American Economic*

Policy, 1921–1933 (Cambridge and New York: Cambridge University Press, 1985) and *Designs within Disorder. Franklin D. Roosevelt, the Economists, and the Shaping of American Economic Policy, 1933–1945* (Cambridge and New York: Cambridge University Press, 1996). He held the presidency of the History of Economics Society during 1989–90.

Yves Breton, born 1942, is Research Director at the CNRS, ERMES, University of Paris 2 Panthéon-Assas, France. He is a specialist in the history of French economic thought (1800–1940). He co-edited *L'économie politique en France au XIXe siècle* (Paris: Economica, 1991) and *La longue stagnation en France. L'autre grande dépression (1873–1897)* (Paris: Economica, 1997). He has also edited a new edition of Ch. Gide, *Principes d'économie politique* (Paris: L'Harmattan, 2000).

José Luís Cardoso, born 1956, is Professor of Economics at the Technical University of Lisbon, Portugal. He has published several articles and books on the history of economic thought in Portugal (*O pensamento económico em Portugal nos finais do seculo XVIII*, Lisboa: Estampa, 1989; *Pensar a economia en Portugal: digressões históricas*, Miraflores: DIFEL, 1997). He is co-author of *A History of Portuguese Economic Thought* (London: Routledge, 1998), general editor of the series *Classics of Portuguese Economic Thought* and co-editor of *The European Journal of the History of Economic Thought*.

Guido Erreygers, born 1959, is Professor of Economics at the University of Antwerp, Belgium. His main fields of research include the History of Economic Thought, Linear Systems of Production and the Economics of Exhaustible Resources. His main publications are: 'On the uniqueness of square cost-minimizing techniques' (*The Manchester School*, 1995); with John Cunliffe, 'Moral Philosophy and Economics: The Formation of François Huet's Doctrine of Property Rights' (*The European Journal of the History of Economic Thought*, 1999); and with Christian Bidard, 'The number and type of long-term equilibria' (*Journal of Economics*, 1998).

Marco E.L. Guidi, born 1958, is Associate Professor of History of Economic Thought at the University of Brescia, Italy. He has published books and articles on Bentham and classical utilitarianism and on Italian economic thought. He co-edited *Le riviste di economia in Italia* (Milano: Angeli, 1996) and *Associazionismo e diffusione dell'economia politica nell'Italia dell'Ottocento* (Milano: Angeli, 2000). He is chief editor of *Il pensiero economico italiano* and a member of the Advisory Board of *The European Journal of the History of Economic Thought*.

Harald Hagemann, born 1947, is Professor of Economic Theory at the University of Hohenheim, Stuttgart, Germany. His main areas of research are Growth, Structural Change, New Technologies and Employment and the History of Economic Analysis. Recent work also focuses on the emigration of German-speaking economists after 1933. He is a co-editor of *The Legacy of Hicks* (London: Routledge, 1994) and of *Money, Financial Institutions, and*

Macroeconomics (Boston: Kluwer Academic Publications, 1997). He is a member of the Executive Committee of the European Society of the History of Economic Thought and of the Editorial Board of *The European Journal of the History of Economic Thought*.

Rolf G.H. Henriksson, born 1937, has taught at the University of Texas at Austin and the Stockholm School of Economics, Sweden. He is presently Senior Lecturer at Stockholm University where he teaches Economic History and the History of Economic Thought. His most recent publications include *Erik Lundberg Studies in Economic Instability and Change* (Stockholm: SNS Forlag, 1994), as well as studies of Eli Heckscher and the rise of the Swedish school of economic thought and policy.

Jiro Kumagai, born 1938, is Professor of Economic History at St Andrews University, Osaka, Japan. He has published many works in Japanese on economic history and on the history of economic thought in nineteenth-century Japan. He has also contributed to S. Sugihara and T. Tanaka (eds) *Economic Thought and Modernization in Japan* (Cheltenham and Northampton: Edward Elgar, 1998).

Vicent Llombart, born 1948, is Professor of History of Economic Thought at the University of Valencia, Spain. He has published several works on the economic thought and policy of eighteenth- and nineteenth-century Spain, among which is *Campomanes, economista y politico de Carlos III* (Madrid: Alianza Editorial, 1992). He is a member of the Editorial Board of *The European Journal of the History of Economic Thought* and of the collection *Economía y economistas españoles* (1999–2000).

Evert Schoorl, born 1940, is Professor of Economics at Groningen University, the Netherlands. He studied economic history and wrote his dissertation on Jean-Baptiste Say (1980). He has also written on Dutch economic history (in R.T. Griffiths (ed.) *The Netherlands and the Gold Standard*, Amsterdam: Kluwer Academic Publishers, 1987) and the history of Dutch economics. He has edited the autobiographies of Emile van Lennep (Leiden: Stenfert Kroese, 1991, English edn, 1998) and Willem Drees (Amsterdam: Balans, 2000).

Keith Tribe, born 1949, is Reader in Economics at Keele University, UK. His main fields of research are the History of German and British Economic Thought in the Eighteenth and Nineteenth Centuries. He has published, among others, *Land, Labour and Economic Discourse* (London: Routledge & Kegan Paul, 1978) and *Strategies of Economic Order. German Economic Discourse, 1750–1950* (Cambridge: Cambridge University Press, 1995). He has edited *Economic Careers. Economics and Economists in Britain 1930–1970* (London: Routledge, 1997) and co-edited *The Market for Political Economy. The Advent of Economics in British University Culture* (London: Routledge, 1993). He is a member of the Editorial Board of *The European Journal of the History of Economic Thought*.

Preface

This book is the outcome of a research project on 'economic associationism in the Nineteenth Century' that concluded with an international conference held in Pisa on 14th–16th October 1999. The conference, devoted predominantly to the presentation of a systematic investigation of the Italian case, opened with a session providing a comparative international overview, during which papers were read that were later expanded into the chapters composing this book.

Research on nineteenth-century economic associations forms part of a broader international focus on several closely inter-related economic themes, which seek to acquire an understanding of the social nature of economics, the role of institutions in the dissemination of political economy and the professionalisation of the economist. Starting out from the pioneering research by Bob Coats on these subjects (collected in Coats 1993), in the early 1980s Piero Barucci and Istvan Hont set up an international working group in order to undertake an investigation of the processes that had led to the rise and increasing importance of political economy within the university system.[1] Several extensive and penetrating studies on the institutionalisation of political economy in America, Japan and Europe sprang from the individual and collective efforts of the working group.[2] The wealth of information and insights offered by the results of this research prompted the historians of economic thought to expand the range of historiographic and methodological issues explored, in the awareness that the channels through which economics had gradually spread and gained increasing esteem varied considerably from country to country. A series of study meetings were thus held in Italy, Spain, Portugal and France, addressing such issues as the 'national styles of political economy', relations between the different national traditions, and the international circulation of economic ideas.[3] One of the channels for the dissemination of political economy – periodicals – subsequently formed the object of specific research, which likewise involved scholars from a number of different countries.[4]

This in turn kindled the desire to achieve a more detailed reconstruction of the complex routes through which economics spread to various parts of the world, underwent increasing specialisation and was finally crowned by the professionalisation of the economist. We thus decided to focus on that which had emerged as one of the most significant aspects: the economic associations of the nineteenth century.[5]

The chapters composing the present volume portray the birth and evolution of the first economic societies in various European countries, the USA and Japan during the period stretching from the end of the eighteenth century up to World War I. Inevitably, a diversity of approaches between the different chapters can be perceived. In some cases, the chapters represent the first systematic exploration of the history of economic associations in a given country. In other cases, they build on research conducted by other scholars over recent decades, incorporating the latest findings and offering historiographic reflections. From the methodological point of view, the essays display a plurality of approaches, a feature we believe to represent the lively and dynamic status of international research on the theme of economic societies. The introductory chapter aims to attempt a first, if incomplete, international comparison of the phenomenon of nineteenth-century economic associations in different countries.

Certain editorial choices require a brief explanation: to avoid pointless verbosity, the names of the associations cited have been translated only when the root of the words contained in their titles differs from the corresponding English root; in contrast, all citations have been translated into English for ease of reading. For the same reasons, it was decided not to encumber the texts or the notes with biographic profiles of the authors and historical figures mentioned, dates or references to historical events occurring in the different countries. Finally, insofar as possible, the secondary literature has been limited to the theme of economic associations.

We wish to thank all those who have contributed to the fulfilment of this achievement. We are indebted to all the authors of the present book for their useful advice during the preparatory work for this collection. We express our thanks to Rachel Costa for her competent assistance in the English-language revision and translation of parts of this book. We also thank Annabel Watson and Simon Whitmore of Routledge and their staff, Carol Baker and the anonymous Routledge referees for their valuable advice during the preparation of this book.

Pisa, 20th September 2000
Massimo M. Augello and Marco E.L. Guidi

Notes

1 The theme of the project, which was also the title of an international conference held in the spring of 1986 at S. Miniato, Italy, was 'The Institutionalisation of Political Economy: Its Introduction and Acceptance into European, North-American and Japanese Universities'.

2 See Le Van-Lemesle 1986; Barber 1988; Augello *et al.* 1988; Waszek 1988; Sugiyama and Mizuta 1988; Kadish and Tribe 1993.

3 Worth mentioning, among others, are: the 1992 international conference at the Fondazione Einaudi of Turin on 'Political Economy and National Realities' (see

Albertone and Masoero 1994); the Encontro Iberico sobre Historia do Pensamento Economico held in 1992 (Fundação Calouste Gulbenkian, Lisbon); the conference held in September 1993 at the Ecole Normale Supérieure of Fontenay-St-Cloud on 'La diffusion internationale de la Physiocratie' (see Delmas, Demals and Steiner 1995); the 1988 conference on 'La tradition économique française' (University of Lyon II) (see Dockès *et al.* 2000), the Italo-French conference held in September 1999 at the University of Parma on 'I reciproci influssi tra la Francia e l'Italia del XVIII secolo nel campo della scienza economica' (see Bianchini and Tiran 2000).

4   One may cite the conference held in 1994 at Parma and Reggio Emilia on 'Periodical Press and Political Economy in the Nineteenth Century' (see Augello, Bianchini and Guidi 1996; Bianchini 1996) and the 1995 conference in Toulouse on 'Les revues d'économie politique en France' (see Marco 1996).

5   The results of research on the Italian case are presented in Augello and Guidi 2000.

References

Albertone, M. and Masoero, A. (eds) (1994) *Political Economy and National Realities*, Torino: Fondazione Luigi Einaudi.

Augello, M.M., Bianchini, M., Gioli, G. and Roggi, P. (eds) (1988) *Le cattedre di economia politica in Italia. La diffusione di una disciplina 'sospetta' (1750–1900)*, Milano: Angeli.

Augello, M.M., Bianchini, M. and Guidi, M.E.L. (eds) (1996) *Le riviste di economia in Italia (1700–1900). Dai giornali scientifico-letterari ai periodici specialistici*, Milano: Angeli.

Augello, M.M. and Guidi, M.E.L. (eds) (2000) *Associazionismo economico e diffusione dell'economia politica nell'Italia dell'Ottocento. Dalle società economico-agrarie alle associazioni di economisti*, 2 vols, Milano: Angeli.

Barber, W. (ed.) (1988) *Breaking the Mould. The Development of Academic Economics in XIX Century America*, Middletown, CT: Wesleyan University Press.

Bianchini, M. (ed.) (1996) *Political Economy in European Periodicals, 1750–1900*, special issue of *History of Economc Ideas*, 4, 3.

Bianchini, M. and Tiran, A. (eds) (2000) *La Francia, l'Italia e la formazione dell'economia politica (secc. XVIII–XIX)*, special issue of *Il pensiero economico italiano*, 8, 2.

Coats, A.W. (1993) *The Sociology and Professionalization of Economics, British and American Economic Essays*, London and New York: Routledge.

Delmas, B., Demals, Th. and Steiner, Ph. (eds) (1995) *La diffusion internationale de la physiocratie (XVIIIe–XIXe)*, Grenoble: Presses Universitaires de Grenoble.

Dockès, P., Frobert, L., Klotz, G., Potier, J.-P. and Tiran, A. (eds) (2000) *Les traditions économiques françaises 1848–1939*, Paris: CNRS Editions.

Kadish, A. and Tribe, K. (eds) (1993) *The Market for Political Economy. The Advent of Economics in British University Culture, 1850–1905*, London: Routledge.

Le Van-Lemesle, L. (ed.) (1986) *Les problèmes de l'institutionnalisation de l'économie politique en France au XIX siècle*, special issue of *Economies et Sociétés*, série Oeconomia, PE n. 6.

Marco, L. (ed.) (1996) *Les revues d'économie en France. Genèse et actualité (1751–1994)*, Paris: L'Harmattan.

Sugiyama, C. and Mizuta, H. (eds) (1988) *Enlightenment and Beyond: Political Economy Comes to Japan*, Tokyo: University of Tokyo Press.

Waszek, N. (ed.) (1988) *Die Institutionalisierung der Nationalökonomie an deutschen Universitäten*, St. Katharinen: Scripta Mercaturae Verlag.

1 Nineteenth-century economic societies in a comparative approach

The emergence of professional economists

Massimo M. Augello and
Marco E. L. Guidi*

A well-established tradition of studies has clarified that the rise and evolution of national economic societies in the nineteenth century[1] is not an issue that can be dismissed as simply a form of historical erudition. Rather, it involves crucial aspects of the history of modern economics: the academic institutionalisation of political economy,[2] the professionalisation of economists, the origins of specialist economic journals,[3] the international circulation of ideas and the relations between economists, politics and public opinion. It is not necessary to make a leap of faith and proclaim belief in Kuhnian and Rortyan epistemology in order to underline that knowledge of these institutional developments, which shaped the dialogic relations between economists and their scientific community, is often of vital importance for an understanding of the evolution of economics and the success or failure of rival paradigms within this field.

So far, however, there has been considerably less awareness that political economy, since its scientific origins, has been characterised not only by analytical rigour and theoretical consistency but also by a strong pedagogic and popularising commitment (see Steiner 1998), embodying an implicit desire to win over the consciences of those active in the 'public sphere' (Habermas 1989), in order to fulfil its own nature as a 'political' science. Such a science could continue to be 'a branch of the science of a statesman or legislator' (Smith 1976: 500), provided it was recognised that it was none other than 'the study [...] of the nature and functions of the different parts of the social body' (Say 1843: 1). It is thus hardly surprising that the enthusiastic nineteenth-century acolytes of political economy felt the need to found clubs and societies in which, through debate with politicians, journalists and businessmen, they could convey the message of reform that was part and parcel of this new science. In this perspective, the economic associations were but one of the tools singled out by nineteenth-century economists to educate public opinion and the world of politics – together with pamphlets, journals and the many 'catechisms of political economy' which in that period abounded.

This book presents a series of studies on the first economic societies that arose in nineteenth-century Europe, America and Japan, investigating the motives that inspired their founders and organisers, the activities undertaken, and the reasons for their success and for their decline. This introductory essay aims to provide a tentative overview of the phenomenon of associations among economists and offers an international comparison outlining the historical meaning of the experiences described, the analogies and differences between the various models, and finally the effects of the associations on the development of economic studies. In this context, the much-discussed theme of the birth of the professional figure of the economist forms a natural focus of investigation. Section 1 analyses some historiographic problems that come to the fore when considering the nature and goals of the early economic societies. Section 2 is devoted to the direct antecedents of the first debating societies that held gatherings explicitly in the name of political economy. Section 3 is devoted to the numerous societies that were set up in various countries, starting from the Political Economy Club (founded in London in 1821) and the Paris Société d'Economie Politique (founded in 1842), the main aim of which was to disseminate Smithian political economy and its *laissez-faire* implications; both of these societies became models that were widely imitated in other countries. Finally, Section 4 concentrates on the origins and the first activities of the economic associations set up in the closing decades of the nineteenth century. These associations were formed to pursue the aims of social reform, to promote positive study of economic events and policies or to support the establishment of scientific journals. Some of these societies would in the following century become an essential component of the scientific community of economists and of their scientific identity.

1 Economic societies, the spread of political economy and professionalisation: preliminary remarks

The studies by Bob Coats on the British Economic Association (hereafter: BEA) and the American Economic Association (hereafter: AEA) represent the benchmark of investigation in this field, by virtue of their wealth of documentation and the breadth of their interpretative framework. These studies form part of a more extensive inquiry into the institutionalisation of political economy and the professionalisation of the economist. According to Coats, the rise of the economics profession was a long drawn-out and ambiguous process, whose main precondition was the existence of a specialist training which aspiring economists should receive. It is therefore evident that the emergence of professional economists depended above all on the progress of the institutionalisation of political economy in universities. However, Coats argues that the foundation of economic associations in the closing decades of the nineteenth century – together with the creation of specialised journals – likewise constituted a precondition of professionalisation (Coats 1991).

One query that arises spontaneously for those who seek to enquire more closely into the history of economic societies in the nineteenth century is whether the link between the rise of these societies and the phenomenon of the professionalisation of economics is legitimate and heuristically fertile. For instance, the paper by Keith Tribe in the present collection voices a number of doubts that deserve attention. Tribe suggests that the connection between economic societies and professionalisation may contain certain interpretative limitations. Firstly, it may be flawed by a retrospective bias which takes for granted that societies still in existence today and now characterised by 'quasi-professional status' must necessarily have been set up with characteristics and aims analogous to those of today. Secondly, the introduction of a conceptual line of demarcation between 'pre-professional' debating societies such as the Political Economy Club and the first 'professional' societies towards the end of the century could prove to be artificial. But there are, in Tribe's view, two rather more substantial reasons for casting doubt on the approach of professionalisation: on the one hand, it cannot automatically be taken as given that the founders of the first economic societies had in mind the same notion of 'economist' as that which prevails today; on the other, the modern sociological notion of 'professionalisation' – which has in turn given rise to a consolidated historiographic tradition in different fields (see Burrage and Torstendahl 1990; Malatesta 1995) – can only with some difficulty be adapted to the identity of the economist.

Let us start with the latter point. The notion of professionalisation, which has been applied to categories such as lawyers, physicians, engineers, etc., is grounded on the assumption that the birth of a profession involves certain typical stepping stones: most crucially, the establishment of public regulations for access to professional status (educational qualifications and admission only upon approval by independent professional associations);[4] and secondly the practice for the state to delegate 'public' tasks to the body of 'professionals', to be performed either privately or in state-run organisations. It can readily be seen that such characteristics are still absent from the 'profession' of the economist even today, whether the profession is practised in a university environment, in private organisations or in public agencies. Granted, common features do exist: economists are awarded professional recognition through a mechanism of cooptation based on examinations, and their assessment is carried out mainly by academic economists, who also represent the central nucleus of economic societies. Furthermore, the academic profession of the economist is regarded as a 'public service' in which insiders have a virtually exclusive right to select the outsiders. However, not only have economic associations never sought to acquire legal power of selection of the 'professionals' of the field, but also – as Coats himself has pointed out (1993: 399) – there exists no specific educational qualification (like the Ph.D) that constitutes a prerequisite for recruitment of economists to public and private organisations (only the regulations for access to university posts generally impose more rigid criteria).

Such limitations could simply be taken as indicating that the professionalisation of economists is still incomplete at the present time, or alternatively that there are perhaps more deep-seated reasons why it cannot proceed beyond a certain limit. It is worth pointing out, first of all, that there is a looser meaning of 'profession' which does appear more suited to the concept of the professionalisation of economics: this is the meaning Coats tends to fall back on when contending with the above-described difficulties. This meaning is particularly evident in the adjective 'professional' as opposed to 'amateur' (Coats 1993: 403). According to the far less sophisticated definition used by Stigler, the two essential prerequisites of the economics profession should be seen as 'specialization' and 'persistence', i.e. 'continued application to this defined area' (Stigler 1965: 32). For Stigler this means that 'it is difficult to be a professional outside, and easy to be one inside, the field of one's livelihood' (Stigler 1965: 32). In addition to these criteria, Coats places emphasis on specialistic training. Doubts can certainly be cast on the legitimacy of using the accepted notion of 'profession', yet one of its merits resides precisely in highlighting the fact that application of the sociological notion of 'professionalisation' to a learned or scientific profession may be misleading in part.

Indeed, in the case of the profession of economics (and in particular that of the academic economist), the term that best expresses the aims pursued in recruitment of outsiders is not 'professionalism' or 'competence' but 'scientific quality'. For what is at stake is no less than the admissibility of the candidate to the *scientific* community of economists. In this regard, modern economic societies have mirrored the function of universities and played a by no means purely subsidiary role: by offering scholars the opportunity to present and discuss the results of their research, they have controlled and sanctioned the scientific quality of their members. To this end they have often adopted a screening criterion for enrolment of members or – if a deliberate policy of broader-based membership is pursued – for choice of members to be appointed to official boards. The screening mechanisms have quite naturally been those in use in the academic world.[5] Professionalisation is thus also a quest for more rigorous scientific standards among economists.

These reflections now allow us more easily to set in a historical perspective the phenomenon of economic societies established in the nineteenth century. We may begin by agreeing with Tribe's concern that the 'professional' function of economic associations has not always been an intrinsic feature of their existence, and that the terms 'pre-professional' and 'professional' societies do not provide a correct key to understanding their development. It thus becomes important to engage in painstaking reconstruction of contextual history in order to study the nature and functions attributed to these associations in different periods of history, the activities they undertook and the different aspects of the economic discourse that arose within them. At the same time, however, the question as to when and to what extent the economic societies of the nineteenth century established the premises for the growth of the 'professional' identity of the economist must certainly be addressed. The evidence provided by this collection reveals that most of these societies strengthened this identity not only through scientific meetings but also by enhancing the profile of academic economists, favouring the institutionalisation of political economy, contributing to building up the 'professional ideology' of economists, etc. The fact that the professional self-awareness of economists did not assume its present-day character until the mid-twentieth century by no means excludes the hypothesis that the premises for this situation may have been laid long before, partly within the framework of economic societies. This may at times have come about as the unintentional consequences of choices made for quite different reasons (prestige, objectivity, pluralism, authoritativeness) At other times, it may have been the result of the conscious and far-sighted commitment of some economists, who regarded the societies both as a tool to reinforce the scientific nature of political economy and to favour the professionalisation of the economist.

In a nutshell, while it may be questionable to attribute the nature of professional societies across the board to all economic societies of the nineteenth century, yet it is unquestionable that in very many cases these associations did favour the rise of the 'professional' profile of the economist. This is not to deny that profound differences can be found among the various national patterns towards professionalisation. Thus in some cases – for instance England, Sweden or Portugal – the delayed institutionalisation of political economy ruled out any possibility of a professional function of the economic societies, while in other cases – the USA, Germany, Italy or Japan – the inter-relations between economic associations and professionalisation are as evident as they are diverse; in yet other cases – France, Belgium, Spain – the dissociation between institutionalisation and the history of associations can be attributed to a number of different causes.

Whatever the reasons, the comparative perspective adopted here allows the overall statement that the history of the economic societies of the nineteenth century is a phenomenon that cannot be restricted to the question of professionalisation. In the nineteenth century the 'spirit of association' was one of the ideals shared by all those who found the scientific and modernising language of political economy highly persuasive: scholars, politicians, journalists, businessmen, educators – and this list could be extended, testifying to the very broad appeal of these societies. The founders of economic societies wished to create a forum for debate not only on the theoretical aspects but also, and above all, on the means by which economics could illuminate the political and social issues of the day. Economists sought to spread their ideas through the daily press and cultural and scientific journals, and they engaged in a veritable apostolate vis-à-vis the politicians (who were largely involved in the movement), urging those in power to endorse the conclusions that seemed to spring naturally from scientific analysis. How to achieve the proper balance between the scientific dimension on the one hand and the practical orientation on the other was an issue that consistently formed the crux of heated debate and out-and-out battles. But for all the members of these societies the 'spirit of association' was a necessary component part of the political-economic discourse. It is precisely this aspect that makes them into such a thought-provoking object of study, because it leads the enquiring mind directly into the very heart of political economy, opening up fascinating vistas into the reasons for its ambivalent yet alluring success in contemporary society.

In other words, while the history of economic associations cannot disregard themes and issues forming part of sociological history, it must at the same time maintain close contact with the analysis of economic idioms.

2 Enlightenment, patriotism and progress: economic associations at the outset of the nineteenth century

The first associations or academies to bear the adjective 'economic' in their denomination or goals were set up in the mid-eighteenth century in the major centres of Europe, as a direct result of Enlightenment culture. The Dublin Society for Improving Husbandry, Manufactures and other Useful Arts (1731), the Accademia Economico-Agraria dei Georgofili (founded in Florence in 1753) and the Society for the Encouragement of Arts, Manufactures and Commerce (inaugurated in London in 1754) represented the first manifestations of a new zeal for the development of manufacturing arts and agriculture as well as for the reform of economic legislation that soon gained popularity among European cultured elites.[6] The model chosen by the Georgofili – soon followed by further experiences in Milan, Turin and other Italian cities – was that of the scientific academies which had flourished since the seventeenth century, whose members were predominantly drawn from the more illuminated sectors of the aristocracy that hoped to play a vital role in the reform policies set in motion by the European courts. The novelty was represented by the new object on which members were urged to focus when presenting their memoirs and debating. A similar model was followed in France, where the Sociétés Royales d'Agriculture began to spread starting from 1757 (Roche 1978), and then in the Swiss Canton of Berne, where the Ökonomische Gesellschaft – which would become famous for its competitions that mobilised the cream of European scholars – was set up in 1759, and in Russia, where the Imperial Free Economic Society was established at St Petersburg in 1765. In that same year, the first Reales Sociedades Económicas de Amigos del País appeared in Spain, later to be imitated, but with unequal success, both in Spanish America and in Portugal from the 1780s onwards.[7] Finally, in Germany the Hamburgische

Gesellschaft zur Beförderung der Künste und nützlichen Gewerbe [Hamburg Society for the Promotion of Arts and Useful Trades] was founded in 1765, and in Holland the Oeconomical Branch of the Dutch Academy of Sciences in 1777.

Set up through private initiative, often in environments that were clearly inspired by Masonic ideas, or else created by *diktat* from above, these 'economic societies' soon received a somewhat double-edged recognition from eighteenth century reform-minded sovereigns. The latter, as well as the Napoleonic regimes some decades later, tried to demonstrate through their patronage that they welcomed the public usefulness of these associations[8] but also aimed to keep control over debates and initiatives that touched on potentially explosive social, fiscal and legislative questions. In countries like England or Holland, where, at least up to the French Revolution, there existed a climate of greater protection of civil liberties, such associations recruited a more 'bourgeois' public, encouraging the spirit of free debate and 'patriotic' social commitment.

These associations were held in considerable esteem by the main European economists of the time, who worked for their advancement. Thus in Italy there was Antonio Genovesi (1803: VIII, 20–3), whose influence extended throughout the Iberian world, and Melchiorre Gioia (1818: vol. I, 329); in Spain, Pedro Rodriguez de Campomanes (see Llombart 1992: 277–91); in the United Kingdom Jeremy Bentham (1952: 184). Such economists recognised that the associations were an important tool for economic progress, above all through dissemination of knowledge and encouragement of innovations.

The promoters of these economic societies cherished a multiplicity of goals: reform of public finance and economic legislation, dissemination of scientific agronomy and technical and commercial skills, education of peasants and craftsmen and economic education of the upper classes,[9] promotion of technical innovations, organisation of industrial exhibitions,[10] and extensive empirical investigations of the economic situation in different areas. All these objectives were basically designed to encourage economic development and fight poverty and backwardness with indirect and 'immaterial' tools, in an era in which the virtues of free competition and emulation were becoming increasingly popular. Therefore one of the characteristics of the debates that took place within these societies was the development of an economic discourse of a 'political', technical and practical nature, which sometimes also availed itself of the theoretical results achieved by the political economy of the day, even though in an instrumental manner. For economic discourse was still profoundly rooted in the moral and practical aspects of Aristotelian *oikonomìa* and Latin agronomy (Brunner 1968: ch. 6; Frigo 1985) and in the traditional conception of political economy as the 'art of the sovereign' (Perrot 1992). Yet it had to some extent been modernised by authors such as Genovesi, Bentham and Gioia, who had highlighted the role of knowledge and inclination, in addition to the material element of capital, in promoting the wealth of nations and had emphasised the economic function of education, statistics, prizes and awards for inventors (see Guidi 2001).

The Economic and 'Patriotic' Societies continued to engage in intense debates and economic promotion during the early decades of the nineteenth century, favouring the dissemination of political economy throughout society. In some cases these associations have survived to the present day, although they have acquired a more academic and ritual character. Thus they remained active even after the foundation of the first societies of political economy, and many of their protagonists also figured prominently in the creation of the latter. On balance, the economic societies of the eighteenth century represented a model that was at least partially to be imitated, not only as regards their general aim, which was always to further social and economic improvement through the spread of economic knowledge, but also as far as certain specific purposes were concerned, such as the promotion of prizes and the publication of journals, proceedings and memoirs, which summarised their activities.

Finally, it should not be overlooked that academies (Italy, Spain), clubs and debating societies (United Kingdom, Portugal) also displayed a lively interest in political economy in the closing decades of the eighteenth century and the early nineteenth century, although ideas were exchanged more freely in certain periods than others in relation to the cyclical phases of repression and liberalisation characterising contemporary political events.

3 The political economy societies: economic education, *laissez-faire* and public opinion

The clubs and societies that arose in the central decades of the nineteenth century – whose denomination proudly bore the term that identified the young science of political economy – were fellowships composed of a heterogeneous public of men of letters, journalists, politicians and economists. These associations had been set up with the aim of discussing and spreading knowledge of the basic tenets of economic policy as expounded in the works of Smith, Say and Ricardo: free trade in international exchanges and a plentiful dose of *laissez-faire* in the domestic affairs of each country.

The first of these associations was the Political Economy Club (hereafter: PEC), founded in London in 1821 on the initiative of Thomas Tooke, and conceived as 'a means [...] through which men of affairs could become better acquainted with the theoretical underpinnings of free trade' (Tribe, pp. 38–9). James Mill was responsible for the drafting of the club's by-laws, and Torrens, Malthus, Ricardo and Grote became members of the society. But perhaps the association that exerted the greatest influence as a model and sometimes as a direct stimulus for the establishment of similar experiences was the Paris Société d'Economie Politique (hereafter: SEP), mainly by virtue of the cosmopolitan atmosphere that reigned in the French capital and was reflected in the membership of the association itself. Founded in November 1842 by Joseph Garnier, Adolphe Blaise, Eugène Daire and Gilbert-Urbain Guillaumin, it began its activity with Charles Dunoyer as its 'first president'. This group of economists, commonly referred to as the French liberal school, claimed to be the direct heirs of Jean-Baptiste Say; through the *Journal des économistes* and the publishing activities of Guillaumin (see Laurent and Marco 1996; Le Van-Lemesle 1996) these economists promoted the doctrine of *laissez-faire*. The ideals and the associative model of SEP provided the inspiration for the foundation, in rapid succession, of the Società di Economia Politica of Turin, established in 1852 by Francesco Ferrara and presided over by Count Cavour[11] (the architect of the political unification of Italy), the Société Belge d'Economie Politique established in Brussels in 1855 by the economist Charles Le Hardy de Beaulieu and the ultra-liberal French–Belgian economist Gustave de Molinari, and presided over by the Italian Giovanni Arrivabene,[12] the Sociedad libre de economía política de Madrid, set up in 1856 through the initiative of L. Figuerola, M. Colmeiro and G. Rodríguez.[13] In that same year, a Political Economy Society was also active in St Petersburg. In 1858 the naturalised Prussian John Prince-Smith, formerly a British citizen, founded the Kongreß der deutschen Volkswirte [Congress of German Economists], which became the organisation of free-trade economists and exerted strong influence at German universities and in the governments of the German states. There followed, albeit with a slight delay, the Danish (1872) and Swedish (1877) Economic Societies, which likewise drew their inspiration from the French SEP. In contrast, the PEC model provided the inspiration towards the end of the nineteenth century for the American Political Economy Club (1883), presided over by Simon Newcomb with J. Laurence Laughlin as secretary,[14] and the Tokyo Political Economy Club (1887–1923), 'a sort of non-governmental academic society whose purpose was the diffusion and progress of political economy from the viewpoint of the British liberal school' (Kumagai, p. 200). This picture could be completed by taking into account the spread of the SEP model in Latin America and the experience of the Greek Society for the Freedom of Trade (1865–7).

One rather effective approach in examining the nature of these associations consists in seeking to determine what the opportunity of periodical gatherings to discuss political economy must have meant for persons who were active in politics, culture and business. Insight into this aspect can be gleaned by analysing both the aims of the associations as they were expressed in their manifestos and constitutions and in their internal debates, as well as by comparing the new attitude towards political economy with that prevailing in the economic societies examined in the previous section. The main novelty that can be perceived is that political economy was by now universally considered as a scientific body of principles and laws that had been fully clarified by authors such as Say or Ricardo. It was believed that these principles and laws provided a rigorous interpretation of the systemic and self-referential attributes of market mechanisms. There was now a firmly rooted conviction that the 'recipes' of economic policy sprang from the objective laws of political economy – via that which was later to be termed a 'naturalistic fallacy'. *Laissez-faire*, in particular, was no more than the most visible aspect of this conceptual framework.

Knowledge of the laws of political economy thus became an advantage, and indeed a necessity, for anyone playing a public role. For this science indicated constraints that restricted the spectrum of choices available to governments, and highlighted the existence of mechanisms of adverse selection and adverse incentives, awareness of which was essential in order to ensure the efficacy of economic legislation. Consequently, the central aims of mid-nineteenth century Political Economy Societies were to foster discussion and dissemination of political economy, and in particular to spread knowledge of the means of applying it to issues of economic development and social reform. It is important to underline that a sort of logical reversal of the relation between economics and polity had come about. No longer was economics to be considered as a mere tool aiding government decisions: rather, it was the latter that now had to accept the dictates of political economy.

One of the most frequent conclusions reached in the essays on Political Economy Societies presented in this collection concerns the absence of debate on theoretical questions within these societies, whose discussions focused instead almost exclusively on what we now term 'applied economics'. Among historians of economics there is still a widespread tendency to dismiss these discussions as pre-professional or marginal as compared to the evolution of 'high theory'. But anyone who has had the patience to read the proceedings of the meetings of these societies will be well aware of the degree to which these supposedly 'practical' discussions were rich in theoretical content.

On closer inspection, this should come as no surprise. Firstly, in the political economic discourse, the relation between economic theory and applied economics was conceived as a continuum, whereas the real distinction was widely felt to lie between the science of political economy (positive and normative) and the art of economy, delegated to politicians and subordinated, depending on the point of view, either to 'higher maxims' or 'sinister interests' (Winch 1983; Steiner 1997). Secondly, once the spirit of systematic analysis of political economy had been embraced, it was logical to expect that debate on concrete problems of protective tariffs, public finance, money and social policy would lead economists to discover previously unexplored theoretical connections. Indeed, as has been shown in the recent rediscovery of authors such as John Rae, Charles Babbage or the Marshall of *Industry and Trade* (Becattini 1989; Rosenberg 1994; Maneschi 1998), it was precisely the theoretical results achieved in the field of applied economics in the nineteenth century that gave rise to some of the most important aspects of economic theory today. Suffice it to mention the enormous debt owed by modern welfare economics or law and economics to those early debates on the railways, smuggling, property rights, commons and forests, which were often at the heart of discussions within the economic societies.

But one can go a little further along this line of interpretation. Not only did those who engaged in discussion on practical problems eschew any hypothesis of a clear-cut discontinuity with the theoretical content of political economy, but political economy itself was seen first and foremost as a practical science. As a result, the ability to translate the messages conveyed by this science into operational proposals was viewed as the ultimate test of its social function. Paradoxically, the criterion of verification of political economy was more its practical applicability than the empirical validation of its theoretical laws. This may contribute to explaining why political economy became such a fashionable science among the nineteenth-century elites, so *à la mode* indeed that many felt duty bound to accept the rites and obligations of bourgeois sociability in order to engage in discussion on this subject and flaunt their knowledge: demonstrating an understanding of the problems of 'applied economics' meant having all the appropriate prerequisites for governing, directing public affairs, illuminating public opinion, and so forth. Furthermore, it was precisely on account of this social and political function – rather than by virtue of its theorems – that political economy gained prestige in the academic, social and cultural world of the nineteenth century, a position it was to hold into the following century as well.

One important aspect to be considered in this context is that many of these associations were repeatedly faced with the problem of how to maintain a proper balance between scientific discussion of economic questions and political propaganda, in particular in favour of free-trade policy. This balance was not always sustained: in some cases, as for instance in the Società di Economia Politica of Turin in the 1860s, the tendency towards political lobbying gained the upper hand. But in general the climate of scientific discussion was upheld. Often the chosen strategy was to opt for personal or group participation in the activity of 'parallel' political propaganda associations. But attitudes varied: while in Italy Ferrara and the other economists bade the Society to attend to its scientific duties, in France Joseph Garnier and Léon Say challenged Frédéric Bastiat by defending the view that SEP should stand aloof from the militant free-trade activism of the parallel Association pour la Liberté des Echanges created by Bastiat himself in 1846. Breton, in the essay published in the present collection, argues that prudence towards the government – which was often hostile to the Société – featured strongly among the causes of this attitude, as did the desire to maintain internal cohesion among members, which would have been undermined had the society become involved in political lobbying activity. In England the role of free-trade 'agitprop' was carried out independently by the Anti-Corn-Laws League, founded in Manchester in 1839, and by the Cobden Club. An exemplary case is that of the Belgian Society (see Chapter 5), which was very active in its early years in launching a movement in favour of free trade while avoiding out-and-out identification with this campaign, and exploiting the Association pour la Réforme Douanière as its 'militia'. In Spain it was the very members of the Madrid Society who created a parallel association, the Asociación para la Reforma de Aranceles de Aduanas [Association for the Reform of Customs Tariffs] (1859), while in Greece the situation was reversed, with the Society for the Freedom of Trade aiming to be granted the status of scientific society. A slightly different situation can be found in Germany, where the Deutsche Freihandelsverein [German Free-Trade Association], founded in Berlin in March 1847 by John Prince-Smith on the model of Bastiat's association, began its activity eleven years before the creation of the Kongreß der deutschen Volkswirte. Even in the case of Sweden (see Chapter 10) it appears that, although the threat of a return to protection-ist policies represented the main motivation of the group of politicians and scholars who founded the Economic Association in 1877, the desire for an unbiased approach to economic policy in its internal debates was the driving force that induced the leading figures of the association to found a separate society named Föreningen emot Livsmedelstullar [Society Against Food Tariffs] in 1885, designed to wage the battle for free trade.

Cobden's triumphant journey in Europe shortly after the victory of the League in 1846 offers a classic example of this ambivalent relation of distinction and blurring between economic societies and free-trade associations: his most acclaimed speeches were precisely those he held in the academies and the learned societies that had awarded a privileged role to political economy. In effect, the differentiation between scientific and propagandistic association was often more formal than substantial, not only because the protagonists were the same but also because, whatever the underlying truth, their convictions were not presented as the fruit of class interests but rather as the rigorous prescriptions of political economy – prescriptions that the advocates of protectionism apparently ignored. Besides, an analysis of the discussions that took place in these associations reveals how far removed their economic ideas were from the 'night watcher' stereotype: rather, they favoured a joint effort of the government and the economic and philanthropic associations in fields such as canal-building and the railways, education, prison reform, poor relief (typically organised according to the 'less-eligibility principle'), universal exhibitions, etc.

However, this does not mean that political economy was to be identified in practical knowledge. The inclusion of political economy among the issues discussed in the scientific and literary academies in France, Italy and elsewhere sparked the expectation of increased scientific dignity of the discipline and, naturally, of its most highly qualified practitioners. Similar expectations were raised by the establishment in 1833 of a 'Statistical Section' within the British Association for the Advancement of Science (founded in 1831). Significantly, there even emerged a certain dissatisfaction when it became clear that the debating floor of the Association's annual meetings was composed mainly of scholars lacking specialist training and that the subjects addressed were of an excessively practical nature.[15]

We thus need to analyse more closely the nature of the mixed constituency that characterised mid-nineteenth century Political Economy Societies. For one of the features to emerge from the contributions in this book is that those who could, according to the canons of the age, be defined as 'economists' were decidedly in the minority. In PEC the majority of members were MPs and bankers; SEP was peopled by businessmen, journalists, civil servants and politicians from an urban background, while landowners were conspicuous by their absence. The latter were, however, present in the associations of the other Latin countries. The German Kongreß attracted an elevated number of businessmen and industrialists. But it is important to note that there were rigid selection criteria such as nomination by existing members and the ballot, and that even more exclusive criteria were applied to the appointment of the secretary or the Committee, whose task was to draw up the agenda, lead the discussion and decide who should be called upon to present memoirs and lectures. An outcome of the application of these selection criteria was a situation in which the 'economists' occupied leading positions in the associations and provided authoritative opinions and proposals, while the other groups of members participated more passively – driven above all by the desire to engage in economic education (Breton, p. 57) – or only took an active part in more practical discussions: this was a mechanism that would be repeated by late nineteenth-century economic associations.

But who were these economists who sat on the official boards of the societies? It is clear that in the central decades of the nineteenth century their identity was defined more on the basis of what they wrote (and sometimes these were authors who were far from being specialised exclusively in political economy) than on their professional qualifications. However, the gradual onset of the institutionalisation of political economy in the universities was beginning to bring a few subtle changes. If in the case of England the main economists were not academics, while in Belgium there was a sharp distinction between the protagonists of the Political Economy Society and university professors, in Italy, Spain and Germany, on the other hand – and to some extent in France as well – it was precisely those who held chairs in political economy who were appointed to key posts in the various associations created in the mid-nineteenth century. Such appointments sometimes created a situation that allowed spirited interaction between the prestige of economists, the aims of the associations, the discussions internal to the latter and the institutionalisation of political economy. For instance, debate focused on the possibility of strengthening the teaching of economics in the universities and in other secondary or higher education institutions, or on the criteria for recruitment of university professors, and it was not unknown for such debates to correspond to actions (and sometimes even conflicts) centring on the creation of chairs of political economy and the choice of professors. The comparative approach adopted here suggests one cannot rule out the hypothesis that from as early as the mid-nineteenth century the Political Economy Societies may in some cases have contributed to the evolution of the economist towards a more 'professional' physiognomy strongly rooted within the university.

There remains the fact that these associations certainly had a heterogeneous membership, and this very circumstance explains their primary function: that of acting as a forum for exchange of ideas and information between economists, politicians and the protagonists of public opinion. The types of associative bonds among members are a further testimony of this situation. Thus all of these societies shared similar sociability rites (Agulhon 1979) that were clearly distinct from the later model of the scientific society: the club, the dinner at a restaurant, the *impromptu* drawing up of the agenda at the beginning of the meeting,[16] a degree of informality in the regulations and management of the Society, at least in the initial stages. Requests for these procedures to be modified long remained minority proposals, indicating that the regulations in force reflected the overall wishes of the associations' constituencies.

The Political Economy Societies were thus an integral part of the public sphere, whose functions embraced both self-education for the members of the social and political elites and the task of orienting public opinion and the political establishment. The economists saw themselves as called upon to become the 'competent' interpreters of public opinion at a time when the first social conflicts emerging in the industrial world were undermining impartiality of judgement (Habermas 1989). Furthermore, they appealed to public opinion in their endeavour to reinforce their social prestige and their role as privileged advisors of political leaders (Church 1974). At the same time, however, the economists also cherished the ambition of becoming an integral part of the world of politics as MPs and ministers, as shown by the careers of the leading figures of some of the Political Economy Societies. The contacts they established with politicians in the associations also contributed to the success of this aspiration, which should be considered not so much as the fruit of individual ambition but rather as a consequence of the missionary zeal the political economic discourse inspired in all who adopted it.

This having been said, the relation between Political Economic Societies and the political sphere was not always serene. For instance, relations between the SEP and the government were frequently troubled both in the period of the Second Empire and under the Third Republic, and the Committee members were forced on several occasions to act with extreme prudence in order to avert suppression of the Society. This case suggests a more general consideration: the creation of these societies was probably slowed, or in some cases actively discouraged, as a result of the 'suspicion' aroused by debates calling into question existing legislation and political choices. This was particularly true of the illiberal regimes set up after the Restoration, but not only these. In the United Kingdom, after the suppression of the Jacobin clubs in the 1790s, serious limitations on the possibility of free expression within associations were introduced, and when the PEC was founded in 1821, it was composed of a selected group of people who engaged in debates behind closed doors. By contrast, in Holland the absence of any suspicious attitude towards political economy led to the flowering of a variety of associative experiences. It would therefore appear, in a historical perspective, that one of the conditions for the emergence of Political Economy Societies is the existence of a liberal political regime.

The desire to influence public opinion was manifest in all the activities undertaken by the societies. Consider for instance the efforts of the SEP and other associations to offer opportunities for economic education as an alternative to the elite-oriented university lectures. But this desire was most clearly voiced through specialist journals founded by the societies in order to make public the results of their meetings and host broader debates on themes concerning political economy. Sometimes, as in the case of England, journals hosting economic debates antedated the birth of associations, such as the *Edinburgh Review* founded in 1802. In France the paucity of means at first prevented the SEP from establishing a journal of its own, but SEP members could avail themselves of the *Journal des économistes* and the *Annuaire de l'économie politique*, which were run by the same group of liberal economists.[17] In Italy, the Società di Economia Politica of Turin was unsuccessful in attempting to found its own periodical, but it nevertheless published the minutes of its meetings in respected journals such as the *Rivista Contemporanea*, the *Annali Universali di Statistica* and *Il Politecnico*. It was not until the association was transformed into the Società Italiana di Economia Politica in 1864 that it finally succeeded in creating its own journal, taking over *Il Commercio Italiano* which was already published in Turin. The Société Belge d'Economie Politique published the *comptes-rendus* of its meetings in *L'Economiste belge* from 1855 to 1868, and, from 1890, in the *Revue économique* edited by Louis Strauss. The Sociedad Libre de Economía Política of Madrid utilised *El economista* (1856–7), *La tribuna del economista* (1857–8) and the *Gaceta economista* (1861–3). The Danish Nationaløkonomisk Forening [Economic Association] founded its own journal in 1873 (*Nationaløkonomisk Tidskrift*). In Holland both the economic journal *De Economist*, founded in 1852 by J.L. De Bruyn Kops, and the literary journal *De Gids*, founded in 1837, performed a similar function. The common intention shared by all these journalistic experiences was to create a pulpit, as it were, from which to convey the message of political economy to as wide an audience as possible.

Finally, one noteworthy characteristic of the mid-nineteenth century Political Economy Societies was their remarkably transnational membership and the international circulation of memoirs, journals and persons. This characteristic should be underlined, because by the end of the century the economic societies had acquired a rather more evident national character, and in fact it would not be until the late decades of the twentieth century that economists would once again feel the need to establish links through international societies.[18] The international dimension of the mid-nineteenth century Political Economy Societies thus appears as an original element, which can be explained more convincingly and more directly in terms of the marked cosmopolitanism that was inherent in the political economic discourse itself (Winch 1994) rather than as a result of free-trade language urging the brotherhood of peoples and *paix perpétuelle*. This early internationalism of economic associations engendered a network whereby some 'social entrepreneurs' acted as a crucial link between different national experiences. One may cite such figures as the Portuguese Francisco Solano Constâncio, a member of the SEP, the Spaniard Manuel García Quijano, who was also member and treasurer of the Parisian society, the Italian Giovanni Arrivabene, President both of the Société Belge and the Società Italiana, and Gustave de Molinari, active both in Belgium and France. The primacy for energy and drive in organising conferences and international meetings perhaps belongs to Belgium: the Congrès des Economistes held in Brussels, 16th–18th September 1847 and the Congrès International des Réformes Douanières, also held in Brussels from 22nd to 24th September 1856, were a big success and awakened the stimulus in some delegations, such as the Spanish delegates, to create their own national society.

4 Social reform, statistics and the beginnings of 'professional' economic societies

From the 1870s or thereabouts, the Political Economy Societies that followed the *laissez-faire* orientation began to show signs of decline. The first to close, in 1868 after several years of sluggish activity was the Madrid Society. At the beginning of the 1870s, conflicts within the Italian Society led first to a slow-down in the pace of activities and then to a prolonged suspension; the attempts made in order to relaunch the activity of the Society in the late 1870s did not go beyond a couple of meetings, the last of which was held in March 1882 (Asso 2000). This was followed in 1885 by the disbanding of the Kongreß der deutschen Volkswirte. In contrast, the PEC, SEP and the Belgian Society survived: the French Society – reformed by Gustave de Molinari in 1887 – displayed an intense level of activity until the inter-war period and still exists today, albeit with a lower profile.[19] The Belgian society likewise still endures today, transformed in this case into a professional society under the name of Société Royale d'Economie Politique de Belgique.

During the period under review, the latter two societies succeeded in maintaining their strength and doctrinal creed intact thanks to a sizeable and compact group of economists who were determined to defend *laissez-faire* orthodoxy. But in France, this faithfulness to their origins came at the cost of increasing isolation vis-à-vis not only the government but also the younger heterodox economists recruited by virtue of the *agrégation* of the

Faculties of Law instituted in 1889. Even the group of free-traders who had founded the Swedish Economic Association was snubbed in the political and electoral arena at the end of the 1880s, thereby failing in its attempt to resist the powerful protectionist lobby. It also had little success in seeking to involve the few academic economists of the time, but it nevertheless survived thanks to its activity in organising lectures of a commendable scientific level, which were held mainly by members of the board. The PEC, on the other hand, enjoyed continuing prestige as a forum for selective evaluation of economists (Henderson 1983) and this – rather than any ideological commitment – is one of the reasons why the British Economic Association, established in 1890, elected in its early years not to hold annual meetings among its members.

The underlying causes of the gradual decline of these associations are multiple, and, as already noted, do not follow a uniform pattern. But certain common phenomena can be found in the different national experiences:

1   a crisis of the 'classical' economic paradigm which came to the fore *sub specie* of a dispersion of economists into different schools of thought and sparked controversies on the method of economics;
2   a parallel crisis of *laissez-faire* ideology in the wake of both the 'social question' and the powerful economic interests favourable to protectionism and extensive government intervention;
3   the rise of new associations which embraced the new theoretical orientations and the demands for social reform, and which antagonised the Political Economy Societies;
4   the growth of the 'critical mass' of academic economists, which ushered in changes in the economic societies such as the increased influence of academic economists in official boards, the elimination of votes on motions addressing the most controversial issues of economic policy and the attempt to exercise control over academic policy.

It would be beyond the scope of this chapter to conduct an in-depth examination of the first two of the above-listed aspects. However, it is worth pointing out that study of the economic societies reveals at least three peculiarities of the evolution of economics in the closing decades of the nineteenth century. First and foremost, it should be noted that the classical paradigm was challenged from a number of different standpoints. While the influence of the German Historical School played a significant role in Italy and the United States, the role of Catholic social economy in various countries should not be underestimated. Catholic social doctrine introduced the principle of 'subsidiarity' as a criterion to evaluate the type and extent of state intervention necessary to correct the distributive bias of the market economy. This was the case in Spain, for instance, where Christian social economy obtained some support among academic economists; likewise in Italy, where the exponents of the social doctrine of the Church set up the

Unione Cattolica per gli Studi Sociali in 1889 (Pecorari 2000); a similar situation arose in Belgium, where Catholic economists stood aloof from the Société d'Economie Politique and founded their own association in 1881, the Société d'Economie Sociale.

The debates within the economic societies also reveal a second characteristic of the new intellectual climate. True, there was a renewed interest in protectionist policies, a new concern for social reform, a more critical attitude towards the deductivist and nomothetic approach of classical political economy and a denial of the independence of economics by those who supported the *Staatswissenschaften*: yet these developments by no means resulted in mistrust of the scientific status of economics or a return to a more pragmatic viewpoint. Quite the contrary: the rise – not only in the Germanic area – of a *Methodenstreit* and a *Werturteilsstreit* marked the outset of genuine research into the scientific foundations of economics. Furthermore, as clearly emerges from the Platform of Richard T. Ely for the AEA, partisan though it may have been (Barber, p. 223), a widespread feeling at that time was that the theoretical scope of economics could no longer be enclosed within the restricted number of canonical principles and methods of classical political economy. Economics was still a young science, in search of its theoretical foundations, and it was now considered inadmissible for a young scholar imbued with a sincere spirit of scientific investigation to remain anchored in the past. Indeed, even the advocates of protectionism sought to improve their reputation as scholars, advancing arguments endowed with greater theoretical dignity such as the 'infant industry argument' championed by John Rae, Friedrich List and Henry C. Carey. The fact that during this period debates within the societies focused almost exclusively on themes of applied and social economics was certainly not an innovation and cannot in itself be considered a symptom of the decline of economics.

A third characteristic of the new phase is well illustrated by the attitude of economists who took an active part in the foundation of associations. One of the motivations that indirectly impelled scholars to seek new paths to build up and strengthen the scientific status of economics was the success of socialist doctrines after 1848. Providing answers to social alternatives that frequently assumed the guise of a veritable 'scientific' theory became a 'must' for practitioners of a discipline that aspired to enhance its status as the science of the legislator. In this perspective, although the associations founded by the German 'chair socialists' and their followers abroad were peopled by a constituency that was both socially and politically heterogeneous, they did lay the groundwork for one of the main features of the profession of economist in the twentieth century: the ambivalent blend of a socially conservative orientation and a more pragmatic modernising and reforming inclination averse to any intellectualistic attitude.

New associations sprang up in response to this widespread desire to move with the times by revising the method of economics and devoting greater attention to social problems. The first to enter into action had once again been the British, who as early as 1833 founded Section F of the British Association for the Advancement of Science, dedicated to statistics. In 1856 this section was transformed into the Section for Economic Science and Statistics. In the minds of those who set up this institution, statistics was a positive science capable of endowing political economy with an inductive foundation, an idea that closely matched the approach favoured by Richard Jones and also that of the Historical School and positivist sociology abroad. The sharply hostile reactions voiced in 1877 to Francis Galton's proposal for suppression of Section F show how popular this institution had become, composed as it was of politicians and philanthropists but also of scientists, and dedicated to the discussion of practical papers suffused with an ideal of social reform. At the same time, however, Jevons' decision to present his innovative 1862 paper 'Notice of a General Mathematical Theory of Political Economy' at the Cambridge meeting of Section F – as well as the prestigious presidency of Marshall in 1890 – reveals how far this institution had now come in acting as a forum open to general discussion of political economy, worthy of attracting the attention of a still relatively small cluster of young economists.

A similar evolution can be seen in the Vereeniging voor de Statistiek founded in Holland in 1857 and transformed in 1892 into the Political Economy and Statistics Society.[20] Created with the aim of publishing a general statistical overview of the Dutch situation, this society was likewise inspired by an interest in analysis of the economic and social problems of the country and a concern for social reform, which had been a constant feature of economic culture in Holland ever since the eighteenth century. Study of these problems was undertaken by a heterogeneous group composed of statisticians, agriculturists, geographers and physicians, as well as politicians and businessmen. In the 1870s, the advent of a new generation of economists guided by N.G. Pierson infused an increasing economic content into the society's debates, to the point that in the twentieth century the Vereeniging was transformed into a professional economic association.

A greater practical tendency was also evinced by the National Association for the Moral and Social Improvement of the People, founded in London in July 1857, later better known as the Social Science Association. Its aim was to exert pressure for reform on central and local government. This model was once again emulated in the United States, where an American Social Science Association was created in 1865 in the 'post-Civil War flush of enthusiasm for social reforms' (Barber, p. 216). In 1862 the founder of the British society, Lord Brougham, together with Michel Chevalier, Garnier Pagès and a group of Belgian philanthropists also attempted to create an International Association for the Advancement of Social Sciences, which organised four conferences in the period from 1862 to 1865. Later, in Brussels, the Société d'Etudes Sociales et Politiques, founded in 1890, effectively rose from the ashes of the international association. It has to be said, however, that in these associations as well as in the statistical associations analysed above, the prevailing tendency was continuity with the past. Neither the foundations of classical political economy nor *laissez-faire* doctrine were disputed: the general assumption was that study and dissemination of the 'social question' would be sufficient to mobilise the action of private individuals, associations and local institutions in a common effort to solve social problems through philanthropic and economic initiatives.

In other countries, on the other hand, new and more aggressive associations arose as an outcome of generational change and the strengthening of the institutionalisation of political economy. These associations entered into the fray of social reform, bringing forward their dissatisfaction with the method of classical economics and *laissez-faire* ideology, and opposition to socialism. The 'mother of all these associations' was the Verein für Sozialpolitik, founded at a conference in Eisenach on 13th October 1873, after a preliminary conference on the 'social question' which had been held a year earlier in the same city. The Verein was founded by a group of social reformers, the so-called '*Kathedersozialisten*' who were opposed both to *laissez-faire* positions and Marxist socialism. The three leading figures in the first decades of the Verein für Sozialpolitik were Gustav Schmoller, Adolph Wagner and Lujo Brentano. Although all its members shared the same underlying outlook, the life of the Verein was far from calm: numerous controversies flared up between a 'centre' represented by Schmoller and Nasse, a 'left' guided by Brentano and Karl Bücher (and later by Max and Alfred Weber and Werner Sombart), and finally a 'right' with which Wagner and most industrialists sided. The period of genuine agitation in favour of social reform lasted from 1873 to 1881, the year in which, as we will shortly see, steps were begun to transform the Verein into a more scholarly association. The board was composed of academic economists, although the majority of Verein members belonged to other professional categories. One peculiar feature which was partly responsible for the later developments of the Association was that various members of the Kongreß also joined the Verein, despite the contraposition between the two associations.

The influence of the German chair socialists was particularly strong in Italy, the United States and Japan, where new associations arose with the aim of imitating the Verein and propagating its doctrines. Similarly, in Denmark the Economic Society founded in 1872 also underwent an evolution from the SEP model to that of the Verein.

In Italy, in the mid-1870s, a controversy on method broke out. It was triggered by several articles of Vito Cusumano, who had completed his specialisation in Germany and was an outspoken supporter of the positions of the chair socialists, and Francesco Ferrara, who defended the naturalistic and *laissez-faire* viewpoint of classical economics. This led to a split among economists and consequently to the birth of two parallel associations, expressing opposite visions of economics and economic policy. The first to be created was the Società Adamo Smith, founded in Florence in 1874 by Francesco Ferrara and several liberal politicians belonging to the group of the so-called 'Tuscan moderates', which was rooted in the principles of *laissez-faire* and championed an abstract and deductive approach to economics; the opposing association was the Associazione per il Progresso degli Studi Economici, instituted in Milan in 1875 by a group of senior economists also active in politics, among whom were Luigi Cossa, Fedele Lampertico, Luigi Luzzatti and Antonio Scialoja. These economists advocated the inductive method of the Historical School and embraced a paternalistic ideal of social reform inspired by the German Verein. It would be the latter approach – supported by such figures as Luzzatti who were active in the field of social policy – that went on to acquire greater favour, leading to a generational change among academic economists; as a result, the Ferrarian economists were gradually ousted from universities and other scientific and institutional circles.

In the United States the influence of the German *Kathedersozialisten* was on the contrary the reflex of a generational phenomenon that began in the 1880s. Given the paucity of opportunities for specialist studies in economics in American universities, many young scholars chose to complete their training in Germany. Once back home again, these 'Young Turks' accused the 'old school' of stuffy conservatism for having remained faithful to Anglo-French political economy. Similar charges were also levelled against the American Social Science Association, regarded as incapable of embarking on courageous debate concerning social reform. After a failed attempt in 1884 to create a Society for the Study of the National Economy that would replicate the German Verein, a movement arose within the Johns Hopkins University, resulting in the 1885 foundation of the AEA, upon the initiative of Richard T. Ely, who had obtained a doctorate at the University of Heidelberg. Significantly, the Platform circulated by Ely – in contrast with one of the objectives the association had planned to pursue, namely the 'encouragement of perfect freedom in all economic discussion' – voiced the criticisms raised by the young generation of 'Germanised' economists against classical political economy and *laissez-faire* as well as the request for greater state involvement in social policies. However, Ely's most radical proposals were not incorporated within the Statement of Principles adopted at the first conference, held the same year in Saratoga; in addition, the Statement itself was suppressed just a few years later. Therefore, as will be shown below, the association achieved such outstanding success that it rapidly led to the loss of the militant and generational tones that had been a feature of its foundation.

The case of late nineteenth-century Japan revealed a close connection between the creation of new pro-German associations and the internal political affairs of the country. The role of Richard Ely was played here by Noburu Kanai, a professor of the Tokyo Imperial University with a background of study in Germany under the guidance of Gustav Schmoller. In 1891 Kanai deplored the prevalence of the British classical approach in Japanese academic circles, despite the influence of German economic culture in Japan for about a decade: the Society for German Studies had been founded in 1881 by Kowashi Inoue, a government councillor who was firmly convinced that the Japanese economic model resembled that of Germany. After fighting a vigorous political battle to achieve a favourable reception for his protectionist and interventionist ideas, Inoue founded this association in order to propagate the approach of the German *Staatswissenschaften*, which rejected the independence of economics from politics. In contrast, the Society for State Sciences, set up as a branch of the department of political science of Tokyo Imperial University in 1887, had a more academic nature. The aim of this association was nevertheless similar to that of its predecessor. But the most important event was the 1891 foundation of the Nihon Shakai Seisaku Gakkai [Japanese Association for the Study of Social Policy], on the model of the Verein. This society provided the impetus for the 'social policy school' headed by Noburu Kanai, which dominated economic debate and the Japanese academic world for several decades.

Broadly speaking, the associations founded in the late nineteenth century shared many aspects with those stemming from the earlier period: their constituency was still mixed and the majority of their members were composed of politicians, businessmen and civil servants. Furthermore, the common goal of these somewhat disparate groups of people was a genuine desire to explore and spread a message believed to spring from economics. However, for many countries there was one new feature, represented by the increase in the number of academic economists[21] and the progressive increase in the number of graduates who had received training in economics. This development could not fail to alter the internal balance of these associations and, at least in part, their aims and internal activities as well. After all, given the ends pursued by these associations, it was inevitable that academic economists would assume the leadership of the official boards and organise the internal debates. Just as it was equally inevitable that they would bring with them a whole host of concerns pertaining to the university world and relations with the academic and political authorities. Without going so far as to say that they were moved by their own private interest alone, it is undeniable that the very logic of the scientific causes championed by the associations required economists to be aware of the possible repercussions on the professional and institutional plane.

A general overview of the evidence presented in this volume suggests a hypothesis which, while certainly limited, does capture some important analogies between different cases. We might call it the 'two stage' hypothesis: during the first stage the division of economists into the 'old' school versus the 'new' school actually favoured a strategic commitment of the associations towards enhancing the institutionalisation of economics and the academic profession of the economist, in order to modify the power relations between the opposing camps; in the second stage, on the other hand, this division was felt to be an impediment both to the growth of scientific rigour and to the expansion of academic positions in the field of economics, and so the associations were transformed into an impartial forum for exchange of ideas open to all schools of thought and oriented towards more scholarly enquiry. Naturally, not all countries followed this route: some did not experience the first stage, while others did not succeed in establishing a more ecumenical atmosphere among economists until well beyond the middle of the twentieth century.

The existence of a correlation between divisions in theoretical matters and the efforts of academic economists in promoting associations and favouring the institutionalisation of political economy is demonstrated for the Italian case by the endeavours of the two above-mentioned rival associations in the mid-1870s, as they struggled to boost the presence of economics in the universities. The case of Germany is more complex. The year in which the Verein was founded coincided with the apogee of free-trade policies and the Kongreß, the latter being extremely influential both in the university world and in government circles. However, many congressmen joined the Verein and from the outset attempts to cooperate prevailed on both sides. As a clear demonstration of this, suffice it to note that it was a Congressman, Rudolf von Gneist, who was elected the first Chairman of the Verein. But the diatribe then surfaced again within the association itself, with a contraposition between a 'liberal' left favourable to free trade, headed by Nasse and Brentano, and a more moderate position favourable to Bismarckian protectionism, whose leader was Schmoller. The 1879 meeting represented the dramatic culminating point of these smouldering confrontations, ending in a victory for the conservatives. However, the extent to which these events were correlated with power struggles in the academic world is less clear. The presence of academic economists in the Verein and above all in its leading group was evident, although they did not constitute the majority of the members. What is certain is that episodes of discrimination occurred: the Berlin academic environment was highly conservative and it is no coincidence that 'most leading representatives of the liberal current within the Verein had professorships outside Prussia, like Brentano in Vienna, Leipzig and Munich, Bücher in Basel, Karlsruhe and Leipzig, Max Weber in Freiburg and Heidelberg, and Alfred Weber in Prague and Heidelberg. On the other hand, most of the leading conservatives were teaching at Prussian universities' (Hagemann, p. 155).

As far as the United States is concerned, it is worth pointing out the presence, as early as the 1880s, of a substantial critical mass of scholars who had undergone training in economics. While this did not in itself result in the immediate demand for a professional association of economists, it does go some way towards accounting for the importance of links between economic associations and professionalisation. It is interesting to note that the *Methodenstreit*, which began to gather pace around the mid-1880s, was characterised by the harshness of the accusations hurled at each other by the opposing parties, as if the mere fact of belonging to the rival camp was a sure sign of a total lack of even the most rudimentary requisites of scientific rigour. For instance, Barber points out that 'Ely's decision to launch the American Economic Association (AEA) in 1885 contained an element of opportunism' (p. 221), given the in-fighting between himself and Newcomb at Johns Hopkins and Ely's fear of being deprived of his teaching position.

In Japan, as well, the various activities promoted by the associations had close links with developments in the academic world, so that the clashes between pro-British and pro-German associations reflected and in some sense evolved side by side with the university institutionalisation of political economy.

Interestingly, a further demonstration of the nexus between doctrinal disagreements and institutionalisation comes from evidence of the inverse situation, namely the difficulties, mentioned earlier, encountered by the surviving societies of *laissez-faire* persuasion in seeking to establish relations with the new generation of academic economists. Thus in France the SEP was compelled to acknowledge the preference of Third Republic governments for heterodox economists such as Paul Cauwès and Charles Gide, and failed to recruit any academic economists of the younger generation. In Sweden the Economic Association exerted no influence whatsoever over the academic institutionalisation of political economy. The Association also had no part in the foundation of the *Ekonomisk Tidskrift* and the Institute of Social Science in Stockholm.

Despite this, the phase of militant conflict was soon succeeded by a quest for appeasement and mutual tolerance among the different schools of thought. In the Verein für Sozialpolitik the decision taken in 1881 no longer to put sensitive questions of economic policy to the vote, after the dramatic 1879 split on the issue of protectionist tariffs, signalled the first step towards the search for a compromise among the different streams of thought present in the association. It was hoped this would lead to a more scholarly and neutral climate of debate, while not relinquishing the policy-oriented nature of the Verein. A further step in this direction was taken when, after another crisis in 1905, Schmoller pressed for a compromise between the younger generation influenced by Marxism and the older liberal generation. And changes did indeed follow, even becoming excessive, in that the greater ecumenism came at a cost of increasing apathy and indifference towards debates, accompanied by widespread absenteeism. Such a development could in fact be considered symbolic of the evolution of economic associations in the nineteenth century: an economics which for reasons of prudence and academic respect had been deprived of its most practical and concrete aspects could hardly attract an audience that had turned to the associations to improve itself and create means of bringing pressure to bear on political circles.[22]

Developments within the AEA unfolded according to a similar pattern. In 1892 Ely was forced out of his position as secretary of the organisation, testifying to a widespread desire to bring economists together in order to strengthen the position of economics in a university world – both public and private – that was undergoing a period of extraordinarily rapid expansion. For there was an insidious risk underlying jobs entrusted to economists: most of them could be threatened with reprisals by private donors or public administrators if the economists took up a controversial stance on some of the most burning issues of the day.[23]

In the Far-East, the Japanese Association for the Study of Social Policy also assumed a distinctive scientific and professional role at the beginning of the twentieth century. Some commercial schools and private educational institutions aspired to acquire university status, and sent their economists to study abroad in order to increase the scientific prestige of these rising scholars. Thus the association, and in particular its annual meetings, became a glittering occasion to parade their scientific accomplishments. This in turn encouraged a growing desire to make the society into a forum for Japanese economists of all persuasions, in order to demonstrate the authority of economic studies in Japan. However, the Association was eventually dissolved in 1924, partly as a result of ideological clashes similar to those within the Verein (Marxists against liberals), and partly because the academic economists were dissatisfied with the emphasis placed on political issues rather than theoretical questions during debates.[24]

The first period of the BEA, founded by Marshall in 1890 and transformed in 1902 into the Royal Economic Society (RES), presents some similarities with the cases analysed above, although also displaying unique characteristics. British economic debate had been affected only marginally by the opposition between the different schools of thought characterising the other European countries and the United States. Furthermore, the society had been founded with the main aim of providing an organisational structure that would guarantee proper management of the *Economic Journal*, first issued in 1891. The Association's aim was to ensure the new journal would not be monopolised by any school or tendency. Thus the BEA/RES shared with other late nineteenth-century associations the objective of impartiality and a willingness to be open to all schools of thought. It is also interesting to note that although membership of the society was open to anyone, the editorial committee of the journal was composed chiefly of academics, 'setting a pattern in the relationship between the structure of the membership of the Association and that of its officers which persisted into the later twentieth century' (Tribe, p. 47).

In Italy, all attempts made in the early 1880s to unite economists under the banner of the Società di Economia Politica Italiana foundered, and neither of the two rival associations survived for long. Among the various reasons for this failure one may cite the fact that 'Germanised' economists not only obtained a quasi-monopoly over the university teaching but also secured prestigious posts within the government, and in advisory commissions and local institutions also. This meant that the main exponents of this approach found they no longer needed an association as a launch pad for their school within academia or in the world of politics; moreover, they themselves embarked on a series of projects in the sphere of publishing, politics, and economic and social affairs which promised to be more fruitful than mere internal debate in the associations.[25]

Finally, a few words should be said on the case of Spain and Portugal. The peculiarity of the Spanish case is that although the closing decades of the nineteenth century did indeed see the increasing academic institutionalisation of political economy, there was a dearth of initiatives in the field of economic associations. This may be explained by noting that while a number of opinion-maker economists who had been well-known figures for over half a century retired from the scene because of advancing age, the new generation of university professors of economics did not shine either in specialisation or abundance of scientific publications or even in commitment to public office, limiting themselves instead to their teaching activities. Revival did not begin until 1914, whereupon, however, economists opted to emulate the German model of university seminars as their preferred form of scientific and professional debate. Such a tradition to some extent continues to the present day, thus partly accounting for the absence of a general association of economists. Portugal, on the other hand, would have to wait until the 1940s for the advent of any substantial professionalisation of economics, when the Instituto Superior de Ciências Económicas e Financeiras was transformed into a modern school of economics, followed by the establishment of the Sociedade de ciências económicas in 1941.

In conclusion, by the end of the nineteenth century many economic associations had contributed in various ways to promoting the institutionalisation of economics and the academic professionalisation of economists, and while remaining anchored to their original characteristics, they had set in motion some of the transformations that led them during the twentieth century to take on the attributes of modern scientific and professional associations.

5 Concluding remarks

The economic societies that arose between the second half of the eighteenth century and the end of the nineteenth century were different both in nature and aims from the modern scientific and professional associations of economists, yet in many ways they laid the groundwork for these associations. They provided economics with the stamp of authority as a discipline that was at one and the same time a science of the public sphere and a science of the legislator. They offered economists a forum to assert and champion their ideas. They also contributed to the institutionalisation of political economy and the rise of the academic profession of the economist.

Three stages can be distinguished in the development of these associations. The first was that of the Societies for the Encouragement of Arts and Agriculture, whose main aim was the spread of knowledge on economics.

The prevailing approach in these societies was that of practical and policy-oriented economic knowledge, in comparison to which political economy played a purely instrumental role. The second stage was that of the Political Economy Societies, which can be considered a natural product of the enthusiastic reception of Smithian political economy and *laissez-faire* doctrine in mid-nineteenth-century European culture; the members of these associations – politicians, businessmen and a minority of economists, of whom only a part were university professors – shared a common zeal for the dissemination of political economy in governmental spheres and in public opinion. The same function and the same social background also character-ised the Economic Associations that arose in the final decades of the nineteenth century, which were influenced by new economic perspectives such as chair socialism, the Historical School, positivist social science and Catholic social economy. In many cases these societies were established against the backcloth of a situation that had seen a marked increase in the critical mass of academic economists. While this at first resulted in a generational conflict and clashes between different schools of thought, which had controversial repercussions on the institutionalisation of political economy within the universities, it subsequently encouraged economists to adopt a more 'ecumenical' strategy and a more detached scientific approach in order to further the overall growth of the academic profession of the economist. It was in particular after this new orientation had been embraced that the goals of popular enlightenment and opinion-making previously pursued by the economic societies began to fade into the background, and the societies themselves became instruments to strengthen the professionali-sation of the economist.

Throughout these developments, one of the most striking features was the international circulation of ideas and models among different national contexts. Seen from the vantage point of the economic associations, economics – despite its distinctive 'national styles' (Coats 1988) – appears from the very moment of its origins as a self-expanding and cosmopolitan science.

Notes

* The authors wish to thank Pierfrancesco Asso and the contributors to this volume for their useful comments on a first draft of this introductory chapter. Although the general structure of this chapter was composed jointly, M. Guidi drafted sections 2 and 3, and M. Augello section 4. Sections 1 and 5 were written in common.

1 The most widely studied cases are those of the United Kingdom, the USA and Italy. See Coats 1993, which gathers together the numerous essays on this subject written by the author from the 1960s onwards; Barber 1987; Augello 1989; Augello and Guidi 2000.
2 On this theme, P. Barucci and I. Hont coordinated a research project in the 1980s, which was completed with an international conference held in spring 1986 at San Miniato, Italy, entitled 'The Institutionalization of Political Econ-omy: Its Introduction and Acceptance into European, North-American and

Japanese Universities'. The papers presented at this conference were subsequently incorporated into various national collections: Le Van-Lemesle 1986; Barber 1988; Augello *et al.* 1988; Waszek 1988; Sugiyama and Mizuta 1988; Kadish and Tribe 1993.

3   See Augello 1995; Augello, Bianchini and Guidi 1996; Bianchini 1996; Marco 1996.

4   The official justification was that this would reduce the disadvantages generated by one of the most classic cases of asymmetric information.

5   As shown by the essays published in this book, the history of the Latin nations which experienced totalitarian regimes in the twentieth century provides evidence *against* this evolution. Only in the case of Portugal did economists create an association of their own (the ephemeral Sociedade de ciências económicas founded in 1941). In Italy, the reluctance of economists to take this step has been explained by such phenomena as the desire to avert the transformation of an association into a corporatist trade union, with all the consequences this would have entailed in terms of political interference in the scientific (and academic) selection of candidates. The case of Spain is even more emblematic. Here, from 1947 onwards, economists were granted recognition of their professional status in a corporatist organisation (the Colegio de economistas), but for reasons analogous to those of their Italian colleagues they refused to create an association of a scientific nature.

6   For a survey of the literature on these issues up to the 1960s, see Torcellan 1964: 534–43.

7   In addition to the contributions by S. Almenar and V. Llombart and by A. Almodovar and J.L. Cardoso in this book, see also Enciso Recio 1996.

8   These societies were attributed official duties such as advisory functions, collection of statistical data, training civil servants and granting patents of invention.

9   In the Spanish case the economic societies created the first chairs of political economy.

10   It is worth recalling that the London Society of Arts was the organiser of the Great Exhibition of 1851.

11   After a period of suspension the Società di Economia Politica of Turin was re-founded in 1860, with Giovanni Arrivabene as its President and Gian Giacomo Reymond as its secretary.

12   In Belgium, the Association Belge pour la Liberté Commerciale, headed by Charles de Brouckère (President), Giovanni Arrivabene and Fr. Basse (Vice-presidents), had already been in existence since 1846.

13   As documented below in the essay by Almenar and Llombart, the mobilising ability of the *laissez-faire* doctrine is clearly demonstrated by the failure of an association – the Sociedad de hacienda y crédito público (1841) – which, although inspired by the model of PEC or SEP, proposed to consent to pluralism among its members on the crucial theme of customs tariffs and state intervention in the economy.

14   As W. Barber underlines in the chapter published in this book (p. 219), '[a]n ideological purity test, however, was not a precondition for election' in this club.

15   It is important to note that in Italy, where an Association for the Advancement of Science was not created until the beginning of the twentieth century, the Congresses of Scientists that were held annually starting from 1839 (see Fumian 1995) did not admit a section devoted to economics, despite repeated requests. In the section on agrarian sciences, in which some economists took part, great disappointment was expressed at the low level of the papers presented.

16   In the case of the Madrid society, the agenda of the next meeting would be drawn up at the end of each meeting.

17 It should be pointed out that one of the aims of Gustave de Molinari's reform of the constitution of SEP in 1887 was precisely that of founding a periodical, the *Bulletin de la Société d'économie politique*.
18 For a background study on the internationalisation of economics see Coats 1996.
19 The current professional society of French economists is the Association Française de Science Economique, founded in 1950 as a partner of the International Economic Association.
20 The association is still in existence as the Royal Netherlands Economic Society. See the essay by Schoorl in this book.
21 In this respect, the United Kingdom represented an exception that was only partially offset by the quality of its scholars.
22 Today the Verein is the association of German-speaking economists (including Austrian and Swiss economists). In 1956 the name of 'Gesellschaft für Wirtschafts- und Sozialwissenschaften' was added, 'to steer clear of misinterpretations of its name and activities in the narrow sense of social policy' (Hagemann and Trautwein 1999: 8).
23 This association – without doubt the best known and the one having the largest membership – has nowadays a scientific and professional character.
24 The Japanese Economic Society was established in 1934.
25 The Società Italiana degli Economisti was founded as late as 1950. See Quadrio Curzio 1998.

References

Agulhon, M. (1979) *La République au village. Les populations du Var de la Révolution à la IIe République*, Paris: Seuil.

Asso, P.F. (2000) 'La Società italiana di economia politica di Firenze (1868–1882)', in Augello and Guidi (2000).

Augello, M.M. (1989) 'The Societies of Political Economy in Italy and the Professionalization of Economists (1860–1900)', *History of Economics Society Bulletin*, 11, 1: 99–112.

—— (ed.) (1995) *L'economia politica nell'Italia di fine Ottocento. Il dibattito sulle riviste*, special issue of *Il pensiero economico italiano*, 3, 2.

Augello, M.M., Bianchini, M., Gioli, G. and Roggi P. (eds) (1988) *Le cattedre di economia in Italia (1700–1900). La nascita di una disciplina 'sospetta'*, Milano: Angeli.

Augello, M.M., Bianchini, M., and Guidi, M.E.L. (eds) (1996) *Le riviste di economia in Italia (1700–1900). Dai giornali scientifico-letterari ai periodici specialistici*, Milano: Angeli.

Augello, M.M. and Guidi, M.E.L. (eds) (2000) *Associazionismo economico e diffusione dell'economia politica nell'Italia dell'Ottocento. Dalle società economico-agrarie alle associazioni di economisti*, 2 vols, Milano: Angeli.

Barber, W.J. (1987) 'Should the American Economic Association Have Toasted Simon Newcomb at Its 100th Birthday Party?', *Journal of Economic Perspectives*, 1, 1: 179–83.

—— (ed.) (1988) *Breaking the Mould. The Development of Academic Economics in XIX Century America*, Middletown, CT: Wesleyan University Press.

Becattini, G. (1989) 'Sectors and/or Districts: Some Remarks on the Conceptual Foundations of Industrial Economics', in E. Goodman and J. Bamford (eds) *Small Firms and Industrial Districts in Italy*, London: Routledge.

Bentham, J. (1952) [1787] *Defence of Usury*, in W. Stark (ed.) *Jeremy Bentham's Economic Writings*, vol. 1, London: Macmillan.

Bianchini, M. (1996) *Political Economy in European Periodicals, 1750–1900*, special issue of *History of Economc Ideas*, 4, 3.

Brunner, O. (1968) *Neue Wege der Verfassungs- und Sozialgeschichte*, Göttingen: Vandenhoeck & Ruprecht.

Burrage, M. and Torstendahl, R. (eds) (1990) *Professions in Theory and History. Rethinking the Study of the Professions*, London: Sage.

Church, R. (1974) 'Economists as Experts. The Rise of an Academic Profession in the United States, 1870–1920', in L. Stone (ed.) *The University in Society*, vol. 2, Princeton: Princeton University Press.

Coats, A.W. (1988) 'National Styles in Contemporary Economics: Some Introductory Remarks', *History of Economics Society Bulletin*, 10, 2: 145–6.

—— (1991) 'Economics as a Profession', in Coats (1993).

—— (1993) *The Sociology and Professionalization of Economics, British and American Economic Essays*, London and New York: Routledge.

—— (ed.) (1996) *The Post-1945 Internationalization of Economics*, annual supplement to vol. 28 of *History of Political Economy*, Durham, NC and London: Duke University Press.

Enciso Recio, L.M. (1996) 'Las Sociedades Económicas de Amigos del País', in *Le società economiche alla prova della storia (secoli XVIII–XIX)*, Atti del Convegno Internazionale di studi, Chiavari, 16, 17, 18 maggio 1991, Rapallo: Azienda Grafica Busco.

Frigo, D. (1985) *Il padre di famiglia. Governo della casa e governo civile nella tradizione dell''economica' tra Cinque e Seicento*, Roma: Bulzoni.

Fumian, C. (1995) 'Il senno delle nazioni. I congressi degli scienziati italiani dell'Ottocento: una prospettiva comparata', *Meridiana. Rivista di Storia e Scienze Sociali*, 24: 95–124.

Genovesi, A. (1803) [1766–7] *Lezioni di economia civile*, in *Scrittori classici italiani di economia politica*, vols VII–IX, Milano: Destefanis.

Gioia, M. (1818) *Del merito e delle ricompense*, Milano: Gio. Pirotta.

Guidi, M.E.L. (2001) 'L'industrie inventive dans les premières réflexions de Bentham sur l'économie politique (1778–1787)', in A.L. Cot (ed.) *L'utilitarisme: analyse et histoire*, Lille: Presses Universitaires de Lille.

Habermas, J. (1989) [1961] *The Structural Transformation of the Public Sphere. An Inquiry into a Category of Bourgeois Society*, Cambridge, MA: MIT Press.

Hagemann, H. and Trautwein, H.-M. (1999) 'Verein für Socialpolitik – the Association of German-speaking Economists', *Newsletter of the Royal Economic Society*, 107: 7–9.

Henderson, P.J. (1983) 'The Oral Tradition in British Economics: Influential Economists in the Political Economy Club of London', *History of Political Economy* 15, 2: 149–79.

Kadish, A. and Tribe, K. (eds) (1993) *The Market for Political Economy. The Advent of Economics in British University Culture, 1850–1905*, London: Routledge.

Laurent, E. and Marco, L. (1996) 'Le *Journal des économistes*, ou l'apologie du libéralisme (1841–1940)', in Marco (1996).

Le Van-Lemesle, L. (ed.) (1986) *Les problèmes de l'institutionnalisation de l'économie politique en France au XIX siècle*, special issue of *Economies et Sociétés*, série *Oeconomia*, PE n. 6.

—— (1996) 'Nineteenth-century economic reviews in France', in Bianchini (1996).

Llombart, V. (1992) *Campomanes, economista y politico de Carlos III*, Madrid: Alianza Editorial.

Malatesta, M. (ed.) (1995) *Society and the Professions in Italy, 1860–1914*, Cambridge: Cambridge University Press.

Maneschi, A. (1998) *Comparative Advantage in International Trade. A Historical Perspective*, Cheltenham and Northampton, MA: Elgar.

Marco, L. (ed.) (1996) *Les revues d'économie en France. Genèse et actualité (1751–1994)*, Paris: L'Harmattan.

Pecorari, P. (2000) 'L'Unione cattolica per gli studi sociali in Italia dalle origini (1889) alla fine dell'Ottocento', in Augello and Guidi (2000).

Perrot, J.-C. (1992) [1988] 'Economie politique', in *Une histoire intellectuelle de l'économie politique (XVIIe–XVIIIe siècle)*, Paris: Editions de l'Ecole des Hautes Etudes en Sciences Sociales.

Quadrio Curzio, A. (ed.) (1998) *Gli economisti italiani nella loro Associazione. Materiali per 50 anni della SIE*, Ancona: Società Italiana degli Economisti.

Roche, D. (1978) *Le siècle des Lumières en province. Académies et académiciens provinciaux 1660–1789*, Paris: Mouton.

Rosenberg, N. (1994) 'Charles Babbage: Pioneer Economist', in *Exploring the Black Box: Technology, Economics and History*, Cambridge : Cambridge University Press.

Say, J.-B. (1843) *Cours Complet d'économie politique pratique*, Bruxelles: Société typographique belge.

Smith, A. (1976) [1776] *An Inquiry into the Nature and Causes of the Wealth of Nations*, R.H. Campbell, A.S. Skinner and W.B. Todd (eds), Oxford: Oxford University Press.

Steiner, Ph. (1997) 'Politique et économie politique chez J.-B. Say', *Revue française d'histoire des idées politiques*, 3: 23–58.

—— (1998) *Sociologie de la connaissance économique. Essai sur la rationalisation de la connaissance économique (1750–1850)*, Paris: Puf.

Stigler, G. (1965) 'Statistical Studies in the History of Economic Thought', in *Essays in the History of Economics*, Chicago: University of Chicago Press.

Sugiyama, C. and Mizuta, H. (eds) (1988) *Enlightenment and Beyond: Political Economy Comes to Japan*, Tokyo: University of Tokyo Press.

Torcellan, G. (1964) 'Un tema di ricerca: le accademie agrarie del Settecento', *Rivista storica italiana*, 76, 2: 530–52.

Waszek, N. (ed.) (1988) *Die Institutionalisierung der Nationalökonomie an deutschen Universitäten*, St. Katharinen: Scripta Mercaturae Verlag.

Winch, D. (1983) 'Higher Maxims: Happiness versus Wealth in Malthus and Ricardo', in S. Collini, D. Winch and J. Burrow, *That Noble Science of Politics. A Study in Nineteenth-century Intellectual History*, Cambridge: Cambridge University Press.

—— (1994), 'Nationalism and Cosmopolitanism in the Early Histories of Political Economy', in M. Albertone and A. Masoero (eds) *Political Economy and National Realities*, Torino: Fondazione L. Einaudi.

2 Economic societies in Great Britain and Ireland

Keith Tribe

In Britain public discussion of political economy and economic issues was during the later eighteenth and early nineteenth centuries something that for the most part took place in print. The suppression of Jacobin and revolutionary clubs in the mid-1790s had deterred respectable literary and philosophical societies from debating matters bearing on politics, a taboo which lasted well into the post-war period; public discussion of political economy, it was thought, might all too readily become socially divisive, or even seditious. When in 1821 the Political Economy Club (hereafter: PEC) formed in London it was a dining club limited to thirty members. Discussion was therefore conducted behind closed doors and between a select group of elected members and their guests. Not until the 1830s did respectable people moot the possibility of systematically diffusing political economy through open meetings, by which time the movement for social and political reform had once more established itself in the mainstream of public life. These restrictions did not apply however to the publication of pamphlets and books or, with the foundation of the *Edinburgh Review* in 1802 (Fontana 1985; Fetter 1965), to periodicals which reviewed recent books. Later in the century the work of political economists appeared in literary publications such as the *Fortnightly Review*, emphasising the lasting importance of general periodicals for an educated reading public in the dissemination of the work of Jevons (1876) and Cairnes (1872), for example. In addition to this, the *Journal of the Statistical Society of London* regularly published papers related to economic affairs, where of course the focus was upon practical and policy matters, and not the development of economic theory. For political economy was widely understood in the early nineteenth century to be a practical, rather than a theoretical, science.

The first specialist economic publication, the *Economic Journal*, appeared shortly before the end of the century;[1] although distinguished by its specialised appeal, it was from the first committed to representing all leading contemporary schools and opinions (Tribe 1992). This intent was effected through the formation of the British Economic Association (hereafter: BEA; from 1902 the Royal Economic Society; hereafter: RES) as its parent organisation. Departing from the example provided by the

Quarterly Journal of Economics (published from Harvard since October 1886), the principle purpose of the Society was to establish a management committee and appoint an editor answerable to a broad membership, and not to any one department or organisation. The founders had considered the possibility of staging regular open meetings of the Society, but rejected this on the grounds that many members did not live in London, while for those that did the opportunity for discussion was already available at the PEC and the Statistical Society.[2] Not until the formation in the mid-1920s of the Association of Teachers of Economics was there in Britain a regular annual forum for open discussion among academic economists. As we shall see, academics were originally in a small minority among the membership of the BEA, although its organ, the *Economic Journal*, quickly established a reputation for academic respectability and impartiality, and the leading positions in the Association and Society were from the beginning over-whelmingly held by senior academics.

1 The chronology in outline

The early history of the BEA has been outlined in a number of articles by Bob Coats (1968, 1970, 1973), heavily coloured however by his strong comparative interest in the role played by economic societies in the emergence of an economics 'profession'. From this perspective the early history of economic societies in Britain can be quickly recounted in the following manner (see Henderson 1996). In 1821 the PEC was formed by Thomas Tooke as a private dining club which would meet on a regular basis to debate matters relating to political economy, especially the desirability of free trade. Meetings of the Club were attended over the course of the century by eminent economists, but the membership was always dominated by politicians and businessmen whose grasp of the developing corpus of economic principles was often tenuous. The formation of the British Association for the Advancement of Science in 1831 represented a more significant development, for it was an organisation dedicated to promoting scientific discussion among the intelligentsia, doing so by staging an annual conference in the cities and towns of Britain. The British Association provided the first national, open forum for such discussion, and its peripatetic, annual representation of this principle was the original model for the modern academic conference. In 1833 the Association was due to meet in Cambridge, which brought the Belgian statistician and sociologist Adolphe Quetelet in contact with Richard Jones, as a friend of Babbage and of Whewell. Jones was also on good terms with Malthus, who at that time lived and taught at the East India College in nearby Hertford, and so a meeting was organised in Jones' rooms, chaired by Malthus, to discuss the formation of a 'statistical section' of the British Association. 'Section F', as it became, had its founding meeting in late June as part of the British Association (Cullen 1975: 77–82). This created a more public forum for the discussion of practical and theoretical issues connected with political economy, especially after 1856, when it became the 'Section for Economic Science and Statistics'.

A more specialised forum was created in 1834 with the foundation of the London Statistical Society, a society whose principal purpose was progressive social reform, the framework within which the work of political economy was primarily conceived by those interested in it. In 1838 the London Society began regular publication of a journal, and although other provincial statistical societies were founded, the London Society quickly assumed the role of a national organisation dedicated to the discussion of issues related to social reform. In 1887 it became the Royal Statistical Society, and as Coats noted, Marshall for some time nurtured the idea of the BEA as a sub-group of the Statistical Society in a relationship analogous to that between the British Association and its Section F. Although the Royal Statistical Society offered a more specialised and permanent constituency for economists than the British Association and the annual meeting of Section F, the breadth of its concerns remained a problem for an emergent discipline seeking to establish its own forum capable, not least, of communicating on equal terms with similar associations forming in the United States and continental Europe. The creation of the BEA, itself one element of Marshall's strategy for the promotion of economic science, provided such a forum, and with it, so the story goes, a vehicle for the professionalisation of economics.

2 The problem of 'professionalisation'

Although this outline provides a rough-and-ready background to the development of the RES as a national economic association, the habit of conceiving this story in terms of the rise of a professional economics supposes that university economics is 'professional' economics and that, therefore, 'professional economists' are academically qualified practitioners of the subject, primarily teachers of the subject. Embedded in this 'professionalisation' model is an assumption that the aspirations and purposes of those who founded the BEA have been fully realised in the structures with which we are familiar today. For Coats, a 'professional' economist is a university-trained economist, and it appears natural that the history of 'professionalisation' of economics in Britain should therefore centre upon the formation of the BEA/RES as a vehicle for the dissemination of academic economics. This was the first organisation formed so to do, and its success can be read out of the eminence that the organisation today enjoys as the national association for academic economists. Coats does note the fact that for much of its early life the RES was dominated by members who had neither a university qualification in economics, nor indeed any specific academic links, but this is not treated as something requiring any special explanation. In fact, it was not until perhaps the mid-twentieth century that in Britain 'economist' became an occupational description for a person with a university qualification in the subject and who was employed to teach it; hitherto it had denoted a person interested in, and with opinions upon, economic affairs, whatever their qualification or employment – a self-description which reaches back to the original members of the PEC. It is the development of university institutions in the later nineteenth and early twentieth century which effects this transition in the definition of an economist; the RES plays a part in this transition, but it is not the motive force itself.

Furthermore, some consideration has to be given to the plausibility of the sociological model of 'professionalisation' that governs Coats' approach. In the labour market, the status of 'profession' is something aspired to by occupational groups seeking legitimacy and exclusivity of practice. But adoption of this terminology overlooks the awkward fact that there remain ineradicable differences in the practical significance of skills, the ease with which competences are acquired and tested, and, once certified, practitioners regulated. Hence while the British Medical Association and the Royal College of Surgeons can with some justice be regarded as medical trade unions, they are much more than this, and very different in kind from the RES. Sociologists who themselves cannot be said to possess specialised knowledge, the acquisition and exercise of which requires particular talent and skill, are inclined to discount the (unfashionable) view that we need to be protected from negligent doctors, engineers and lawyers in a way that we do not need to be protected from bad sociologists or economists. There is indeed an extensive literature on professionalisation, but it is best disregarded in favour of two basic principles.

1   A profession is a skilled, specialised lifetime occupation, membership of which is controlled by a self-regulating association with an established monopoly over its field of expertise, from which other practitioners can be excluded, or existing members stripped of the rights and privileges conferred by membership of their association through the removal of a practising certificate, or similar sanction.
2   Emergent occupational groups aspire to the labour market advantages enjoyed by established professional groups such as lawyers, barristers, engineers and surgeons. However, while the organisations which these groups establish seek to emulate the exclusivity enjoyed by established professional associations, none of them exercise the kind of self-regulation of membership typical of the Law Society or the Institution of Electrical Engineers. *Ergo* there is no such thing as an 'economics profession'.

We need to distinguish *claims* to be a profession from the *recognition* and *legitimacy* enjoyed by genuine, self-regulating professional associations. When Coats links the formation and growth of the RES to the 'profession-alisation' of economics in Britain, the process to which he is pointing is better conceived as linked to the emergence of the modern university and the transformation of practical knowledges into academic disciplines. Henceforth identification as a 'real' mathematician or economist is linked to the study and practice of an appropriate university discipline, while 'science' becomes the impetus which shapes the subsequent growth and development of the discipline. It was the expansion of the university system in the later nineteenth century which redefined what it meant to be 'an economist', and it was this cultural mutation which prompted the creation of the BEA, and its later transformation into the RES.

3 Societies and the Enlightenment – a sketch

Although political economy had been part of formal educational structures since the early nineteenth century – at the East India College, at University College, London, and as an element of the London BA degree – during the greater part of the century familiarity with its principles was not formally acquired. When in the 1880s Sidgwick complained about the level of discussion at the PEC, he acknowledged of those members who were bankers that it would be

> [...] an exaggeration to say that they know no Political Economy; I think they read Mill some time ago and look at him from time to time on Sundays.
>
> (PEC 1921: 315)

This was a not inaccurate judgement; for the greater part of the century it was considered that an adequate knowledge of political economy could be gained through the reading of one or two books, and that the limited number of principles thereby acquired could henceforth be applied to discussion of the economic issues of the day. Not that it was in any respect unimportant for an understanding of the world; it was just not thought to be arcane or specialist knowledge. As with the political issues of the day, anyone was free to air their opinion on economic issues, and the principles of political economy consequently formed an important element in popular movements for social reform. To understand the propagation of political economy during the first two-thirds of the nineteenth century we should therefore look to those organisations formed to further social improvement. This takes us back to the societies of the mid-eighteenth century, and the project of social progress through discussion, the improvement of industry and agriculture, and popular enlightenment.

The Dublin Society for Improving Husbandry, Manufactures and other Useful Arts was among the first of such foundations, originating in 1731 and providing a model for many similar societies. The object was entirely practical, descriptions of good technique being disseminated in discussion and publication. The most enduring and successful of these foundations was the Society for the Encouragement of Arts, Manufactures and Commerce,[3] inaugurated in 1754 and generally referred to as the 'Society of Arts'. Those present at its first meeting noted that cobalt and madder, basic to the dyeing of textiles, were currently imported at great expense, and a prize was offered to anyone discovering a source of cobalt in Britain and successfully cultivating madder (Hudson and Luckhurst 1954: 8). During the first one hundred years of its existence the Society offered many such prizes and reported on their outcome. Based in London, membership quickly reached 2,500, the *Museum Rusticum et Commerciale* and then later *Memoirs of Agriculture and other Oeconomical Arts* summarising its activities. In the 1840s the Society sponsored exhibitions of manufactured goods, culminating in the Great Exhibition of 1851; and then from 1856 set the first national examinations in modern and commercial subjects, written examinations being sat in forty centres in 1858 (Hudson and Luckhurst: 251). The provision of these national examinations, together with the later Cambridge local examinations, formed an important bridge in provincial Britain to the new London University BA, which was in turn the examination initially offered by most of the new city colleges of the last third of the century.

Besides the Society of Arts, dedicated to improvements in technique and practice, societies dedicated to public debate flourished in the latter part of the eighteenth century, such as the Robin Hood Society in London, the Manchester Conversation Society and the Amicable Debating Society in Birmingham (Fawcett 1986: 216–9). The broad purpose of these and many similar societies was to bring together men who, on the basis of their reading, could exercise their understanding of what they had read through public discussion. These societies were not simply vehicles for mutual education, but also for training in argument and persuasion; the Edinburgh Speculative Society was a noteworthy example of this, with a purpose-built debating chamber and a membership limited at first to twenty-five. Here Francis Horner and his contemporaries self-consciously honed their rhetorical skills before making their transition to London in the early 1800s (Fawcett 1986: 223).

The gagging acts of 1795, prompted among other things by the activities of London Jacobin clubs, had put paid to discussion of politics, and by extension political economy, in most provincial clubs and societies – and this proscription survived, self-imposed, into the 1820s and 1830s, when Mechanics' Institutes explicitly excluded discussion of political issues from their proceedings.[4] Seen in this context, it is perhaps more understandable that the public dissemination of political economy in the nineteenth century developed along two broad paths: as a subject of theoretical discussion among the members of closed dining clubs; and as a form of didactic public enlightenment. When for example John Barrington discovered that workmen at his Dublin firm had combined together with the intent of raising wages, his response was to endow a series of public lectures on political economy for the purpose of informing workers and others of their true interests. Established in 1834, administration was transferred to the Dublin Statistical Society in 1849,[5] lecturers being required to give annually eight lectures in Dublin and not less than twenty-four in four or more other Irish towns and villages. The venues at which these lectures were delivered were provided by a broad range of mechanics' institutes, literary and philosophical societies and other mutual improvement societies (Boylan and Foley 1992: 100–4). The 'diffusion of useful knowledge' in the first half of the nineteenth century was facilitated by a dense network of societies and associations of this kind in both principal cities and the provinces (Inkster 1981).

In the second half of the nineteenth century the University Extension movement assumed many of these functions, becoming in the process an important medium for the diffusion of political economy, peripatetic lecturers running courses in numerous centres throughout the country (Kadish 1993). Classes were often provided in association with the lectures, although the classes were mostly attended and essays written by students drawn from a clerical background taking this opportunity to begin working towards local examinations and, perhaps, a London BA. Those courses with predominantly working-class venues typically reported well-attended lectures, but there was little regular involvement in the associated classes. Political economy as a vehicle of social enlightenment was never therefore simply a conscious middle-class strategy for the containment of the masses, but this was the typical form in which working people approached the subject and engaged with it.

Open, public discussion of political economy was directed not to its basic principles, but was instead dominated by practical matters, linked to social reform and free trade, issues where broad public coalitions could be created. The constituency for regular and detailed discussion of the principles of political economy was generally quite small in the first half of the century; not much greater, we might suppose, than the original membership of the PEC.

4 The PEC

Although Thomas Tooke was the initiator of the PEC when it formed in April 1821, Henry Higgs surmises that the original moving spirit was David Ricardo, who had been holding regular 'economic breakfasts' at his London home in 56 Upper Brooke Street since becoming an MP. Tooke's own initiative can be traced back to a small dinner party to discuss matters relating to free trade that took place in January 1820 at the house of S.C. Holland, a Baring & Co. partner. Tooke was taken aback to find that, although all present professed allegiance to the principles of free trade, three or four of his fellow-diners had a very rudimentary grasp of political economy, and the more they talked, the greater the number of exemptions from its principles for this or that good they proposed.[6] He concluded that a means was required through which men of affairs could become better acquainted with the theoretical underpinnings of free trade. The following year a small group met in mid-April, and determined to form a society for the promotion of political economy, James Mill being responsible for the drafting of a club constitution before the next meeting on 30th April 1821. Of the seventeen men present at that meeting only six names are today readily recognisable as practising political economists: Torrens, Malthus, Ricardo, Mill, Tooke and Grote. James Mill introduced his proposed rules, beginning with the restriction of the number of members to thirty and the reservation of the first Monday of each month, December to June inclusive, for their meetings, at which they would debate questions tabled by members, all for an annual fee of 5 guineas. The member present agreed to his proposals that

> The members of this Society will regard their own mutual instruction, and the diffusion among others of just principles of political economy as a real and important obligation.
> [...] It shall be considered the duty of the Society to study the means of obtaining access to the public mind through as many as possible of the periodical publications of the day, and to influence as far as possible the tone of such publications in favour of just principles of Political Economy.[7]

However there were a number of proposals made by Mill to which the members did not agree. For example, a decision on this proposal was 'suspended':

> At each meeting the Chairman shall put to each of the members present the following questions:

> Have you read or heard of any book or other writing lately published likely in your opinion to interest the members of this Society and can you give any account of it?

> In the course of your reading or intercourse have you met with any facts or speculations which appeared to you important as regarding Political Economy?

> Have you been engaged in any conversation or discussion on subjects of Political Economy an account of which would be useful for the purposes of this meeting?

Members clearly did not wish to be quizzed too closely on their levels of activity with respect to the principles of political economy. Likewise, although it was agreed that the Press was a powerful force for good or evil to which attention should be paid, members rejected the idea that a standing committee should, between meetings, monitor newspapers and periodicals with the objective of giving effect to these sentiments. Mill clearly hoped that the PEC would be characterised by rather more missionary zeal than the founding members in fact possessed; disappointed, he later ceased attending.[8]

Membership of the PEC was by nomination and ballot, a two-thirds majority of members present being required for acceptance. Visitors were permitted, but naturally as guests of existing members. The chief function of the Club was to discuss questions proposed by members, any member being able to table as many questions as he wished, the existing list being then read out at the conclusion of each meeting, and discussed in the order that 'may seem good to the Club' (PEC 1899: 69). The published minutes record the list of questions, but not the related discussion, and so no direct assessment can be made of the tenor or quality of argument. It is clear however that questions were initially tabled faster than they could be discussed, and the fact that by the mid-1830s the minutes record only one or two questions suggests that these represent those actually discussed. It is also from about this time that the great majority of those responsible for tabling questions can consistently be identified as 'economists' rather than MPs or bankers; from which date the pattern is set that the minority of 'economists' propose the questions and, we might suppose, guide discussion, notwithstanding the constant predominance of members from the world of commerce and politics.[9] Which, as we shall see, is not far off the norm for the membership of the BEA. But first we need to deal with the relation of political economy to statistics.

5 Social reform, political economy and statistics

The British Association marked a clear break with existing societies and associations for the promotion of knowledge, formed as it was to support the staging of an annual conference whose venue altered from year to year. Its programmatic commitment to the diffusion of scientific knowledge was therefore reinforced by its peripatetic character, bringing its commitment to a succession of provincial cities whose populations were therefore exposed to national debates and issues. The first meeting was held at York in 1831, under the auspices of the Yorkshire Philosophical Society, one of the strongest of the provincial societies. York was a suitable provincial location for other reasons too: it was accessible from the major centres of population, and had strong Anglican and Dissenting traditions. The Association had in its early years a federal character, linked to the existing network of literary and philosophical societies, but its independence of any one organisation was assured by the manner in which, in the course of the annual meeting, the President and Secretaries for the following year were selected, securing the Association from domination by any one region or interest (Morrell and

Thackray 1981: 92–3). In 1833, as outlined above, the 'Statistical Section' was added. As with the Association as a whole, the Presidency of this new Section was for one year only, conferring on the incumbent organisational responsibility for the conduct of proceedings for that year, as well as the opportunity to compose a Presidential Address in which '[…] the progress of the sciences in which the members specially attached to this section are the most interested' (Chadwick 1862: 502). Here again, the very mixed constituency before which papers were read and presidential addresses delivered is an important element in appreciating the level and rate of diffusion of economic argument in nineteenth-century Britain.

'Statistics' in the sense used in the title of Section F was defined in 1833 by Sedgwick as concerned with

> […] 'matters of fact,' 'mere abstractions,' and 'numerical results', constituting what might be called 'the raw material to political economy and political philosophy,' by which perhaps 'the lasting foundations of those sciences may be ultimately laid'.
>
> (Guy 1865: 482)

This coincided of course with Richard Jones' project for an inductively founded political economy, recalling an earlier understanding of the subject as the 'anatomy of nations'. The range of topics involved was outlined in a paper presented to Section F in 1838, in which a series of categories to be used by local societies in collecting data was proposed, classified according to the following heads:

I   Physical Statistics; relating to Topography, etc.

II   Vital Statistics; relating to the Physical Being of Man.

III   Mental Statistics; relating to the Intellectual and Moral being of Man.

IV   Economic Statistics; relating to the Social Condition of Man.

V   Miscellaneous.

(Hare 1838: 427)

In the early years of the Association there was little control over who presented papers, in many sections a 'first come, first served' principle prevailing. For Section F the outcome was decidedly mixed, most of the papers being extremely descriptive, prompted by no discernible agenda. As with the PEC, those attending the annual meetings of Section F were drawn from diverse backgrounds, although teachers of political economy were always present, if not as presenters of papers. It is sometimes said that the vitality of political economy in Britain reached a low point in the 1870s, citing as evidence for this a proposal in 1877 to dissolve Section F, on the grounds that it represented interests not properly part of an organisation devoted to the advancement of science (Winch 1990: 7). The proposal came from Francis Galton, but his argument was in fact not explicitly directed against political economy; his chief complaint concerned the entirely heterogeneous nature of the statistical papers presented to the sessions of Section F. The issue first arose at the annual meeting in June 1877, and later that year Galton submitted his comments on the matter to the Council. His first line of attack was that

> The principles on which Statistics are founded are derived from the theory of probabilities, and have exercised, and will still exercise, the ingenuity of many generations of the ablest mathematicians.
>
> (Galton 1877: 469)

This is disingenuous, at best. Few articles on statistics in this modern sense were published anywhere before 1900. In the late 1890s the *Journal of the Royal Statistical Society* carried accounts of descriptive statistics broadly continuous with its coverage of the 1840s; at most Galton, Edgeworth and one or two others would have at this time have had any understanding of this line of argument (Stigler 1986: chs 7 & 8).

Secondly, Galton listed, in just under two pages, the titles of papers read before Section F between the years 1873 and 1875. This is a mélange of topics loosely related to economic matters not seriously different in overall scope to the papers which appeared in the early years of the *Economic Journal*, and simply reflects the prevailing diffuse interest in matters of social and economic reform.[10] His third line of argument was that the subjects 'commonly brought before Section F cannot be considered scientific in the sense of the word that is sanctioned by the usages of the British Association' (Galton 1877: 472). If the Section was suppressed, he suggested that discussion would readily find a forum at the congresses of the Social Science Association, where there 'will always be a larger gathering of experts in these subjects'.

The other paper submitted to the Council pointed out that the papers listed by Galton belonged in the long line of 'vital statistics', named as such first by Laplace. A letter appended, from Giffen and Chubb as secretaries of the Section, underlined this objection, also noting that Section F was, more than the other sections, exposed to the attentions of non-specialists:

> Its subjects are also those of practical politics and philanthropy, and this brings to the discussion people who are politicians and philanthropists, but who are not men of science. For the same reason, the discussions on

such subjects, whether scientific or not, are likely to be better reported than purely scientific discussions.[11]

A further defence of Section F was published in *The Economist* for 8th September 1877, signed 'F. R. S.' The important point was made here that, while the next incumbent President of the British Association was nominated one year in advance, this was not the case for the individual sections, where the individual Section Heads were sometimes appointed just a few weeks in advance of the annual meeting. They were not therefore in a position to choose their speakers, let alone a common theme for discussion, and as a consequence papers were presented by those who happened to turn up on the day. In the case of Section F, this writer also made the entirely sensible suggestion that the London Statistical Society should establish a standing committee charged with providing assistance to the President-elect of the Section, enabling a programme of papers to be determined in advance and to arrange that each session was attended by those capable of sustaining scientific discussion.

The proposal to exclude Section F from the meetings of the British Association turns therefore not upon the lack of development of political economy, but rather on an organisational problem that reveals something rather different about the condition of political economy in later nineteenth-century Britain than customarily assumed. There was indeed widespread interest in the subject matter with which it dealt; but popular understanding linked it firmly to social reform, and did not regard it primarily as a theoretical enterprise whose principles required extensive public debate. Galton's listing of the papers presented over a three-year period unintentionally lends insight into the contemporary vitality of interest in political economy. As the University Extension movement of the later nineteenth century demonstrated, there was indeed a wide interest in economic issues; but this interest was informed by only the most rudimentary knowledge of economic principles. The early economic societies reflect both this interest and the generally low level of economic debate; a condition that has not, after all, altered a great deal over the last one hundred years. What has changed in the last one hundred years, of course, is that modern economics is academic economics, an elaborated university discipline based around a set of principles on which several generations of students have been drilled. But this substantial educational programme has, by and large, failed to make a significant impact upon popular political culture. In fact, one could reverse the assumptions usually made concerning the relentless progress of the sciences and suggest that the movement for social reform in the latter half of the nineteenth century was in important respects more broadly based and better informed on economic matters than its modern counterparts. This might seem a rash judgement, until one reflects that much of modern public discussion on issues of social and economic policy is heavily coloured by economic ideologies of one shade or another. True, nineteenth-century reformers had in common a belief that social improvement resulted from the intervention of public (primarily municipal) institutions. But then the principles of free trade have little worthwhile to contribute to the provision of clean drinking water or unadulterated bread. The papers presented at the Social Science Association provide a clearer idea of these practical concerns associated with political economy in the latter half of the nineteenth century.

The National Association for the Moral and Social Improvement of the People was founded at Brougham's London house in July 1857; the term 'social science' was only introduced shortly before the first meeting in Birmingham later that year (Goldman 1987: 139). This initiated a series annual, peripatetic week-long meetings modelled on the practice of the British Association, the organisation finally dissolving in 1886. Its deliberations were divided among five sections: 'Jurisprudence and the Amendment of the Law', 'Education', 'Punishment and Reformation', 'Public Health' and 'Social Economy' (later the 'Economy and Trade' Department) (Goldman 1986: 97). Whereas the purpose of the British Association was to diffuse an understanding of science, the emphasis in the Social Science Association was to provide a forum through which pressure could be brought to bear upon central and local government for reform. The inaugural General Committee, for example, included eighteen peers, twenty-eight MPs, Edwin Chadwick, Kay-Shuttleworth, Mill, Ruskin, Kingsley and Maurice. Its formation resulted from the convergence of three areas of interest: in penal reform, in the legal emancipation of women and in the reform of legal procedure. Despite some adverse comments from Sidgwick, who found the level of debate at the meetings extremely low, it attracted perhaps a less disparate range of speakers than Section F, presumably because of its orientation to social science (i.e. 'reform') rather than statistics. Papers presented to the Social Economy section at the 1862 meeting in London, for example, were arranged in groups such as 'Employers and Employed', 'Co-operation', 'Condition of the Working Classes', 'The Poor Laws' and 'Taxation', an altogether narrower range than that typical at a contemporary meeting of Section F.

That Jevons chose Section F that year as the appropriate forum for the presentation of his paper on mathematical economics, and not the meeting of the Social Science Association, confirms however that this was not a forum open to general discussion of political economy. Issues of theoretical principle would at most appear in the addresses given by the President of each section, as for example did Bonamy Price in 1882 in Nottingham, where he contrasted the respective merits of 'free' and 'fair' trade, rehearsing principles that would have probably been entirely familiar to Tooke some sixty years earlier (Price 1883). The existence of the Association does however underline the presence of a substantial constituency for the discussion of social improvement in later nineteenth-century Britain, a constituency which in all likelihood accepted Brougham's contention in his inaugural address that 'social economy' is the section 'most of all connected with the sister departments' (Brougham 1858: 14). If it draws attention to the breadth of interest in political economy at this time, it does also testify to the general lack of depth in that interest, a feature underscored by the small number of students that Marshall was attracting to his teaching on the Moral Sciences Tripos in Cambridge in the later 1880s and 1890s. Contemporary reports of the formation of the BEA attest to the interest which it aroused, as do newspaper summaries of current *Economic Journal* articles that are collected together in the RES archive.[12] But, as with the PEC, academic economists were here once more in a very definite minority.

6 The BEA

The BEA, chartered as the RES in 1902, had a very different function from all of the bodies discussed so far. Its primary purpose was to provide an organisational structure that would prevent monopoly of its new journal by any one school or tendency. An additional function was to perform the role of a reprint society for economic treatises, a function which the Society continues today. The editor of the *Economic Journal* was to be responsible to an editorial committee answering to a national association, not to a publisher or to an independent editorial board as was the case with other new journals of the time. Moreover, the BEA was in turn, as the opening lines of the first issue of its journal stated, 'open to all schools and parties. [...] The most opposite doctrines may meet here as on a fair field'.[13]

Definite proposals for the formation of an economic society and the publication of a specialist journal date from the early 1880s, when Foxwell roughed out a plan for a new association. He did not however have the institutional weight necessary to realise the plan, and it was Alfred Marshall, President of Section F in 1890, who eventually adopted the scheme and brought it into being. Early proposals had invoked the model of *Mind* and the *English Historical Review* (Kadish and Freeman 1990: 32 fn. 2); but by the time Marshall circulated a paper to the Committee of Section F of the British Association containing proposals for the establishment of an economic society and journal, appropriate examples both of an association and a journal were to be found in the United States. Some months later, when the formal invitation to the inaugural meeting of the BEA was issued,[14] this proposal to found a journal was elaborated in terms of the need for an 'easy means of communication' among English economists, and it was suggested that the future journal might be made up of a long article, two or three shorter articles, reports from foreign correspondents and a bibliography of recent economic literature.

In his flysheet Marshall argued the need for a new journal in the following terms:

> The need of an economic journal has long been felt in England. Every other country in which economic studies are pursued with great activity,

offers facilities for the publication of thorough scientific work by persons who have not the time, or are unwilling, to write a formal treatise. Since isolated pamphlets, however able, seldom obtain any considerable circulation, Englishmen who have something to say that is too technical for the ordinary magazines, and too short for a book, are sometimes compelled to give their views to the world in the columns of a foreign periodical, or as a publication of the American Economic Association; but more frequently they put it aside till an opportunity should offer for working it out more fully and publishing it as a book; and that opportunity too often does not come. A strong and widespread feeling that English economists, and especially the younger men among them, are thus placed at a great disadvantage through the want of any easy means of communication with one another, has led to the holding of many private meetings and discussions on the subject in Oxford, Cambridge, London, and possibly elsewhere; and lately the matter has come under consideration of the Committee of Section F (Economics and Statistics) of the British Association.[15]

Besides the proposal to issue reprints of scarce economic tracts, Marshall suggested that the proposed association could perhaps be later extended in scope by staging regular meetings and even supporting economic investigations of a kind not easily conducted by government departments, on the lines presumably of the Verein für Socialpolitik.

The inaugural meeting, held at University College, London on 20th November 1890, attracted around 200 people, a detailed report and a leading article appearing in *The Times* of the following day. The first resolution was read out by Goschen, Chairman of the meeting and Chancellor of the Exchequer:

That it is expedient to form an association for the advancement of economic knowledge by the issue of a journal and other printed publications, and by such other means as the association may from time to time agree to adopt.[16]

In proposing the motion Marshall noted that he was speaking first on the subject because he happened to be the Chairman of Section F that year. Although the matter had been under discussion for some time, he was not of the opinion that the delay in forming an English society was a cause for great concern, that it was something that should properly have been done many years before. He suggested that there had indeed been a lack of impetus among English economists, but attributed this to the death of four leading representatives of the science in the early 1870s, all of them dying prematurely – Cairnes, Jevons, Bagehot and Cliffe Leslie. Happily, he went on, there was now a large number of able young men at Oxford and

Cambridge, a typical case of Marshall's habit of justifying his arguments by reference to empirical facts of dubious veracity.

Giffen seconded the motion, which was carried unanimously. Leonard Courtney then went on to move the second resolution, concerning membership:

> That any person who desires to further the aims of the association, and is approved by the council, be admitted to membership; and that the annual membership be fixed for the present at one guinea.

Seconded by Edgeworth, this was likewise carried unanimously, establishing the important principle that membership of the BEA/RES was open to anyone who cared to pay the appropriate fee, subject to formal approval by the Council, whose membership was the next item on the agenda. Foxwell moved that those present constitute themselves as members of the BEA and proceed to elect from among themselves a committee to draft its rules, the members of the committee being the founding Council members. The list of nominees for membership of this committee were however unrepresentative of the meeting as a whole, being composed chiefly of academics and teachers of economics, setting a pattern in the relationship between the structure of the membership of the Association and that of its officers which persisted into the later twentieth century.[17] A printed list of members from later in 1891 underlines this discrepancy; including some 470 names, it includes only eleven women, few foreigners,[18] a minority of teachers of economics and thirty-one MPs.

The Committee immediately held a brief meeting at which Goschen was elected President, Edgeworth provisionally nominated as editor of the new journal and an executive committee formed.[19] This new, smaller, committee then met a few days later in Giffen's Whitehall offices and began a series of meetings which were devoted to drafting rules, soliciting members, determining levels of subscription and, interestingly, deciding upon the level of payment for contributors to the *Economic Journal*.[20] Coats estimates that by the time the new journal appeared in late March 1891 membership was around 500, rising by the end of 1891 to 710. Broken down into broad occupational categories, the structure of the membership for late 1891 looks remarkably similar to that of the constituency for political economy that we have noted above – diverse, unspecialised, with teachers of economics at any level in a distinct minority (Coats 1968: 37):

Business	113
University teachers[21]	86
Law	51
Bankers	48
Civil service	44
Administration	29

Landowners, etc.	22
Accounting	16
Church	16
Journalism	16
Misc.	14
School and college teachers	13
Government	12
Army	8
Insurance	7
Medicine	6
Total	501

Any detailed study of the RES membership over the years is hampered by lack of information on occupation and educational background in the records, but even a casual survey of the records shows that this early structure, in which a non-specialist constituency dominated the membership which was in turn dominated by a small number of academic economists, persisted well into the twentieth century. On the other hand, the journal which the BEA was formed to oversee established a high academic reputation from the outset. Seven years after the foundation of the Association, the Council was able to summarise its position as follows:

[The Association] has made economists better known to each other than before; it has brought many of them into conference in the pages of the Journal, and it has multiplied their opportunities for personal acquaintance. [...] A mere glance at the Contents of the seven volumes will be enough to show that the spirit of the Journal has been the spirit of the founders of the Association. As was said on the first page of the first number, both Association and Journal are 'open to all schools and parties'. This toleration has been a discipline for the authors as well as for the Editors, and (it may be hoped) for the readers. The effect has been not to accentuate, but gradually to tone down, the acrimony of partisanship. Writers have become aware that they are addressing not only their own friends, but friendly, and even unfriendly, critics, as well as a number of readers to whom their ideas are entirely novel and incredible. On the whole there have been few pitched battles. Economic instruction has proceeded in the safer though less exciting way of constructive essay, not of course uncritical or uncriticised.[22]

7 Concluding remarks

Although academic economists were in a distinct minority in the BEA, it was nevertheless run for their benefit alone and no advantage was taken of the evident heterogeneity among the membership, which might well have focused attention on the real tasks of *internal* education that the organisation faced. Sidgwick might complain about his bankers at the PEC, but there was never any intention of using the BEA as a vehicle to address this important problem. Instead, the journal which it had been founded to promote followed an entirely academic path of development, edited by academics for the consumption of academics. In this respect it might be suggested that the BEA broke with the conception of an economic society as a focus of discussion and popular enlightenment that has been traced above, reaching back into the eighteenth century.

Notes

1 Discounting the *Economic Review*, which appeared in January 1891 shortly before the first issue of the *Economic Journal* (in March 1891); the *Review* was a publication of the Oxford University Branch of the Christian Social Union dominated by contributions from members of the University, was dedicated to social and ethical questions, and ceased publication in 1914. I am also of course excluding *The Economist*, which has always reported on current economic affairs from a liberal perspective; it is not an economic journal in the sense used here; see Edwards 1993.

2 Marshall responding to Hyde Clarke at the inaugural meeting, *The Times*, 1890, 21st November; 'Proposed English Economic Association', Royal Economic Society Minute Books, vol. I 1890–1921 f. 2 (British Library of Economic and Political Science Archives, Royal Economic Society Papers 2/1/1; henceforth BLPES RES Archive).

3 In 1908 this became the Royal Society of Arts.

4 George Birkbeck, opening the London Mechanics Institution in 1823, stated that 'All intention of interference with political questions we do therefore disclaim. [...] If indirectly we shall be supposed to exercise any influence, – and education may extend the views of the Mechanic, – I am persuaded we shall invigorate the attachment which must ever exist to every wise and well-constructed system of legislation' (Kelly 1970: 122).

5 See Daly 1997 for an account of the Dublin Statistical Society.

6 H. Higgs, 'Introduction' to PEC (1921): x.

7 Meeting of 30th April 1821, Freemason's Tavern, in PEC 1921: 3, 5.

8 As noted by Mallet in his diary for 15th April 1831, in PEC 1921: 224.

9 The first meeting of the Club in 1900, on 2nd February, was attended by fifteen members, only four of whom (Llewellyn Smith, Hewins, Foxwell and Higgs) could be described as 'economists' in the modern sense. (Llewellyn Smith was at this time First Commissioner for Labour in the Board of Trade.) (PEC 1899: 127).

10 For example, 'Industrial Schools', 'Education Statistics of Bradford', 'Prevailing Mode of Preparation for Competitive Examinations', 'Economical Aspects of Endowments of Education and Original Research', to select four successive titles at random.

11 R. Giffen, H. Chubb, letter of 13 July appended to 'Considerations, in the form of a Draft Report, submitted to Committee, favourable to the maintenance of Section F. By Dr. W. Farr', in *Journal of the Statistical Society of London*, 1877, vol. 40, September, p. 475.

12 The volume 'Newspaper cuttings 1890–1895' (BLPES RES Archive 1/3/2) is for the most part composed of resumés of articles in the latest issue of the *Economic Journal* which appeared in the contemporary press.

13 'The British Economic Association', *Economic Journal*, 1891, vol. 1, p. 1.

14 The RES files contain four successive printed versions of the flysheet drafted over the summer.
15 A. Marshall, 'Proposal to Form an English Economic Association' (24th October 1890), flysheet in 'BEA 1890 – correspondence', BLPES RES archive 1/1/2.
16 'Proposed English Economic Association', *The Times*, 1890, 21st November.
17 *The Times* report listed the nominees as: A.H.D. Acland, James Bonar, Charles Booth, John Burnett, John Burt, Prof. Edward Caird, Leonard Courtney, Rev. Dr. Cunningham, Prof. Edgeworth, T.H. Elliott, Sir Thomas Farrer, Prof. Foxwell, Robert Giffen, Mr. E.C.K. Gonner, G.J. Goschen, George Howell, Prof. Ingram, J.N. Keynes, Sir John Lubbock, Prof. Marshall, J.B. Martin, Prof. Munro, Prof. Nicholson, Mr. Inglis Palgrave, Mr. L.L. Price, Rev. L.R. Phelps, Sir Rawson Rawson, Frederick Seebohm, Prof. Sedgwick [sic], H. Llewellyn Smith, Rev. Philip Wicksteed; *The Times*, 1890, 21st November.
18 The list includes the names of Emile Cheysson, Lujo Brentano, Gustav von Schmoller, Frank Taussig, and Léon Walras – 'List of Members of the British Economic Association 1891', BLPES RES Archive 1/1/1.
19 Meeting of Committee, 20th November 1890, Royal Economic Society Minute Book 1890–1921, BLPES RES Archive 2/1/1 f. 3; the Executive Committee was composed of Foxwell, Marshall, Munro, Sidgwick, Bonar, Cunningham, Elliott, Giffen, Martin, Palgrave and Price.
20 These were fixed at 10s. a page for an article, and 5s. for reviewers and translators – meeting of 10th April 1891, RES Minute Book 1890–1921 f. 4.
21 Note that at this time in England there were only three economists who could be considered full-time – Marshall, Flux and Gonner. This category should not therefore be read as representative of 'university teachers of economics', but includes all members who were associated with university institutions in one way or another.
22 Council of the British Economic Association, 'After Seven Years', *Economic Journal*, 1898, vol. 8, p. 1.

References

Boylan, T.A. and Foley, T.P. (1992) *Political Economy and Colonial Ireland*, London: Routledge.
Brougham (1858) 'Inaugural Address by the Right Honourable Lord Brougham and Vaux, President of the Association', *Transactions of the National Association for the Promotion of Social Science. 1857*, London: Longmans, Green and Co.
Cairnes, J.E. (1872) 'New Theories in Political Economy', *Fortnightly Review* 11: 71–6.
Chadwick, E. (1862) 'Opening Address of the President of Section F (Economic Science and Statistics) of the British Association for the Advancement of Science, at the Thirty-Second Meeting, at Cambridge, in October, 1862', *Journal of the Statistical Society of London* 25: 502–24.
Coats, A.W. (1968) 'The Origins and Early Development of the Royal Economic Society', *Economic Journal* 78: 349–71.
Coats, A.W. (1973) 'The Changing Social Composition of the Royal Economic Society 1890–1960 and the Professionalization of British Economics', *British Journal of Sociology* 24: 165–87.
Coats, A.W. with Coats, S.E. (1970) 'The Social Composition of the Royal Economic Society and the Beginnings of the British Economics "Profession", 1890–1915', *British Journal of Sociology* 21: 75–85.

Cullen, M.J. (1975) *The Statistical Movement in Early Victorian Britain*, Hassocks: Harvester Press.

Daly, M.E. (1997) *The Spirit of Earnest Inquiry*, Dublin: Dublin Statistical Society.

Edwards, R.D. (1993) *The Pursuit of Reason. The Economist 1843–1993*, London: Hamish Hamilton.

Fawcett, T. (1986) 'Eighteenth-Century Debating Societies', *British Journal of Eighteenth Century Studies* 3: 216–29.

Fetter, F.W. (1965) 'Economic Controversy in the British Reviews 1802–50', *Economica* 32: 424–37.

Fontana, B. (1985) *Rethinking the Politics of Commercial Society: The 'Edinburgh Review' 1802–1832*, Cambridge: Cambridge University Press.

F.R.S. (1877) 'The Proposed Discontinuance of Section F, Economic Science and Statistics, at the British Association', *Journal of the Statistical Society of London* 40: 631–3.

Galton, F. (1877) 'Economic Science and the British Association', *Journal of the Statistical Society of London* 40: 468–73.

Goldman, L. (1986) 'The Social Sciences Association, 1857–1886: A Context for mid-Victorian Liberalism', *English Historical Review* 101: 95–134.

—— (1987) 'A Peculiarity of the English? The Social Science Association and the Absence of Sociology in Nineteenth-Century Britain', *Past and Present* 114: 133–77.

Guy, W.A. (1865) 'On the Original and Acquired Meaning of the term "Statistics", and on the Proper Functions of a Statistical Society: also on the Question Whether There be a Science of Statistics; and if so, what are its Nature and Objects, and what is its Relation to Political Economy and "Social Science" ', *Journal of the Statistical Society of London* 28: 478–93.

Hare, S. (1838) 'Abstract of Outline of Subjects for Statistical Enquiries', *Journal of the Statistical Society of London* 1: 426–7.

Henderson, J.P. (1996) 'Emerging Learned Societies: Economic Ideas in Context', *Journal of the History of Economic Thought* 18: 186–206.

Hudson, D. and Luckhurst, K.W. (1954) *The Royal Society of Arts 1754–1954*, London: John Murray.

Inkster, I. (1981) 'The Public Lecture as an Instrument of Science Education for Adults – The Case of Great Britain, *c.*1750–1850', *Paedogogica Historica* 20: 80–107.

Jevons, W.S. (1876) 'The Future of Political Economy', *Fortnightly Review* 26.

Kadish, A. (1993) 'The Teaching of Political Economy in the Extension Movement: Cambridge, London and Oxford', in A. Kadish and K. Tribe (eds) *The Market for Political Economy. The Advent of Economics in British University Culture, 1850–1905*, London: Routledge.

Kadish, A. and Freeman, R.D. (1990) 'Foundation and Early Years', in D. N. Winch (ed.) *A Century of Economics*, Oxford: Basil Blackwell.

Kelly, T. (1970) *A History of Adult Education in Britain*, 2nd edn, Liverpool: Liverpool University Press.

Morrell, J. and Thackray, A. (1981) *Gentlemen of Science. Early Years of the British Association for the Advancement of Science*, Oxford: Oxford University Press.

Political Economy Club (1899) *Minutes, Members, Attendances, And Questions. Seventeen Years, 1882 to 1899*, London: PEC.

—— (1921) *Minutes of Proceedings, 1899–1920. Roll of Members and Questions Discussed, 1821–1920. With Documents Bearing on the History of the Club*, vol. 6, London: Macmillan.

Price, B. (1883) 'Address on Economy and Trade', *Transactions of the National Association for the Promotion of Social Science. Nottingham Meeting, 1882*, London: Longmans, Green and Co.

Stigler, S.M. (1986) *The History of Statistics. The Measurement of Uncertainty before 1900*, Cambridge, MA: Harvard University Press.

Tribe, K. (1992) 'The *Economic Journal* and British Economics, 1891–1940', *History of the Human Sciences* 5: 33–58.

Winch, D.N. (1990) 'A Century of Economics', in D.N. Winch and J.D. Hey *A Century of Economics. 100 Years of the Royal Economic Society and the Economic Journal*, Oxford: Basil Blackwell.

3 The Société d'Economie Politique of Paris (1842–1914)

Yves Breton

A preliminary question that should be addressed before examining the history of the Société d'Economie Politique (hereafter: SEP) is whether any association concerned exclusively with political economy existed in Paris before its creation in 1842. This would have been unlikely before the 1830 revolution, since the Restoration was highly mistrustful of economists (Le Van-Lemesle 1991: 360–1). Nor was this state of affairs modified by the institution of the so-called 'July Monarchy' in July 1830, although in the starting period of the new regime all seemed to confirm the possibility of a change of attitude. During its first two years the new regime created a chair of political economy at the Collège de France, to which Jean-Baptiste Say was appointed (12th March 1831). The year after, the Académie des Sciences Morales et Politiques was restored and political economy was reinstated at the Institut (edict of 26th October 1832). Nevertheless, Louis-Philippe maintained an attitude of profound mistrust towards economists during the first ten years of his reign. Meetings with political economy on their agenda were treated with great suspicion and were placed under police surveillance: for example, those held in Paris between 1834 and 1837 (Courtois 1882: 6).

When the Count of Esterno attempted to create a society of economists at the very beginning of 1842, prudence was still the expedient policy. He judged it was necessary to contact Pellegrino Rossi, who had succeeded Jean-Baptiste Say at the Collège de France in 1833, in order to accomplish his project. Rossi was on better terms with those in power and succeeded in obtaining the support of the Duke of Broglie. This enabled the Esterno-Rossi society to be founded on 1st February 1842 with Charles Dunoyer as Vice-president and the Count of Esterno as Secretary. For various reasons (one was that the tone of the first meetings was judged too academic), the society soon ceased all activities (Garnier 1854: 670).

Discussions were held during the second half of 1842 about the advantages of creating a new society. The idea of meeting once a month in a restaurant where political economy would be discussed after the meal gained rapid acceptance. The new Société d'Economie Politique was created on this basis and its first meeting was held on 5th November 1842. The meeting was attended by Joseph Garnier, Adolphe Blaise, Eugène Daire, Gilbert-

Urbain Guillaumin and a fifth person, who very soon found himself out of place and who ended up arguing against political economy and defending the principle of custom tariff protection! (Courtois 1882: 2–5).

Laissez-faire economists now had at their disposal *Journal des économistes*[1] and a learned society that was to outlast the changing regimes: first the July Monarchy, which met its end in the revolutionary days of February 1848, then the Second Republic, which in its turn was replaced by the Second Empire after Louis-Napoléon Bonaparte's *coup d'état* on 2nd December 1851. The Society continued its activities when, following the defeat of the French troops by the Prussians at Sedan on 1st September 1870, the Second Empire gave way to the Third Republic, which was to last up until World War II.

The founders of the SEP firmly believed in the existence of a set of economic and moral laws whose violation would produce a negative effect on the economic and social state of nations, and the institution of the SEP was inspired by the design to fight against the widespread ignorance of these laws in France, while a parallel goal was to 'attend to the progress of political economy' (Garnier 1854: 670).

The ways in which the SEP accomplished these two missions will be examined by distinguishing between two periods: the period between 1842 and 1887, when the reform of the by-laws of the society promoted by Gustave de Molinari was introduced, and the period which spans from that date to the outbreak of World War I.

1   The SEP between 1842 and 1887[2] : from hope to disillusion

During the period between 1842 and the beginning of 1887 the SEP had neither by-laws nor regulations in a written form; it simply had 'customs, like the English parliament' (Say 1882: 528),[3] and this remained the case until January 1887. The Society members employed various means in order to achieve their aims: the Committee was strengthened and an effort was made to develop external relations (see § 1.1); the number of members was increased, and special attention was paid to the strategy of recruitment (see § 1.2); finally, most energies were employed in the organisation and dissemination of debates (see §§ 1.3 and 1.4).

1.1   *The Committee and its external relations*

The SEP had no Committee until 1845. At each meeting a chairman was designated to direct discussions. When the first Committee was elected in 1845, it was decided – in order to comply with the requests of the government – to include in it two faithful servants of the July Monarchy: Charles Dunoyer (who was elected 'First President') (see Pénin 1991: 37) and Hippolyte Passy[4] (who was awarded the office of 'Second President'). The offices of Vice-president were entrusted to Horace Say[5] and Charles

Renouard, who was also in the service of Louis-Philippe's government (see Say 1882: 530). Joseph Garnier and Gilbert-Urbain Guillaumin were respectively nominated Secretary and 'Questor-treasurer' of the Society.

The Committee immediately felt the need to strengthen its foundations, and for that reason a series of measures were introduced.

1   A rule was introduced establishing that upon the death of one of its members, all members holding a lower office would move up a level; if, for example, the First Vice-president died, then the Second Vice-president would become First Vice-president;

2   The office of Secretary was transformed into that of Permanent Secretary in 1849; Joseph Garnier, the beneficiary of this modification, thus consolidated his power;

3   The number of Vice-presidents was increased. Two extra Vice-presidents, Michel Chevalier and Louis Wolowski, were nominated in 1858. The number of Vice-presidents was increased to five in 1865, seven in 1872, up to a maximum of eight in 1881. Towards the end of the 1880s the number was reduced to five.

(*ASEP*, 1, 1846–53: 27–9)

One consequence of these regulations was that only four men succeeded to the office of President of the SEP during this period – Charles Dunoyer (1845–62), Hippolyte Passy (1862–80), Joseph Garnier (1880–1)[6] and Léon Say (1882–96)[7] – and only two Permanent Secretaries were in office – Joseph Garnier (1849–81)[8] and Alphonse Courtois (1881–98). The uninterrupted presence of these men naturally gave the Society great stability and real cohesion, but was also conducive to inertia.

As the years passed by, the SEP also became increasingly exacting about invitations. At the beginning a guest simply needed to be introduced by one of its members. Later, probably for financial reasons, it was required that invitations should be submitted to the Committee for prior approval (*ASEP*, 1, 1846–53: 20). A certain number of French and foreign[9] corresponding members were associated with the SEP, but their position within the Society was not clearly defined. It was not until the beginning of 1887 that this question was clarified.

1.2 *Membership and recruitment*

The 'regulations' of the SEP required that any member not attending the Society meetings for one year and not presenting a valid excuse should be deemed to have resigned (*ASEP*, 1, 1846–53: 20). The meetings held in December 1842 and in the following months saw an increase in membership, with most members of the ephemeral Esterno-Rossi society and other people joining the SEP (Garnier 1854: 670). Five years after the foundation of the SEP, membership figured at around fifty, and in 1851 at around sixty (Garnier 1854: 670). Then there was a rapid increase. Alphonse Courtois (1882: 18) reports the following figures: eighty members at the end of 1849,[10] 117 in 1859, 165 in 1868, 211 in 1874 and 227 at the end of 1882.

However, this progression was not exempt from shortcomings. For several reasons (the distance from Paris of their domicile, poor health, etc.), not all members of the SEP were able to attend meetings, and the result was that the number of absentees was regularly large, sometimes even overwhelmingly large, as complained of in the minutes of the meeting held on 5th December 1870: 'Only 14 members attended, instead of the 50 or 60 present at the same period in preceding years' (*ASEP*, 8–9, 1869–72: 514).

The minutes of these meetings allow more detailed research into the subject of recruitment, since they document the profession of new members,[11] grouped into general categories. Conventional historical periods will be adopted to simplify analysis of these data.

1.2.1 Before February 1848

During this period SEP recruitment consisted of among the following, in descending order of number: economists[12] (15); politicians (13); businessmen (bankers, stockbrokers, merchants, manufacturers,[13] company managers, representatives of the chambers of commerce, etc.) (9); civil servants (members of the Council of State, bureaucrats, etc.) (9); journalists (4); members or prize-winners of the Institut (2); professors[14] and educators (directors of colleges and institutes, etc.) (2); jurists[15] (lawyers, etc.) (1); and farmers (1).

1.2.2 From February 1848 to 1st December 1851

Very few new members were recruited during this troubled period: politicians (4); civil servants (3); economists (2); jurists (1); engineers (1); journalists (1); physicians (1), etc.

1.2.3 From 2nd December 1851 to the end of 1859

In decreasing order, members were recruited in this period from among the following: journalists[16] (16); businessmen (8); engineers (8); civil servants (7); professors of non-economic disciplines and educators (7); jurists (6); military men (3); economists (2); politicians (2); physicians (2); farmers (2); members or prize-winners of the Institut (1), etc. While the increased number of engineers was the main novelty of this period,[17] the large reduction in the number of politicians probably reflected the hostility of the

SEP towards the new regime. Recruitment amongst farmers remained as low as ever.

1.2.4 *From January 1860 to 3rd September 1870*

During this period – which historians usually identify as 'liberal Empire' – the number of new members substantially increased. Ninety per cent of new members were recruited from amongst businessmen (18); journalists (17); jurists (14); civil servants (13); professors of non-economic disciplines (11); politicians (9); and engineers (8). Recruitment from among economists and farmers remained minimal.[18] The SEP truly opened up towards business, the civil service and the world of politics during this period, and the ease with which new members were recruited from such diverse professions shows that there was a real need for economic education. The French élite, which manifestly suffered the lack of teaching of political economy in universities and 'grandes écoles', endeavoured to replace it with the 'mutual teaching' provided by the debates within the Society.

1.2.5 *From 4th September 1870 to the beginning of 1887*

The size and nature of recruitment in this period[19] – in which the influence of some prominent members[20] can be easily discerned – reveals that the Committee acted under the impetus of three main goals: firstly, it aimed to propagate the principle of *laissez-faire* within the upper ranks of the administrative, political and legal establishment of the new republican regime; secondly, the Committee aimed to circulate these principles amongst the readers of the larger national and regional newspapers; and thirdly, it hoped to gain support from business and university circles.

1.3 *The organisation and contents of debates*

By coming together, the members of the SEP aimed to clarify and popularise the economic laws formulated by Quesnay, Turgot, Smith, Malthus and Jean-Baptiste Say[21] more easily than if they had remained isolated from one another. One of the more peculiar rules in force since the creation of the Society prescribed that the agenda should not be decided in advance, the question to be debated being chosen by the majority of members at the beginning of each meeting. This rule was generally respected during the period, although some proposals to modify it were advanced.[22]

Before analysing the contents of debates, we should consider for a moment a question which was raised during the very first years of existence of the Society. Should the SEP take part in the struggle led by the Association pour la Liberté des Echanges created by Bastiat in 1846? Bastiat himself and several other members of the Society thought that it should. Joseph Garnier was not of the same opinion:

> The Society of economists, solicited for a time by some of its members who urged it to take up a course of agitation, believed that its duty lay in not sacrificing all of its time to the success of one single discussion, however important that discussion might appear to be. [...] Therefore [...] the Society of economists desired to remain an exclusively scientific society and to leave to the Association for free trade the task of winning the favour of public opinion and making reform by the three powers of the state possible.
>
> (Garnier 1847: 238)

From this moment on, Joseph Garnier was a constant advocate of this approach. On 6th November 1882 – the fortieth anniversary of the Society's foundation – Léon Say, who was the current First President of the Society, vindicated the same principle: 'We have been [...] faithful to one of the essential conditions of our institution; we did not engage in politics' (Say 1882: 529). Fidelity to this principle can be explained by the fact that the SEP had very often to tackle the manifest hostility of governments in charge (Say 1882: 529–35), and any intervention in the political arena could end up in a deterioration of these already delicate relationships. Another reason was more internal to the life of the Society: since the SEP brought together men of very diverse political orientations (Garnier 1854: 670–1), any discussion of political questions within the Society could only heighten the existing tensions between members and consequently threaten the existence of the association. A good example is that of the potential conflict between Michel Chevalier, who rallied to the regime of Napoléon III, and other influential members of the SEP, who entered into a more or less manifest opposition to the Emperor.[23] Is it legitimate to conclude that the SEP never debated strictly political questions? For the period covering the Second Republic and the very first years of the Third Republic, the answer is definitely negative.[24]

In order to make their analysis easier, we have grouped the questions debated by the SEP into three categories: (1) questions concerning economics and the teaching of political economy; (2) questions concerning 'social economy': working conditions, welfare, insurance, housing, education, trade unionism, socialism, cooperation, unemployment, social conflicts, etc.; and (3) other questions: demography (population, migratory movements, etc.), colonial policy, world exhibitions, public works, etc. Here too we have adopted conventional historical periodisation.

1.3.1 Before February 1848

The questions of free trade and those relative to the teaching of political economy were the most frequently debated. At the start of the activities of the SEP in November 1842, the question of the corn trade was arousing passions in England. At the time of the parliamentary debate which was definitively to seal the victory of the English free-traders led by Richard Cobden, SEP members voted their unreserved and entire support to the free-traders' programme during the meeting of 10th January 1846, thus earning Cobden's gratitude (*ASEP*, 1, 1846–53: 33–6). When the latter came to Paris in August of the same year, an 'unforgettable' banquet was organised in his honour (*ASEP*, 1, 1846–53: 36–54).

The teaching of political economy also provided a fertile ground for reflection. A special committee responsible for the promotion of the teaching of political economy was designated during the meeting of 15th May 1845. A proposal was addressed to M. de Salvandy, the minister of public education, but the events of February 1848 put an end to this project.

1.3.2 From February 1848 to 1st December 1851

The provisional government was hostile to the teaching of political economy given by Michel Chevalier at the Collège de France, and quickly moved to suppress it (decree of 7th April 1848). This naturally led to extremely animated protest by the members of the Society (*ASEP*, 1, 1846–53: 58–67). Léon Faucher led a delegation that met with Lamartine, who was a member of the government. But all attempts were in vain. It was not until the meeting of the National Assembly on 15th November 1848 that the decree was revoked[25] but Chevalier's chair was not definitively re-established until the decree of 10th December 1848. Obviously, the considerable interest shown in protectionism at the time had not gone unnoticed.

Questions of a more theoretical nature were debated in two meetings devoted to land income. As will be confirmed further on, however, theoretical questions were generally neglected, insofar as the members of the SEP were convinced of the existence of natural laws of economics, which had been discovered by their elders and which they only had to disseminate.

Eight meetings were devoted to questions of social economy: the tasks of the state in social policy (4), working conditions (working hours, weekly day off) (2), welfare (1) and socialism (1). Two meetings were devoted to slavery and colonisation.

1.3.3 From 2nd December 1851 to the end of 1859

To a certain extent, Michel Chevalier, as advisor to the Emperor, was able to protect his colleagues in the SEP. There were, nevertheless, subjects of discussion which could not be raised nor even mentioned. During the first years of the Empire, for example, the teaching of economics fell into this category, since the imperial government was fiercely opposed to it. It was only towards the end of 1856 that the subject could be brought up.[26] Conversely, there was no opposition to subjects which pleased the Emperor. Thus the defence of free trade, to which Napoléon III remained committed after his stay in England, and the corresponding criticism of protectionism were amply debated. Subjects of a technical or scientific nature were equally unhindered. Banking and monetary questions, as well as questions of an epistemological nature,[27] were very frequently on the agenda. Particular attention was paid to the origins and causes of the economic and financial crises which multiplied during the second part of this period.

'State insurance' was one of the few subjects in the domain of social economy to be studied.[28] It should be kept in mind that workers were reduced to silence until 25th May 1864, when the right to strike was recognised. Twenty meetings were devoted to 'other questions': world exhibitions (7), demography (6), public works (4) and colonies (3).

1.3.4 From January 1860 to 3rd September 1870

Undeniably, there was a liberal upsurge during the last ten years of the Empire, insofar as members were now able to include on the agenda of their meetings subjects they previously did not dare to discuss. The issue of the teaching of political economy now became a hotly debated topic. In the two meetings devoted to this subject in the second half of 1863, the government was requested to introduce the teaching of economics into law schools. Grievances were only slightly redressed, for only one chair was created at the Paris Faculty of Law in 1864, thanks to the intervention of the minister of education, Victor Duruy. The first holder of this chair was a member of the SEP, Anselme Batbie. Taxation, money, banking and free trade were also debated. The *octroi* was no longer sufficient as a source of tax revenue for large towns confronted with problems of rapid change and development. The existence of a double (gold and silver) standard for currency and the legal parity between them continued to create great difficulties, despite the signing of the monetary convention – the basis of the Latin Union[29] – on 23rd December 1865, and the subject occasioned numerous debates. The signing of the Franco-British free-trade treaty at the beginning of 1860 did not lay all worries to rest, as 'protectionist agitation' supported by Adolphe Thiers developed at the end of the Second Empire.

The increased freedom to express social and political problems is evinced by the fact that 'questions of social economy'[30] were now more frequently debated than those concerning the teaching of political economy.

Questions about public works (the Suez Canal, etc.), world exhibitions, population (the slow growth of the French population recorded in the 1866 census raised much concern) and the colonies were, in descending order of frequency, the 'other questions' most often debated.

1.3.5 From 4th September 1870 to the beginning of 1887

Shortly after its establishment, the Third Republic was confronted with financial problems created by the payment of war reparations to Germany to the amount of five thousand million gold francs and by the indemnities to be allocated to the victims of the war. The nomination of Adolphe Thiers as prime minister was worrying, since it was by leaning on his authority

> that protectionists made a huge effort, after the war, to make us regress, using the false pretext that we should follow the example of the United States of America. They did not entirely succeed, but it is manifestly true that the Third Republic has not yet done us any favour and that the fervent campaign led by our opponents has left its disastrous imprint on our economic legislation.
>
> (Say 1882: 535)

Therefore, it is easy to understand – considering that the desire of SEP members to promote the teaching of political economy had been only very partially satisfied by the Second Empire – why questions about taxation, free trade and the teaching of economics were at the heart of SEP meetings during the first years of the Third Republic. These subjects – including the teaching of political economy – long remained at the centre of debates, despite the creation in March 1877 of a chair of political economy in the twelve Faculties of Law then existing in the country, a measure which the SEP judged largely insufficient. Three meetings were devoted to the economic and financial crises which developed towards the end of this period,[31] but nobody realised the gravity of the reversal they foresaw.

The most frequently discussed 'questions of social economy' were those raised by social conflicts, the regulation of labour, working-class housing, profit sharing, pensions and alcoholism. However these topics were relatively and, one might add, paradoxically less well studied than in the preceding period. The tone of debates on these questions remained quite restrained, although genuine disquiet could be perceived.

Lastly, in decreasing order of frequency, come the 'other questions': public works, world exhibitions, the colonial question and the demographic state of France.[32]

1.4 *The dissemination of debates*

There are no documents available for the period from 1842 to 1845. A small improvement can be noted in the four following years. The minutes of the large majority of debates are available,[33] but they are very perfunctory. It is only from October 1850 onwards that details concerning the meetings become sufficiently numerous and precise, giving us an exact picture of the debates. The SEP, not yet having its own periodical publication, had to rely on *Journal des économistes* and to a lesser extent on the *Annuaire de l'économie politique* which was first published in 1844. We know that Garnier wished to gather all the minutes together in one collection and to fill in the gaps using his own notes. 'It is unfortunately certain that these notes have themselves disappeared' (Courtois 1889: VIII).

Financial difficulties explain why the SEP did not have its own periodical. Since its foundation, the meagre resources of the Society had been provided uniquely by the annual subscription of 10 francs paid by each member. Therefore, towards the end of this period a radical transformation of the SEP was perceived as increasingly necessary. This was very clearly the opinion of Gustave de Molinari.

2 The SEP between the beginning of 1887 and April 1914: seeking a new lease of life

There was nothing fortuitous about the radical transformation undergone by the SEP. It was the fruit of a long-standing reflection.

2.1 *The reform proposed by Gustave de Molinari*

During the meeting held on 5th February 1883, Gustave de Molinari raised first the question of the procedure for choosing the agenda which

> had presented no inconvenience as long as the members of the Society were few in number and were for the most part professional economists of some sort, and whose studies and habitual work enabled them to discuss without preparation the questions that made up the intellectual menu of meetings, such questions being additionally limited in number. [...] But the Society has considerably increased in size, and its recruits come from very diverse sectors: financiers, industrialists, merchants, engineers, and civil servants; true economists now account for no more than a small minority; at the same time the range of questions to be dealt with has greatly expanded. Would it not be useful, in this new situation, to announce in the letter of convocation the subject to be discussed? [...] The choice of the questions on the agenda could be left to the permanent secretary; we would thus save precious time and increase the chances of obtaining the participation of the most competent men in the domain of each particular question. The speaker then moved on to the subject of the recognition of the Society by the state, an event which would be of great advantage. The Society would then be able to receive donations and legacies, and who knows if the friends of science might not contribute to increasing its resources, which are so limited at present. These resources could be devoted to the ever more necessary popularisation of political economy, to the creation of a library, the establishment of lectures, conferences, prizes, etc.; in a word, to enlarging the sphere of action and the influence of the Society.
>
> (*ASEP*, 14, 1883–4: 12–13)

What was being proposed was nothing less than a complete overhaul of the SEP with the primary goal of giving it a new lease of life. Only the second proposal relating to the by-laws was accepted (*ASEP*, 14, 1883–4: 37–8). It proved to be extremely difficult to finalise them. More than three years passed before the new by-laws and internal regulations were accepted (*ASEP*, 1, 1846–53: 21–6).

2.2 *The new profile of the SEP*

The Committee (article 3) was composed of two Presidents,[34] four Vice-presidents, a Permanent Secretary and a Questor-treasurer. After exercising his functions for four years the First President would be replaced by the Second President, who was in his turn replaced by the First Vice-president. At the end of their four-years in office, the Vice-presidents and Questor-treasurer could, however, be re-nominated to the same post. The consequence was that mobility within the Committee remained very low, a phenomenon accentuated by the exceptional longevity enjoyed by several members (Frédéric Passy, Gustave de Molinari and Clément Juglar).

The number of titular members was not allowed to exceed 250 (article 1 of internal regulations), although membership always remained below this limit.[35] On the other hand, no limit was imposed on the number of corresponding members (article 2). These figures should be considered in the light of the high level of absenteeism that still was characteristic of the Society meetings. On 5th May 1890, out of a total of 308 members (243 titular, 65 corresponding) only 41 signed the attendance sheet (*BSEP*, 1890: 66–7), that is to say, less than 14 per cent of members.

Gustave de Molinari's ambitions in the domain of resources and means of action were satisfied. The impact of his intervention can be appreciated simply by reading articles 8 and 11 of the by-laws. Annual subscriptions were set at 20 francs for titular members and 10 francs for corresponding members. The SEP was permitted to receive donations and legacies as well as grants, and to dispose at liberty of the income of its assets and securities, whatever their nature.[36] According to article 11 of the by-laws the Society's means of action were the publication of a monthly bulletin;[37] the publication of reports and pamphlets; conferences, lectures, competitions, prizes and awards.

2.3 *Recruitment*

It is interesting to consider to what extent recruitment was affected by this reform. Two periods of equal length can be distinguished to this effect.

2.3.1 *From 1887 to 1900*

Restricted by the limit imposed on the total amount of titular members, recruitment was lower than in the preceding period (around 30 per cent). But for this reason it is possibly more significant. New members came from the following categories, in descending order: businessmen (25); journalists (20); civil servants (18); economists (8); jurists (7); engineers (7); professors of non-economic disciplines (5). These categories represented more than 90 per cent of new recruits. As in previous periods, the recruitment of farmers remained negligible.

2.3.2 *From 1901 to July 1914*

During this period recruitment decreased once again by nearly 20 per cent, the largest diminution occurring in the years leading up to World War I. Among the most numerous classes of recruits were businessmen (30), followed by journalists (13), civil servants (13), professors of non-economic disciplines (6), engineers (5), politicians (4), economists (4) and jurists (3); these categories accounted for almost all new members. The strong decline that was observed in the recruitment of politicians after 1887 continued in this period and was possibly evidence of the fact that the liberal order so tirelessly defended by SEP members was encountering less and less favour in political and parliamentary circles. Likewise, the low number of professional economists recruited contrasted with the interest shown by the Committee in candidates for the new *agrégation* of the Faculties of Law. This competitive examination was introduced towards the end of 1899 and although the successful examinees were systematically invited, very few of them were to become members of the Society.[38]

2.4 **Debates**

Article 13 of the internal regulations laid down that 'the Society shall meet every month upon convocation by the permanent secretary to discuss scientific subjects'. This implied that 'political subjects' were excluded, confirming a custom that had been established since the beginning.

2.4.1 *From 1887 to 1900*

A consequence of this attitude was that SEP members had to proceed very carefully, for both the role of the government and that of the town councils, which were political institutions *par excellence*, were more and more often at the heart of their concerns, as a consequence of the steadily increasing interventions of these institutions in the economy. It was perhaps for this reason that the nature of the state was debated on two separate occasions with explicit reference to a pamphlet written by Bastiat in 1848.[39] Despite its growing importance during this period, protectionism was scantily debated. This contrasted with the parallel attitude of the Société Belge d'Economie Politique, in which the subject was raised many times during this period. The SEP made partial amend for its fault by publishing, on three occasions, the minutes of the Belgian debates in full length in the *BSEP*. Only one debate was devoted to the teaching of political economy (meeting of 5th June 1896).

'Questions of social economy' were debated more frequently than ever: fifteen meetings were devoted to this category. The desire to render critiques of social policies increasingly 'scientific' is well illustrated by the more and more 'economic' formulation of the questions proposed for debate.[40]

Among the 'other questions', demography remained the subject most frequently discussed.[41] The issue of world exhibitions, which had so fascinated SEP members in previous times, was now hardly mentioned (for example, those held in Paris in 1889 and in 1900). It must be remembered that the members of the Society were increasingly disregarded by the governments of this period, who showed a marked preference for more heterodox thinkers.[42]

2.4.2 From 1901 to July 1914[43]

Protectionism, taxation, and the crises in the United States and in Germany in 1907 and 1908 were among the most debated economic questions during this period, another interesting subject being represented by the trusts, which underwent great expansion, especially in the two countries just mentioned. The progress of a protectionist opinion in England (meeting of 4th July 1903) and the project for income tax legislation in France (meetings of 5th August and 5th November 1903) caused the Society members grave concern.

But it was once again towards 'questions of social economy' that SEP affiliates more frequently turned their attention. SEP opposition to government social policies grew so strong that its members felt it necessary to emphasise the 'disastrous' consequences of the measures taken by the French government. This explains why the agenda of the SEP became more and more accessible to questions of current affairs. Was the SEP still the learned society of which its founders had dreamt at the time of its creation? Over the years, had it not become, on the contrary, a political society?

3 Concluding remarks

To what measure had the Society achieved the purposes it had set for itself since its creation? As far as the popularisation of political economy is concerned, an evaluation is difficult. How can we measure the influence of the Society's debates on readers of *Journal des économistes*, the *Annales* or the *Bulletin*? Did the debates within the SEP have an impact on the people that had been recruited? This seems more likely, insofar as recruits were, *a priori*, favourably disposed towards the *laissez-faire* ideas promoted by the Society. Conversely, the fact that the Society was mostly ignored by the governments of the time – with some rare exceptions[44] – seems to prove that its efforts to change government economic and social policies were insufficient.

On a theoretical level there is no doubt that the contribution of the Society to scientific debate is non-existent. This failure can be attributed partly to the method of choosing the agenda for debates, which remained unchanged during this period despite repeated requests. The agenda was too accessible to questions of current affairs and consequently not sufficiently open to those theoretical questions which were debated by economists in Europe and the United States. The composition of the Committee and the direction in which recruitment developed did nothing to encourage the choice of complex theoretical questions for the agenda. Lastly, the prizes which had been one of the Society's means of action since 1887 achieved very little, because of their scarcity – less than ten were awarded between 1887 and 1914 – but above all because of the nature of the subjects proposed.[45]

The monthly debates of the SEP nevertheless provide an extremely valuable source of information for the historian of economic and social ideas of the period.

Notes

1   The first issue came out on 15th December 1841.
2   The Société d'Economie Politique was called the Société des Economistes until 1847.
3   These customs gradually became 'regulations' (*ASEP*, 1846–53, 1: 20).
4   Hippolyte Passy was twice Minister of Finance in Louis-Philippe's government.
5   The son of Jean-Baptiste Say.
6   He was a Committee member for 36 years.
7   Léon Say, the grandson of Jean-Baptiste Say and son of Horace Say, came into the Committee in April 1863 as treasurer. He was Fifth Vice-president in 1872, Second President in 1881 and First President in 1882, a post he held until his death in 1896. Thus he was in the Committee for more than 30 years.
8   As a consequence, in 1880–1 Joseph Garnier occupied both the post of President and that of Permanent Secretary of the SEP.
9   One of them was Richard Cobden, a leader of the Anti-Corn-Laws League.
10 The decrease in membership of the SEP between 1849 and 1851 which appears in the figures quoted by Joseph Garnier and Alphonse Courtois was probably a real one, since this was a very troubled period.
11 The interpretation of these figures has sometimes been difficult, since the collection of minutes is incomplete and the profession of new members is not always noted, although the number of these cases is very small compared with those for whom the profession is given. The results obtained are therefore only approximate.
12 Notably Michel Chevalier who taught at the Collège de France and two professors from the Conservatoire of Arts and Métiers: Adolphe-Jérôme Blanqui (Arena 1991: 164) and Louis Wolowski (Lutfalla 1991: 187).
13 It should be noted that throughout the whole period industrialists represented a tiny fraction of this category.
14 Excluding professors of political economy who are already counted in the 'economists' category.

15 Jurists in the Council of State are obviously not counted a second time here.
16 Perhaps to alleviate the restrictions imposed on civil liberties and the freedom of the press.
17 The influence of the *polytechnicien* Michel Chevalier, one of the few members of the SEP to rally to the cause of Napoléon III, can be seen here.
18 The immense majority of farmers, like industrialists, remained protectionist.
19 In decreasing order: civil servants (26); journalists (22); politicians (20); businessmen (19); professors of non-economic disciplines (17); jurists (12); economists (8); engineers (8). These categories represent 95 per cent of new members.
20 Notably that of Léon Say, who remained in close contact with the business world, senior civil servants and certain political circles. During this period he was nominated three times Minister of Finance of the Third Republic.
21 These references were later to expand to include Rossi, Bastiat and Chevalier.
22 Two such propositions were made in 1850 (*ASEP*, 1846–53, 1: 135). More than 25 years later, on 5th December 1877, the procedure for choosing the agenda was once again under discussion. Joseph Garnier was opposed to any change (*ASEP*, 1876–7, 9: 155). He had been the most ardent defender of tradition since the beginning. Molinari well understood this, and was to wait until the death of the 'guardian of the temple' before coming back to the subject (see § 2.1).
23 Amongst whom one should mention Charles Dunoyer, Hippolyte Passy, Jean-Gustave Courcelle-Seneuil, Louis Wolowski, Gustave de Molinari, and Léon Say.
24 The following example should suffice: 'A conversation was held on the best organisation of government' during the meeting of 5th January 1871. From the very brief minutes of this meeting we learn that 'Mr. Alphonse Courtois gave an interesting exposé of the ideas propounded by John Stuart Mill in his works *On Liberty* and *The Representative Government*. Mr. O. de Labry, Léopold Hervieux, Griolet, Boutron, Barberoux, de Renusson and Joseph Garnier – the latter taking the chair – then successively took the floor and presented diverse points of view. The conversation was most interesting and very instructive for the members who attended, and we all regret that it cannot be reported within the framework of our *Annals*' (*ASEP*, 1871–2, 9: 2).
25 Thanks notably to the efforts of SEP members (Léon Faucher, Louis Wolowski, etc.) who were in the Assembly.
26 'On the teaching of political economy' is on the agenda of the meetings held on 5th November and 5th December 1856.
27 Meetings at which this type of question were raised include those of 10th April 1853 ('On the limits of political economy'), 10th May 1853 ('On the definition of political economy formulated by M. Michel Chevalier'), 10th August 1853 ('On the relationship between political economy and statistics').
28 Meeting of 5th September 1857.
29 Four countries participated in this: France, Italy, Belgium and Switzerland. Greece was to join in 1868.
30 The following subjects were debated, in descending order of frequency: teaching (liberty, free education, etc.), social conflicts, profit sharing for workers, pensions for workers, housing for workers, socialism.
31 These meetings were: 6th February 1882: 'The stock market crisis (causes and remedies)'; 5th April 1883 ('On the development of public works during a time of crisis as a means of alleviating the effects'); 5th February 1884 ('Is there a general economic crisis in France?').
32 The meeting held on 5th August 1885: 'On the economic causes of the absence of growth in French population'.

33 We can cite, among the meetings of which no trace remains, those of 10th March and 10th May 1849.

34 Léon Say, Frédéric Passy, Emile Levasseur, Paul Leroy-Beaulieu and Yves Guyot were to hold the post of President during this period.

35 This was the result of a deliberate policy. The Committee was well aware that titular members were members for life, and that too many hasty admissions would make it impossible for them to bring in 'notables' (*BSEP*, 1889: 31).

36 The improvement in the financial circumstances of the SEP enabled Garnier's great editorial project to be achieved between 1889 and 1897. Alphonse Courtois was in charge of the project. The sixteen volumes published under the title *Annales de la Société d'Economie Politique* (*ASEP*) report on all the debates carried out by the Society between 1846 and 1887.

37 The *Bulletin de la Société d'Economie Politique* (*BSEP*) – which appeared for the first time in 1888   replaced the *Annales de la Société d'Economie Politique* (*ASEP*).

38 Only Souchon (1907), Deschamps (1909), Truchy and Germain Martin (1914) accepted the invitation.

39 Meeting of 5th November 1890 ('Does a satisfactory definition of the state exist? is it abstract or something real?'); meeting of 5th August 1899 ('On 25th September 1848 Bastiat wrote "The state is the great fiction through which everybody strives to live at the expense of everybody else". Is this still the case and what will it become in the future?').

40 Meeting of 5th December 1890 ('On the economic effects of work regulations and limitations'); meeting of 5th March 1891 ('On the economic influences of the Sunday day of rest'), etc.

41 Meeting of 5th March 1890 ('On the population'); meeting of 7th March 1896 ('On the influence of civilisation on population growth'); meeting of 5th January 1897 ('On the congress to protect and increase the population in France'); etc.

42 Notably Paul Cauwès and Charles Gide.

43 After Germany's declaration of war on France on 3rd August 1914, SEP discussions were focused on the conflict and its multiple effects (economic, financial, monetary) on the protagonists.

44 For example, the Franco-British free-trade treaty signed on 23rd January 1860.

45 The Frédéric Passy prize of 500 francs awarded to the best work on the life and works of Charles Coquelin (*BSEP*, 1904: 50) and the Alexandre Raffalovich prize of 500 francs awarded to the best presentation of Léon Say's economic and financial doctrine (*BSEP*, 1896: 78) are the most significant examples.

Bibliography

Primary sources

Annales de la Société d'Economie Politique [*ASEP*], 16 volumes relating to the period 1846–87.

Bulletin de la Société d'Economie Politique [*BSEP*], volumes relating to the period 1888–1916.

By-laws of the Société d'Economie Politique approved by the presidential decree of 6th December 1886 recognising the SEP as a state-approved establishment, *ASEP*, 1846–53, 1: 21–3.

Committee of the Society at various periods, *ASEP*, 1846–53, 1: 27–30.

Internal regulations adopted at the general meeting of 5th January 1887, in accordance with article 19 of the by-laws and approved by the prefect of the Seine on the 25th of the same month, *ASEP*, 1846–53, 1: 24–6.

Regulations of the Société d'Economie Politique from 1845 to the end of 1886, *ASEP*, 1846–53, 1: 20.

Secondary sources

Arena, R. (1991) 'Adolphe-Jérôme Blanqui (1798–1854), Un historien de l'économie aux préoccupations sociales', in Y. Breton and M. Lutfalla (eds) *L'économie politique en France au XIXème siècle*, Paris: Economica.

Courtois, A. (1882) 'Notice historique sur la Société d'économie politique', meeting of 6th November 1882, *ASEP* 1846–53, 1: 1–19.

—— (1889) 'Avant-propos', *ASEP* 1846–53, 1: VII–IX.

—— (1892) 'La Société des Economistes de 1792 à 1842', meeting of 5th November 1892, *BSEP*: 180–202.

Garnier, J. (1847) 'La Société des économistes', *Annuaire de l'économie politique*: 233–9.

—— (1854) 'Société d'économie politique', in Ch. Coquelin and G.U. Guillaumin (eds) *Dictionnaire de l'économie politique*, 2nd ed., vol. 1, Paris: Guillaumin.

Le Van-Lemesle, L. (1991) 'L'institutionnalisation de l'économie politique en France', in Y. Breton and M. Lutfalla (eds) *L'économie politique en France au XIXème siècle*, Paris: Economica.

Lutfalla, M. (1991) 'Louis Wolowski (1810–1876) ou le libéralisme positif', in Y. Breton and M. Lutfalla (eds) *L'économie politique en France au XIXème siècle*, Paris: Economica.

Passy, F. (1882) 'Quarantième anniversaire de la fondation de la Société', meeting of 6th November 1882, *ASEP* 1880–2, 13: 528–36.

Pénin, M. (1991) 'Charles Dunoyer (1786–1862). L'échec d'un libéralisme', in Y. Breton and M. Lutfalla (eds) *L'économie politique en France au XIXème siècle*, Paris: Economica.

Say, L. (1882) 'Quarantième anniversaire de la fondation de la Société', meeting of 6th November 1882, *ASEP* 1880–2, 13: 528–36.

4 The associations of economists and the dissemination of political economy in Italy

Massimo M. Augello and
Marco E. L. Guidi*

In the mid-nineteenth century Italian economists, following the path trodden by their English and French colleagues a few years earlier, began to feel the need to establish associations that would act as a forum for economic debates. These associations of economists were designed to act as an important tool for the spread of economics beyond the confines of the learned world. Contributions to this mission came not only from economists but also from a variety of social, professional and political figures. Thus in a historical perspective these associations also expressed an attempt to create a setting favourable to exchange of ideas and interaction with those in charge of the political and administrative affairs of the country.

This chapter seeks to analyse the history of such associations in the second half of the nineteenth century. After a brief examination of the historical antecedents, the subsequent sections will reconstruct the sequence of events that led to the establishment of the first associations of Italian economists and the main stages of their development, also investigating the causes that eventually resulted in the abandonment of these projects. Particular emphasis will be placed on exploring their organisational structure and inquiring into the relations between economists and politicians that arose within the associations. Finally, we will study the impulse given by these societies to the study of economics and their role in the process of professionalisation of economists.

1 Historical antecedents

Political Economy Societies did not represent the first instance of associations created by Italian economists with the aim of furthering economic debate and stimulating interest in economic issues. The genesis of such ventures can be found in the Enlightenment, which was also an epoch of intense theoretical elaboration in the field of political economy (Bianchini 1989, 1994). The protagonists of the Italian cultural renewal played a major role in promoting academies and cultural clubs which hosted lively debate on the great economic works of the century. One need only cite two celebrated cases: the Accademia dei Pugni (literally: 'fists') of Milan and the periodical *Il Caffè* (1764–6), both of which were run by Pietro and Alessandro Verri and Cesare Beccaria (Morato 1996), and the group in Naples headed by Bartolommeo Intieri, whose discussions sparked both *Della moneta* (1751) by Ferdinando Galiani and *Lezioni di economia civile* (1766–7) by Antonio Genovesi (Venturi 1969: 553–66).

But above and beyond these well-known examples, it should be borne in mind that the renewal of the extended network of academies – spurred from the seventeenth century onwards by the Galilean revolution – became more accentuated during the period of reforms that gathered pace in the mid-eighteenth century. The academies were called upon to produce a utilitarian type of science, in accordance with the Baconian model. The utility of science was measured in terms of greater dominion over nature and technical progress, but also in terms of the greater ability of governments to maintain order and increase the wealth and power of nations.

Some academies occasionally hosted presentations on themes of agronomy and political economy. But it was the 1753 foundation of the Accademia Economico-Agraria dei Georgofili in Florence that sanctioned the scientific dignity of economics and identified its message with the reform policies of enlightened sovereigns. Right up to the end of the eighteenth century, this academy was to represent one of the main vehicles for the spread of Physiocratic and Smithian doctrines in Italy (Becagli 2000). The founding of this first institution was soon followed by further experiences, in Milan, Turin, the territories of the Venetian Republic and the Papal State.[1] In most cases, however, only limited scope was awarded to political economy, as governments generally preferred to orient debate towards the more technical themes of agronomy, medicine and mechanics.

An important step forward was taken in the Napoleonic period, despite the regime's mistrust of the new science of political economy. Academies founded during this period, such as the Accademia Pontaniana of Naples, founded in 1808, or the Istituto Nazionale of Bologna (transferred to Milan in 1810) included departments of moral and political science in line with the model of the Paris Institut. In the nineteenth century these departments became an important forum for the proponents of political economy.

Furthermore, during the Napoleonic period the experiences of eighteenth-century agrarian academies prompted the establishment of a network of provincial associations termed 'agrarian societies' or 'economic societies'. Verri, Genovesi and Melchiorre Gioia believed these could act as essential tools for promoting economic development. The economic and agrarian societies were set up by legislative decrees issued by the Republic of Italy (1802) and the Kingdom of Naples (1810, 1812), and in many cases they received an enthusiastic response from the city élites composed of the landed and educated classes. Their links with governments were entrusted to coordinating bodies denominated Istituti di Incoraggiamento, located in the capitals. The economic societies continued their activities even during the decades following the Restoration and expanded from Piedmont to Sicily.

They exerted an important function of stimulating the local economies and raising public awareness (see Aa. Vv. 1996; De Lorenzo 1998; Augello and Guidi 2000: vol. 1).

Despite their eminently practical goals, extensive economic debate was aired within the economic and agrarian societies, above all during the periods of greater political freedom, for instance in the 1830s and 1840s. Discussion naturally focused on applied economics: roads, canals and railways, education, poor relief, landed property, the contractual relationships between landowners and peasants, taxation, the priority sectors within a developmental strategy, the question of free trade versus protectionism. But debate was by no means devoid of in-depth theoretical elaboration, and many of the major economists of the time took part in those issues, convinced that powerful influence could thereby be exerted over public opinion and the government. The economic societies thus gave an important thrust towards the spread of the tenets of economics and favoured the propagation of British and French political economy and *laissez-faire* doctrine.

These semi-official associations entered into decline with the advent of Italian unification between 1848 and 1860. A number of reasons can be suggested. Worth mentioning is the threat of social unrest and the growth and diversification of economic interests, but also the progress achieved in the professionalisation of economists. These aspects led to a change in perception: the old model of society, composed as it was of men of letters interested in political economy and united by a common passion for progress, by now appeared obsolete. Thus while the government was entrusted with an ever-increasing array of tasks, a new type of association began to take shape, with more specific functions. The function of representation of economic interests was assumed by associations established on the basis of profession and class; that of economic promotion was taken over by the chambers of commerce, the professional schools and other bodies; finally, the function of the dissemination of economics was assumed by the societies of political economy.

The academies, on the other hand, although showing some signs of decline, maintained their position as an important means for the diffusion of political economy throughout the second half of the nineteenth century. They also retained their function of sanctioning the scientific status of economics (Augello and Guidi 2000: vol. 2, part 1).

2 The first economic association: the Political Economy Society of Turin (1852–66)

The 1840s saw an expansion of economic studies within the universities, which became more generalised during the following decade. This process was manifested both through the establishment of a course in political economy at several university faculties (such as Pisa, Siena and Turin) and through more selective recruitment of academic staff (Catania, Naples, Palermo), which contributed to overall improvement in the quality of teaching (Augello *et al.* 1988).

Even outside the university world, greater attention began to be paid to political economy, leading to a series of activities promoting and spreading economic studies, including several important achievements in the world of publishers. For instance, in Turin, which was at that time the capital of the Kingdom of Sardinia, the publisher Giuseppe Pomba undertook the publication of the *Biblioteca dell'economista*, edited by Francesco Ferrara, the major Italian economist of the period. This opus, a series containing the Italian translation of the works of the main economists, proved extremely successful, with volumes continuing to appear in the following decades.

It was precisely in Turin that a project began to take shape in the early 1850s, with the aim of setting up a society of political economy. Its promoter was Ferrara himself, who held a teaching position at the University of Turin (Pischedda 1985, 1986; Faucci 1995). Together with a small group of political figures and university professors, most of whom were Piedmontese, Ferrara wrote out the manifesto of the Società di Economia Politica of Turin, presented to the public on 25th June 1852.[2] The Society, formed on the model of similar bodies previously established in England and France, constituted the first attempt in Italy to gather 'economists' together in an association whose mission was defined as disseminating and strengthening economics.

The Society's by-laws laid down that its goals were to be pursued primarily through periodic meetings devoted to debates on economic issues. The impact of the Society's activities was to be boosted by the creation of a journal and by the publication of low-cost economic textbooks. Another important objective was to encourage the establishment of elementary schools of economics.[3] For those wishing to join the Society there was to be no discrimination of a political or doctrinal nature. Furthermore, in addition to the regular members, up to twenty-five honorary members could be nominated, chosen from among foreign economists who had made particularly significant scientific contributions.[4]

The by-laws of the Society represented an important document, marking the first time in Italy that an explicit programme had been drawn up – by politicians and economists jointly – to address the question of the diffusion of political economy. At the same time, it reiterated the independence of economics and the need for the study of this discipline to be free from political interests and untrammelled by practical problems.

At the founding meeting (27th June 1852), Camillo Cavour, who was a member of Parliament and would shortly thereafter become prime minister, was elected President of the Society, with Ferrara as Secretary. The latter was in effect the real driving force of the Society: it was his task to organise the meetings, draw up the agenda for debates, write the minutes and see to their publication, and in general to act as the official spokesman of the Society.

From the very first meeting, Ferrara sought to implement the statutory regulation enshrined in the by-laws that provided for the nomination of honorary members. The names he proposed represented the most eminent figures of economics in his day, including A. Blanqui, H.C. Carey, M. Chevalier, J. Garnier, J.R. McCulloch, J.S. Mill and N.W. Senior. However, his plan to confer professional and scientific prestige on the Society was rejected by the majority of members, who, inasmuch as they were politicians by profession, were more interested in its role as a venue for debates on economic policy.

On 6th January 1853, Cavour held his opening address as President of the Society. He outlined the historical development of economic thought, also dwelling on the Italian tradition, and underlined the significant progress made by economics in the preceding decades; he also pointed out, however, that much remained to be done as far as the diffusion of economic principles was concerned. He confidently hoped that bodies such as the Turin Society would be instrumental in fulfilling this purpose.[5]

This marked the official launch of the Society's activities, which then proceeded auspiciously. The members met regularly at least once a month, dealing with both scientific and organisational issues, and also addressed questions pertaining to the promotion and spread of economic studies.[6] Among the scientific matters considered, particularly noteworthy were the debates concerning taxation on personal property. Other issues which formed the focus of the majority of meetings included the teaching of economics in elementary and secondary schools and the possibility of setting up a journal of political economy. The latter topic was discussed in numerous meetings and was favourably received. Indeed it was on the verge of being accomplished in June 1853, but would shortly be abandoned. This dealt the Society a severe blow and signalled the onset of serious problems, leading to a sharp drop in the frequency of meetings and culminating within a year in the dissolution of the Society.

The causes of this breakdown are to be sought first and foremost in the conflicting conceptions of the model of the Society and its goals. Ferrara preferred the concept of a scientific association, while the majority of members were more inclined towards debate on contingent questions of economic policy and thus tended to transform the association into a political lobby (Augello 2000).

The latter feature was pointed out by Ferrara himself,[7] and was implicitly confirmed through the subsequent history of Italian economic societies. Significantly, no sooner had Ferrara given up his teaching position in Turin and moved to the University of Pisa in 1859–60 than the very persons who had done little, only a few years earlier, to prevent the dissolution of the Turin Society resumed discussion on the appropriateness of establishing an association for the dissemination of economic studies.

As a result, steps were taken for the establishment of a 'new' Society, which in many respects was nothing other than a replica of the previous one.

Its official title (Società di Economia Politica of Turin) was identical, as were its aims, many of its regulations and, to a large extent, its organising members. But it was distinguished from the earlier version by the regulation included in the by-laws requiring debate to focus above all on 'questions of immediate interest' rather than, as had been the case in the past, on 'economic issues to be addressed from a purely scientific point of view'.

Thus on 28th May 1860 the new Society of Political Economy was launched. Its President was the economist Giovanni Arrivabene;[8] its Vice-presidents Carlo Cadorna and Camillo Cavour, political figures who had held high-ranking posts in the earlier association. Gian Giacomo Reymond, a young economist who had been one of Ferrara's students, was appointed to the position of Secretary. Like the first Society, this one aimed to promote in-depth study of economics through periodic debate and to spread information through publication of the minutes of the meetings. Admission to the Society was to be free from any formal constraints linked to professional qualifications or any special status: membership would be conditional simply on acceptance of the rules enshrined in the by-laws.[9]

The initial composition of the Society mirrored its new physiognomy. The majority of members were political figures, high-ranking public officials and jurists; there was a paucity of academic economists. Thus out of sixty-four founding members, no fewer than forty-three were politicians, while the only professors of political economy were Reymond, Pietro Torrigiani (University of Parma), Francesco Trinchera (University of Modena) and Boccardo, who would be appointed professor at the University of Genova the following year (see Benvenuto Vialetto and Ancona 1969). The other professors of political economy did not figure among members of the Society.[10] This absence underscored the feature of regionalism that still characterised the association and also revealed scanty awareness among academic economists of the role of associations. In any case, the association – a typical dining society – wished to be no more than a venue for discussion among its own members, who, irrespective of the professions and activities in which they engaged, represented a heterogeneous array of 'experts' on economic problems and theoretical and practical scholars of political economy.

The Society engaged in intense activity and its meetings proceeded apace.[11] The objective of promoting and spreading economic studies was placed squarely at the centre of its efforts. Its scientific undertakings were disseminated through publication of extensive minutes of the meetings, which also outlined the different positions adopted during discussion. In contrast to the previous experience, in which the reports were published through the daily press, the new association made use of some of the major scientific journals of the period: at first *La Rivista contemporanea* (Turin, 1853–70) and the *Annali Universali di Statistica* (Milan, 1824–71), then, from January 1862, *Il Politecnico* (Milan, 1839–44; 1860–1937), which for a while became its official mouthpiece.

The economic debate that developed in the framework of the Society was not of a particularly elevated level from a theoretical point of view. For an overview of its contents, the subjects addressed can be roughly divided into two groups: those pertaining to political and social issues, and those embodying reflections on the main theoretical categories of economics. The former group was in effect a single general debate in which all aspects hinged on the question of the role of the state in the economy and the related issue of the boundaries of economics. Discussion focused both on the theme of government intervention in healthcare and pension provision and on such matters as compulsory primary education, employment of women, means for improvement of workers' conditions, etc.[12] Members unanimously took up a position against extensive state intervention in the economic and social field. Respect for the principle of economic freedom led members to rule out any generalised recourse to such a strategy, even in those sectors – such as that of charity or education – where certain initiatives were regarded as admissible in special cases.

When addressing theoretical issues, the Society focused attention primarily on monetary questions, commercial treaties, public loans, customs tariffs, credit, etc.[13] These were themes that directly concerned all the main questions of economic policy that the first national governments found themselves facing. Such choice of themes faithfully mirrored parliamentary debate of those years, as also shown, for instance, by the fact that in 1864 the Society's interest centred almost exclusively around two burning issues of the time: the railways and banking.[14] On all the subjects that attracted its interest, the Society engaged in intense and interesting activity.

In the wake of these successful undertakings, an endeavour was made in the spring of 1864 to re-launch the Turin Society on a more solid and genuinely national basis. It was thus renamed the Società *Italiana* di Economia Politica; new members were enrolled and Antonio Scialoja, one of the most authoritative Italian economists of the day (Gioli 1989), was elected Vice-president. In addition, the old plan to endow the Society with a designated publication was revived and implemented, using a periodical, *Il Commercio Italiano*, that was already being published in Turin and was an expression of the liberal political group. Yet despite this organisational thrust, the activities of the Society would shortly slow down considerably, with meetings becoming increasingly infrequent. At the beginning of 1866, the Society was definitively dissolved. The official motivation was that membership had shrunk dramatically after the capital of the Kingdom was transferred from Turin to Florence, since the overwhelming majority of members were politicians.

In hindsight, the Turin Society was far from having achieved the status of an association of economists, despite Francesco Ferrara's initial buoyant expectations. His project was vastly ahead of its time, and therefore suffered from the lack of a well-defined and widely recognised professional figure of the economist. In those years even university professors of political economy (in the few places where this discipline was taught) were typically jurists or politicians who dabbled in economics. They did not yet possess the necessary requisites (in terms of educational background, specialist training, scientific production and academic qualifications) that would enable them to be clearly distinguished from colleagues belonging to other disciplines. As a consequence, the overall community of 'economists' did not yet have sufficient awareness and perception of its role to constitute a distinct professional group.

What the experience of the Turin Society does show is that the function of such associations was better understood in political circles, which featured a number of scholars interested in the diffusion of political economy. The various projects undertaken by the Society, the themes addressed during its scientific meetings and the tendencies revealed during discussion suggest that the Society predominantly took on the character of a lobby that tended to influence, or support, government choices. The very decision to dissolve the association following transfer of the capital confirms this interpretation. Furthermore, its alternating fortunes reflect the close connection and osmosis between the political milieu and university circles, a feature that was to remain a constant characteristic of Italian social and political history in the so-called 'liberal age' (1861–1922). As also underlined by subsequent experiences, relations between politicians and economists have always underlaid the process of dissemination of economic studies in Italy.

3 The Italian Society of Political Economy in Florence (1868–82)

With the political and administrative unification of Italy (1861), the Italian university system accelerated the process of expansion of economic studies. Within a few years almost all the law schools set up a course in political economy, recruiting professors through a system of public open competitions that was managed from within the scientific community itself and was therefore more rigorous than systems adopted in the past, when teachers were directly chosen by the government (see Augello *et al.* 1988).

The increase in number and quality of academics brought a new perspective to the problem of the spread of economic studies beyond the confines of the university world. This was a particularly sensitive problem for academic economists, as they felt they should be awarded a more prominent role than politicians, who had so far been the most active. A number of professors therefore sought to revive the project of an associative structure that would overcome the predominantly 'political' character of the Turin Society while still retaining the positive aspects of interaction with political circles that had been such a striking feature of the first experience.

When work began on this new project, which would ultimately lead to the establishment of the Società di Economia Politica Italiana, the centre of activity was no longer Turin but Florence, by now the capital of the Kingdom. The driving force behind the project was Francesco Protonotari, who some years earlier had been appointed professor of political economy in Pisa (Faucci 1978). Together with a small group of economists and politicians, he drew up the programme of the new Society, distributing it in university circles in order to canvass for membership enrolments among his colleagues.[15]

The by-laws of the Society were definitively approved on 6th June 1868. The initial organisation chart indicated Senator Arrivabene as President and Protonotari as Secretary; the economists Ferrara, Minghetti and Scialoja, who were also members of Parliament, were elected Vice-presidents. The twenty-four founding members were evenly balanced between university professors and politicians.[16] The composition of internal groupings within the Society was likewise carefully designed to ensure interaction between scientific research and political practice in the process of expansion and diffusion of economic studies. In particular, all the main universities were represented by their own economists. These included Boccardo, Marescotti, Reymond and Torrigiani, who had previously belonged to the Turin Society of Political Economy; in addition to these, there were names such as Giovanni Bruno, who taught in Palermo, Antonio Ciccone (Naples), Luigi Cossa (Pavia), Salvatore Majorana Calatabiano (Catania), and Angelo Messedaglia (Padua).[17]

The founding members of the Society did not include any other professors of political economy. However, this should not be read as political or scientific discrimination, for the range of members did express a variety of positions,[18] and in any case there were no illustrious scholars among those excluded. What is important to note is that academic economists were strongly and well represented, which guaranteed proper attention to scientific problems. It is worth noting that the by-laws significantly opened with the statement that the Society's mission was to 'promote and disseminate economic studies'.[19]

While not proposing to follow a specific institutional model, the Society drew its inspiration from the experience of the Société d'Economie Politique founded in Paris in 1842. Its intent was to act as a forum for debate free from any 'gravity of formal procedures', although there was general recognition that in order for the Society to acquire prestige and standing, the number of members should not exceed seventy, to be reached through a rigorous coopting mechanism.

The aim of spreading economic studies was to be further enhanced by a special relation between the activity of the association and the world of publishers, which was to cover works ranging from scientific debate to popularisations on economics. But while the latter aspect never went beyond mere occasional reports of books regarded as suitable for this purpose, the Society achieved considerable success in giving its activities a very high profile. Thus Protonotari systematically published extensive reports on the Society's scientific meetings in *Nuova Antologia* (Florence, 1866–) – a literary and scientific journal that would become one of the most prestigious at a nationwide level – and also provided information and updates on the life of the association.

Initially the Society was extremely active. In barely more than three years, about twenty scientific meetings were held. They featured lively exchange of ideas between economists and politicians on matters pertaining both to theory and economic policy. Among theoretical questions addressed, attention focused on money and monetary systems, commercial treaties and issuing banks,[20] while policy issues included the economic problems of administrative decentralisation, deed fees and stamp duty, and above all the role of government in running the railways.[21] Fervent debate was also stirred by such topics as ownership of the mines and land rent, which were discussed both from the point of view of economic theory as well as that of practical application.[22]

Discussion frequently touched on the profession of the economist, either directly or indirectly, as well as the dissemination of economic studies. Matters such as the problem of agrarian schools and the content of university courses in economics were often on the agenda;[23] and sharply opposing views on the appropriateness of introducing political economy into secondary school curricula were also aired.[24] Debate on these issues habitually provided a framework for animated interaction between scholars and those in charge of government policy.

As a general statement, the Italian Society of Political Economy cannot be considered a professional association of economists in a modern sense, despite already manifesting a number of traits characteristic of such bodies. But neither was it a mere lobby organised around specific political interests, as in its previous embodiment. Economists who took an active part in the life of the Society showed a good level of professional self-awareness, as testified in particular by the fact that the Society's deliberations were presented as the expression of the 'opinion of the scholars of economic science in Italy', independently of the methodological and ideological diversity among members.[25]

These achievements notwithstanding, the aim of conducting in-depth theoretical study and enhancing the professional status of economists soon gave way to issues focusing on parliamentary debate and government economic policy, in spite of the opposition of Ferrara. Once again, it was on the plane of relations between politics and economics that the crisis of economic societies was played out amongst those who were involved in the field of economics. Conflicts concerning the new orientation of the Society's activities arose as early as the beginning of the 1870s, leading first to a slow-down in the pace of activity and then to a prolonged suspension, lasting from January 1873 right up to 1878. During this period, differences of opinion between Italian economists developed into a veritable clash along ideological as well as scientific lines. There had already been disputes previously among members on the object and method of economics and the role of the state in the economy. But disagreement had been contained within the framework of clear-cut scientific debate, the only consequence being the polemical attitude of Ferrara who – isolated in a position of intransigent *laissez-faire* – had resigned from the Society.[26] Now, however, the conflict between economists culminated in the so-called 'debate on the method', a profound opposition that could not fail to be reflected within the Society itself. Indeed, the latter virtually ceased to exist, and the attempts by Protonotari to reconcile diverging views among Italian economists into a single united front by relaunching the activity of the Society[27] in the late 1870s did not go beyond a couple of meetings, the last of which was held in March 1882.[28]

4 The Italian *Methodenstreit*: the Adam Smith Society and the Association for the Advancement of Economic Studies

The process of the professionalisation of economics in the nineteenth century has been viewed by a consolidated historiography (Church 1974; Coats 1993) as a linear evolutionary path, linked to the acquisition of the neutral techniques of marginalist analysis. According to this interpretation, the absence of methodological controversies constitutes one of the main indicators of the stabilisation of the discipline, whose adherents recognise certain fundamental principles as common terms of reference for the profession of economist.

In the Italian historical experience, on the other hand, the professionalisation of economics did not travel along an equally linear path (Augello 1989). For although the spread of marginalism in the closing decades of the nineteenth century certainly influenced the evolution of economics in Italy, the importance of the *Methodenstreit* in this process should not be underestimated, nor the contribution of economists who followed the approach of the 'Historical School'.

As is known, the debate on the method, which developed in Europe after the congress of the *Kathedersozialisten* in Eisenach, also had significant repercussions in Italy, where it exploded in the mid-1870s. The controversy was prompted by the publication of the writings of Vito Cusumano[29] – a follower of Luigi Cossa, who had completed his specialisation in Germany – on the most recent developments in German economics. Francesco Ferrara drafted a biting rejoinder to Cusumano, thereby triggering a polemic that was destined to become a far more sweeping controversy than a mere scientific wrangle (Ferrara 1874a, 1874b).

It was a dispute in which all the major economists and national periodicals became involved. The opposition between different economic, ideological and political conceptions also had an important impact at the professional and academic levels, as the ensuing divisions induced economists to devote greater attention not only to the scientific aspects of the profession (training and specialisations) but also to academic policy (increase in the number of academic chairs, control over open competitions, etc.). This process also resulted in a generation change within the ranks of academic staff, leading to a preponderance of exponents of the Historical School and the demise of the *laissez-faire* doctrine championed by Ferrara. Thus the gradual professionalisation of economists, far from being held back by the division between the two schools, was in effect accelerated by the very consequences of the conflict surrounding the academic development of the discipline.

It was against this backcloth that projects such as the Società Adamo Smith and the Associazione per il Progresso degli Studi Economici arose. The former was set up in Florence in 1874 upon the initiative of a group of economists headed, once again, by Francesco Ferrara and several liberal politicians belonging to the so-called 'Tuscan moderates'. High-ranking positions in the Society were held by Gino Capponi and Giovanni Arrivabene as Honorary Presidents, Ubaldino Peruzzi and Pietro Bastogi, respectively President and Vice-president, with Giulio Franco and Carlo Fontanelli as Secretary and Deputy-secretary.[30]

The aim of the Society was that of 'promoting, developing and defending the doctrine of economic liberties'[31] originally formulated by Adam Smith. Membership of the Society was conditional only upon acceptance of these principles. The by-laws did not provide for subsidiary branches, although a related body was formed in Sicily and was active up to the end of the 1880s (Li Donni 2000). The organ of governance of the Society was the members' assembly, which deliberated on the research and debates to be conducted, prizes to be awarded, as well as the studies to be published in *L'Economista* of Florence, which was the official press organ of the Society. In addition, the regulations required that a general congress be held at least once a year, to act as an overall 'sounding box' for the association's activity.

The Society aimed to assume the character of a scientific body, excluding from debate all that could be more properly described as political. Such an approach was in effect a constant feature of positions favourable to *laissez-faire* in late nineteenth-century Italy, and it would be strongly reaffirmed by marginalist economists. Orthodox Smithian doctrine was presented as the only scientific legitimisation of political economy and the only approach consistent with the reality of economic facts; historicist descriptivism, on the other hand, was judged to be incapable of founding an autonomous science.

Among the fifty-eight founding members[32] there were jurists, politicians and public officials, together with a substantial presence of academic economists. The latter constituted a clearly identifiable professional group in that they represented the first generation of university professors of the post-unification period, predominantly trained in the Ferrarian school.[33] In contrast, young economists who were just embarking on their academic career were few and far between.[34] This meant that the Society was in effect a mouthpiece for the demands and aspirations of older economists with a more traditional training. This characteristic needs to be underlined in order to highlight the academic implications of the 'battle' for *laissez-faire* the Society planned to wage, and also to bring to light the differences as compared to the rival association that was set up the following year (Ferrara 1874b: 561).

Overall, the Società Adamo Smith played a substantial role in organising the opposition of the traditional Economic School towards the new doctrines of the Historical School that were gaining credence in Italy. It was highly instrumental in the dissemination of political economy, even though its contribution to the professionalisation of the economist is open to doubt. It undeniably acted as a tool for growing professional self-awareness among the group of advocates of *laissez-faire*, who perceived their scientific and academic ascendancy to be under threat and felt the need for 'confirmation' of their theoretical approach. But the Society did not succeed in producing an epistemological clarification similar to that which had occurred in other historical circumstances, which would reinforce the profession (Coats 1964). For such a development, Italy would have to await the diffusion and further expansion of marginalism, when a new professional basis for *laissez-faire* economists would be provided (Barucci 1972).

In January 1875 an important scientific congress was held in Milan, at the behest of Cossa, Lampertico, Luzzatti and Scialoja, who had been the protagonists of the debate between advocates of *laissez-faire* and interventionism ever since the Florence Society of Political Economy meetings.

Responding to Ferrara's splinter-group tendency, these economists drew up a document, known as the 'Padua Circular', which marked the start of a counteroffensive by the so-called 'chair socialists'. In this circular, they invited politicians and economists to a congress to discuss the most suitable steps for giving a new boost to economic studies in Italy.[35] The programme of the congress focused principally on the economic role of the state, with particular reference to the 'social question' and the establishment of a new Society of Political Economy.[36]

The congress, attended by roughly two hundred invited participants, opened with an address by F. Lampertico in which the recent conflicts of opinion among Italian economists were outlined. Recalling the traditions of Italian economic science, he specified the concepts that were to form the guiding principles of the new programme of studies. The various sessions, introduced by L. Luzzatti, then touched upon the subjects listed on the agenda, which were concerned with workers' conditions in industry, regulations for the protection of emigrants, the institutions for healthcare and pension provision. The congress closed with the decision to establish study commissions and conduct investigations on the most important aspects of the social question. The final objective was to draw parliamentary attention to the various indications that would emerge from research on the above issues. The main deliberation of the congress consisted in the foundation of the Associazione per il Progresso degli Studi Economici, which designated *L'Economista d'Italia* and the *Rassegna d'Agricoltura, Industria e Commercio* – the latter subsequently transformed into the *Giornale degli Economisti* – as its official press mouthpieces.[37]

The Association set itself the task of building up a programme that would make provision for social studies, to be accomplished partly through extension of its organisational structure to different parts of Italy. The Association was structured into a presidential office, composed of the proponents of the Milan congress, and many local committees to be set up in the major cities, each composed of at least ten members. The President's office coordinated the work of these committees and prepared materials for the general congress of the Association, which represented the climax of the Association's activity. The committees, in turn, assisted the President's office in conducting the research deliberated by the congress; in addition, they were also free to carry out studies under their own initiative.[38] They were required to communicate the results of their activities to the President's office periodically, so that the leaders of the Association were kept constantly informed of the progress of activities within the various peripheral divisions and could exert their coordinating function more successfully (Maccabelli 2000).

The existence of local branches constituted one of the distinctive features of the Association and meant it was able to perform quite detailed social research at grassroots level. This was indeed an ambitious project that harked back to the organisational model of some important surveys requested by the national Parliament. Among these, highly important was the 1870–74 Industrial Survey directed by Antonio Scialoja, prompted by positions in economic circles that did not feel comfortable with free-trade policy (Baglioni 1974: 189–231; Are 1974). The 1875 Congress of Milan voiced these feelings, which eventually gave rise to the political watershed of the following year when the Left headed by Agostino Depretis took over the reins of government.

Within a few months numerous local committees were set up (Bof 2000), some of which were extremely active and survived the central organ of governance of the Association itself, which – as laid down in the by-laws – was short-lived. This was in accordance with the Association's basic mission, namely that of organising a wide-ranging movement of ideas and projects favourable to greater intervention by the state, above all in social affairs.

The Association's activities also had significant follow-on effects in the university world, favouring the influx of a younger generation into the professorial ranks of economists. Thus in the mid-1870s the only professors of economics whose outlook was in tune with the guiding principles of the Milan congress were Cossa, Messedaglia and Boccardo. But just a few years later, the Association featured numerous exponents of the school that adopted the historical approach, among whom one may cite S. Cognetti de Martiis (Turin), A. Loria (Siena), E. Morpurgo (Padua), G. Toniolo (Pisa), and so forth. Their presence overturned the traditional predominance of the *laissez-faire* school and their new vision undermined its scientific basis through their innovative proposals for study and research. This orientation gathered considerable momentum in the following years and would eventually lead to the rise of a new generation of economists specialised in the various branches of applied economics.

The path that was being traced out proved to be of great significance for the professionalisation of the economist, coinciding as it did with the academic recruitment of scholars who, unlike in the past, had undertaken their studies on the basis of specifically economic interests and had received specialist training designed explicitly for the exercise of the profession (Augello 1989). An emblematic case from this point of view is that of the chairs of public finance (introduced into law schools from 1886), where from the very outset leading figures of the Historical School, in its various approaches – positivist, inductivist, sociological – held sway.[39]

The vision embraced by the Association for the Advancement of Economic Studies was thus paralleled by developments in the economic disciplines within the university world and by the shifting balance of power between the two opposing groups. It is partly for this reason that the professionalisation of the economist in Italy appears to be positively correlated with the methodological division endorsed by the Milan congress and also with the research proposals put forward by scholars who had turned away from the Ferrarian school. In effect, even though the late nineteenth-century penetration of marginalism in Italy made the Italian case more similar to that of other countries, it can be stated that Positivism, Lorianism, Christian social doctrine and study of the socialist movement by economists all represent theoretical outcomes of an autonomous process which evolved out of a multifaceted array of positions clustering around the Historical School.

5 The institutionalisation of political economy and the professionalisation of economists at the end of the century

Both of the associations that were established in connection with the 'debate on the method' proved to be short-lived. Their driving force can be said to have waned as early as 1878.[40] At that time, the two opposing groups began to explore the possibility of uniting Italian economists under the flag of the old Società di Economia Politica Italiana, which had held a meeting in that very year (15th May 1878). The sought-after reconciliation was accomplished above all through the efforts of Marco Minghetti – whose name was put forward as the new President of the Society – and met with no resistance either from Ferrara or Luzzatti. But the revival of the Florentine Society was destined never to be carried out.

This phase of the history of economic societies thus came to an end. It had been a phase that had seen the rise of several different societies whose goal was to promote and spread economic studies and, sometimes fairly explicitly, to raise consciousness among scholars of economics that theirs was indeed a genuine profession. A few final offshoots of this phase came into being as late as the 1890s, involving liberal economists in particular, but the nature and aims of these later projects were predominantly political or social, and their by-laws no longer bore any trace of the traditional objectives of the previous experiences, which had to a large extent already been achieved (Michelini 2000; Pecorari 2000).

Overall, the action carried out by associations of economists in the nineteenth century was remarkable in the scope of their work and accomplishments. Meetings were held at very frequent intervals and considerable attention was devoted to institutional aspects concerning the teaching of political economy within universities. Similar attention was dedicated to professional aspects such as the training of economists, although this did not always translate into concrete and enduring projects. Communication of the contents of economic debate that took place within the societies was systematic and accurate, and was achieved through judicious use of the daily press and the major journals. In this regard, the importance of an association-specific publication was frequently underscored: such a publication should be a purpose-designed journal of political economy also capable of acting as a forum for scientific debate. By the mid-1870s, time was ripe for a project of this nature. The Adam Smith Society and the Association for the Advancement of Economic Studies set up their respective journals, *L'Economista* in Florence (later in Rome, 1874–1924) and the *Giornale degli economisti* in Padua (later in Bologna, Rome, and Milan, 1875–), thereby contributing to the process of specialisation of periodicals (Augello and Guidi 1996; Augello *et al.* 1996).

An examination of the subjects that formed the object of debate in these Associations reveals that there was hardly any economic theme that was not exhaustively addressed during the scientific meetings. The main issues of economic theory, as well as the crucial questions of national economic policy, constituted the natural focus of exchange of ideas and discussion: from the theory of rent to that of taxation and methodological problems, from the railways to money and the banks, from the role of the state to the multiple aspects of the social question. Debate was extensive and wide-ranging not only during the periods when the societies were dominated by politicians but also when more professional figures of economists constituted a majority presence.

The net effect of the activities undertaken by these associations over a roughly thirty-year period – from the end of the 1850s to the late 1880s – was that of ushering in a profound change in the institutional set-up of economic studies. The new context transformed the manner of engaging in economic research and saw the gradual emergence of a more clearly defined figure of the economist characterised by specialist training and interests (Augello 1989).

This process was particularly evident in terms of the scientific production of economists. Whereas in the past the issues dealt with had been predominantly political, juridical or social, now attention focused primarily on strictly economic issues, with a clear-cut tendency towards specialisation, at first directed to disciplinary issues and later to specific themes or sectors (Augello 1994). This led to the rise of such professional and academic figures as experts in public finance or statisticians and, subsequently, also to agrarian or industrial economists, transport specialists, experts in monetary problems, economic historians and so forth. There were spillover effects to teaching as well, both in the shape of in-depth study of particular aspects in the framework of courses on political economy and also through the establishment of optional courses on special subjects. It was precisely as a result of this thematic specialisation that these courses would later be introduced as an integral part of the faculties of economics during the twentieth century.

A similar process of specialisation can be seen within the traditional channel of communication of the results of economists' scientific activity, which was represented by periodicals. In the past this function had been performed mainly through scientific and literary periodicals and juridical journals, together with the publications of academies and other learned institutions. The 1870s saw the founding of the first economic journals, which over the following decades took on an increasingly specialist and sectorial character, thereby further contributing to the professionalisation of economics.

As an overall appraisal, the rise of economic societies should therefore be considered as merely one of the threads of a rich tapestry in which the identity of Italian economists was gradually assuming a more distinct shape.

Notes

* This chapter is based on the results of a research project on the history of the economic associations in Italy in the nineteenth century (see Augello and Guidi 2000). The authors are indebted to the contributors to this research for their valuable suggestions, and to Pier Francesco Asso for his comments on a preliminary version of this paper. Although the general structure of this chapter is common, M. Guidi drafted sections 1 and 4, and M. Augello sections 2, 3 and 5.

1 The majority of these experiences is reconstructed in Augello and Guidi 2000, vol. 1.

2 See *Gazzetta Piemontese*, 1852, vol. 3, n. 150, 25 June, pp. 1–2.

3 See the By-Laws of the Society of Political Economy, articles 1–3, in Pischedda 1986, pp. 732–4.

4 By-Laws of the Society of Political Economy, articles 5–7, in Pischedda 1986, pp. 732–4.

5 See *Il Parlamento*, 1853, vol. 1, n. 6, 7 Jan., p. 2; *L'Opinione*, 1853, n. 8, 8 Jan., pp. 2–3. The text of the speech is republished in Pischedda 1986, pp. 136–9.

6 The minutes of the meetings of the Society were edited for publication by Francesco Ferrara in the Turin newspapers *Il Parlamento* and *Gazzetta Piemontese*.

7 A few years later Ferrara observed that in Italy the attempt to set up an Economics Society had very soon turned into a party manoeuvre (Ferrara 1856). On this point see also the correspondence between Ferrara and Giuseppe Todde – a student of his who was to hold a professorship at the University of Cagliari from the 1860s onwards – published in Neppi Modona 1979.

8 Arrivabene had been among the promoters of the Congress of the Economists in Belgium in 1847 and had enjoyed a prolonged acquaintance with Tooke, McCulloch, Mill and Senior in London. On his action as a link between Italian and European economic culture, see Coldagelli 1962.

9 The by-laws of the Association were published in 'Società di economia politica', *La Rivista Contemporanea*, 1860, June, pp. 119–21.

10 The names most significantly absent were Giovanni Bruno (Palermo), Luigi Cossa (Pavia), Placido De Luca (Catania) and Angelo Marescotti (Bologna).

11 From 1860 to 1865 over forty meetings devoted to economic debate were held, in addition to those reserved to discussion on questions of internal organisation and the other activities of the Society.

12 See *Annali Universali di Statistica*, 1861, Jul.–Sept., pp. 41–5; 1862, Jan., pp. 49–58; *Il Politecnico*, 1862, vol. 13, pp. 128–34, 140–8.

13 See *La Rivista Contemporanea*, 1861, vol. 9, Apr. and May, pp. 125–31, 403–20; *Annali Universali di Statistica*, 1861, Apr.–June, pp. 469–75; *Il Politecnico*, 1862, vol. 13, pp. 124–7, 135–9, 358–71; 1863, vol. 17, pp. 325–35.

14 See *Gazzetta di Torino*, 1864, 7, 14 and 21 Jan., 2 and 17 Feb., 18th March.

15 Protonotari's correspondence (Florence, Biblioteca Nazionale) shows that he particularly championed the membership of illustrious economists such as Boccardo, Cossa and Marescotti.

16 In detail, it was composed of ten academic economists, three senators, eight parliamentary deputies, two State councillors and one professor of Law, Luigi Luzzatti, who at that time was the general secretary of the Ministry of Agriculture, Industry and Commerce. See Asso 2000.

17 It should be noted that some of these economists were parliamentary deputies at the time, and others would subsequently also enter Parliament. Among the former, mention can be made of Ciccone, Majorana, Marescotti, Messedaglia, Torrigiani; among the latter, Boccardo, who was nominated Senator in 1877.

18 In the main, the members were supporters of an orthodox version of *laissez-faire*, and some of them had actually been Ferrara's students. But economists of other persuasions were also present – such as Cossa and Messedaglia – who would later take up a stance increasingly unsympathetic to traditional *laissez-faire*.

19 The by-laws of the Society are in Protonotari 1868.

20 The minutes were published by F. Protonotari in *Nuova Antologia*, 1869, vol. 11, n. 6, June, pp. 418–27; 1870, vol. 13, n. 4, April, pp. 847–57; n. 5, May, 196–207; 1871, vol. 17, n. 6, June, pp. 478–83; 1872, vol. 19, n. 1, Jan., pp. 243–50.

21 *Nuova Antologia*, 1871, vol. 16, n. 1, Jan., pp. 246–53; 1871, vol. 16, n. 2, Feb., pp. 504–11; 1871, vol. 17, n. 7, Jul., pp. 716–28; 1872, vol. 20, n. 6, June, pp. 457 ff.

22 *Nuova Antologia*, 1871, vol. 16, n. 3, March, pp. 749–60; n. 4, Apr., pp. 988–1,004; 1871, vol. 17, n. 5, May, pp. 238–47.

23 See the minutes of the session dated 30th May 1870, *Nuova Antologia*, 1870, vol. 14, n. 6, June, pp. 423–30.

24 *Nuova Antologia*, 1868, vol. 7, n. 7, July, pp. 633–44; 1869, vol. 10, n. 2, Feb., pp. 416–25; n. 4, Apr., pp. 858–70. See Bartolozzi 1990.

25 'Società di economia politica italiana', *Nuova Antologia*, 1869, vol. 11, n. 6, June, p. 419.

26 On Ferrara's resignation from the Society, see his exchange of correspondence with Protonotari in Bartolozzi 1990: 764–8. See also Ferrara 2001.
27 See *L'Economista*, 1878, n. 211, pp. 305–6.
28 See *Nuova Antologia*, 1882, vol. 62, n. 3, March, pp. 162 ff.
29 Collected in Cusumano 1875.
30 See 'Società Adamo Smith', *L'Economista*, 1874, vol. 2, n. 27, 5 Nov., p. 729. Fontanelli taught political economy at the Scuola di Scienze Sociali of Florence. See Faucci 2000.
31 'Società di economia politica sotto il titolo di Società Adamo Smith. Atto costitutivo', *L'Economista*, 1874, vol. 2, n. 21, 24 Sept., p. 563.
32 The lists of members who joined the Society later were published in *L'Economista*, 1874, vol. 2, n. 21, 24 Sept., p. 563; n. 22, 1 Oct., p. 601; n. 24, 15 Oct., p. 658; n. 25, 22 Oct., p. 673; n. 26, 29 Oct., p. 701.
33 Among these, mention should be made of the following, who had held professorships for several years: G. Bruno, in Palermo since 1845, A. Marescotti, in Bologna since 1860, G. Todde, in Sassari as from 1860 and subsequently in Cagliari since 1862, P. Torrigiani, in Parma as from 1860 and then in Pisa since 1870, F. Protonotari, in Pisa as from 1862 and in Rome since 1871, S. Majorana Calatabiano, in Messina as from 1867 and then in Catania since 1868.
34 In particular Tullio Martello, Carlo Fontanelli and Jacopo Virgilio, who would later teach political economy at the Higher Schools of Commerce in Venice, Florence, and Genoa respectively.
35 The text of the 'Circular', dated Padua 11 September 1874, is reproduced in Parisi 1978: 339–40.
36 See *L'Economista d'Italia*, 1874, vol. 6, n. 49, 6 Dec.
37 *L'Economista d'Italia*, 1875, vol. 7, n. 2, 11 Jan.
38 For the by-laws of the Association see Parisi 1978: 346.
39 Among others, G. Alessio (Padua), C.A. Conigliani (Modena), A. Graziani (Siena and Naples), A. Puviani (Bologna and Perugia) and G. Ricca Salerno (Pavia and Modena).
40 The Adam Smith Society met very sporadically up to the beginning of the 1880s.

References

Aa. Vv. (1996) *Le società economiche alla prova della storia (secoli XVIII–XIX)*, Rapallo: Grafica Busco.
Are, G. (1974) *Alle origini dell'Italia industriale*, Napoli: Guida.
Asso, P.F. (2000) 'La Società italiana di economia politica di Firenze (1868–1882)', in Augello and Guidi 2000.
Augello, M.M. (1989) 'The Societies of Political Economy in Italy and the Professionalization of Economists (1860–1900)', *History of Economics Society Bulletin* 11, 1: 99–112.
—— (1994) 'L'evoluzione della letteratura economica in Italia: 1861–1900. Una analisi storico-quantitativa', *Il pensiero economico italiano* 2, 1: 7–36.
—— (2000) 'La Società di economia politica di Torino tra politica ed economia', in Augello and Guidi 2000.
Augello, M.M., Bianchini, M., Gioli, G. and Roggi P. (eds) (1988) *Le cattedre di economia in Italia (1700–1900). La nascita di una disciplina 'sospetta'*, Milano: Angeli.

Augello, M.M., Bianchini, M., and Guidi, M.E.L. (eds) (1996) *Le riviste di economia in Italia (1700–1900). Dai giornali scientifico-letterari ai periodici specialistici*, Milano: Angeli.

Augello, M.M. and Guidi, M.E.L. (1996) 'The Emergence of Economic Periodical Literature in Italy (1750–1900)', *History of Economic Ideas* 4, 3: 15–62.

—— (eds) (2000) *Associazionismo economico e diffusione dell'economia politica nell'Italia dell'Ottocento. Dalle società economico-agrarie alle associazioni di economisti*, Milano: Angeli.

Baglioni, G. (1974) *L'ideologia della borghesia industriale nell'Italia liberale*, Torino: Einaudi.

Bartolozzi, S. (1990) 'Francesco Ferrara, la Società di economia politica italiana e il dibattito sull'insegnamento della scienza economica', in P.F. Asso, P. Barucci and M. Ganci *Francesco Ferrara e il suo tempo*, Roma: Bancaria Editrice.

Barucci, P. (1972) 'The Spread of Marginalism in Italy (1871–1890)', *History of Political Economy* 4, 2: 512–31.

Becagli, V. (2000) 'L'Accademia economico-agraria dei Georgofili nell'età della Restaurazione', in Augello and Guidi 2000.

Benvenuto Vialetto, A. and Ancona, G. (1969) 'Boccardo Gerolamo', in *Dizionario Biografico degli Italiani*, vol. 11, Roma: Istituto dell'Enciclopedia Italiana.

Bianchini, M. (1989) 'Some Fundamental Aspects of Italian Eighteenth-Century Economic Thought', in D.A. Walker (ed.) *Perspectives on the History of Economic Thought*, vol. 1, London: Elgar.

—— (1994) 'The Galilean Tradition and the Origins of Economic Science in Italy', in M. Albertone and A. Masoero (eds) *Political Economy and National Realities*, Torino: Fondazione L. Einaudi.

Bof, F. (2000) 'Comitati dell'Associazione per il progresso degli studi economici in Italia (1875–1879)', in Augello and Guidi (2000).

Church, R. (1974) 'Economists as Experts. The Rise of an Academic Profession in the United States, 1870–1920', in L. Stone (ed.) *The University in Society*, vol. 2, Princeton: Princeton University Press.

Coats, A.W. (1964) 'The Role of Authority in the Development of British Economics', *Journal of Law and Economics* 7: 85–106.

—— (1993) *The Sociology and Professionalization of Economics, British and American Economic Essays*, London and New York: Routledge.

Coldagelli, U. (1962) 'Arrivabene Giovanni', in *Dizionario Biografico degli Italiani*, vol. 4, Roma: Istituto dell'Enciclopedia Italiana.

Cusumano, V. (1875) *Le scuole economiche della Germania in rapporto alla quistione sociale*, Napoli: Marghieri.

De Lorenzo, R. (1998) *Società economiche e istruzione agraria nell'Ottocento meridionale*, Milano: Angeli.

Faucci, R. (1978) 'Organizzazione e diffusione della cultura economica in Italia dopo l'Unità. Lettere di L. Cossa e di A. Loria a F. Protonotari 1868–1886', *Economia e Storia* 24, 1: 93–113.

—— (1995) *L'economista scomodo. Vita e opere di Francesco Ferrara*, Palermo: Sellerio.

—— (2000) 'La Società Adamo Smith', in Augello and Guidi 2000.

Ferrara, F. (1856) 'Il Belgio e il Piemonte dall'aspetto economico', *L'Economista. Giornale della Domenica* 14. Repr. in *Opere Complete di Francesco Ferrara*, vol. 7, part 2, F. Caffè and F. Sirugo (eds), Roma: Istituto Grafico Tiberino, 1970.

—— (1874a) 'Il germanismo economico in Italia', *Nuova Antologia* 26. Repr. in *Opere complete di Francesco Ferrara*, vol. 10, *Saggi, rassegne, memorie economiche e finanziarie*, F. Caffè (ed.), Roma: Bancaria editrice, 1972.

—— (1874b) 'La Società Adamo Smith e la circolare di Padova', *L'Economista* 2, 21. Repr. in *Opere complete di Francesco Ferrara*, vol. 8, *Articoli su giornali e scritti politici. Parte terza (1857–1891)*, R. Faucci (ed.), Roma: Bancaria editrice, 1976.

—— (2001) *Epistolario, Opere complete di Francesco Ferrara*, vol. 13, P.F. Asso (ed.), Roma: Bancaria editrice.

Gioli, G. (1989) *Il pensiero economico di Antonio Scialoja*, Pisa: Pacini.

Li Donni, A. (2000) 'La Società siciliana di economia politica dal 1875 al 1888', in Augello and Guidi 2000.

Maccabelli, T. (2000) 'La Società d'incoraggiamento di Padova e l'Associazione per il progresso degli studi economici (1846–1878)', in Augello and Guidi 2000.

Michelini, L. (2000) 'Il movimento anti-protezionistico e l'Associazione per la libertà economica', in Augello and Guidi 2000.

Morato, E. (1996) 'I periodici milanesi dell'età teresiana, *Il Caffè*, l'*Estratto della letteratura europea*, la *Gazzetta letteraria*', in Augello *et al.* 1996.

Neppi Modona, L. (1979) *Francesco Ferrara a Torino. Carteggio con Giuseppe Todde*, Milano: Giuffrè.

Parisi, D. (1978) 'Congresso di Economisti nel gennaio 1875 in Milano', *Rivista Internazionale di Scienze Sociali* 86, 3: 308–50.

Pecorari, P. (2000) 'L'Unione cattolica per gli studi sociali in Italia dalle origini (1889) alla fine dell'Ottocento', in Augello and Guidi 2000.

Pischedda, C. (1985) 'Francesco Ferrara a Torino. La Società di economia politica e un discorso sconosciuto di Cavour', *Studi Piemontesi* 14, 1: 131–41.

—— (1986) 'Francesco Ferrara e la Società di economia politica a Torino', in *Studi in memoria di Mario Abrate*, vol. 2, Torino: Universita di Torino, Istituto di Storia economica.

Protonotari, F. (1868) 'Costituzione della Società di economia politica italiana', *Nuova Antologia* 7, Jul.: 627–31.

Venturi, F. (1969) *Settecento riformatore*, vol. 1, *Da Muratori a Beccaria*, Torino: Einaudi.

5 Economic associations in Belgium

*Guido Erreygers**

Much remains to be done with regard to the history of economic thought in Belgium. There are serious lacunae in our knowledge, especially concerning developments of the discipline in the nineteenth century. This century is particularly interesting, since in Belgium as in many other countries, economics gradually established itself as a separate science. Universities created chairs in political economy, specialised economics journals were founded and economists began to form their own societies and associations. In this chapter I will concentrate on one of these organisations, the Société Belge d'Economie Politique, which dates from 1855 and still exists today.[1] No history of the Society has ever been written; this is a first attempt, which does not claim to be exhaustive, to describe the foundation of the Society and its activities in the nineteenth century.[2]

1 Economics in Belgium before 1845

Throughout the nineteenth century, economics was a rather marginal subject in the Belgian academic system. Universities did create chairs of political economy, but nonetheless at least one prominent contemporary academic lamented that 'the situation long remained highly unfavourable to political economy within the curricula' (Brants 1899: 145). For the history of economic thought in nineteenth-century Belgium one has to look perhaps more at what happened outside academia than at what happened within. Many important writers came from the worlds of journalism, business or government administration. If they lectured, it was often in small and specialised institutions, not in the universities. This highly 'non-academic' character of economics is reflected in the way in which associations and societies of economists were formed in Belgium.

Before Belgium's independence in 1830, the most influential academic economist seems to have been the Dutch economist Jan Ackersdijck, who was professor at the University of Liège from 1825 to 1830.[3] After 1830, the first professors in charge of general courses in political economy in Belgium were Charles de Coux (Catholic University of Louvain, 1834–45), Charles de Brouckère (Free University of Brussels, 1834–8), Philippe De

Rote (State University of Ghent, 1830–52) and C.A. Hennau (State University of Liège, 1830–64) (Brants 1899: 164–5). The most important of these is probably de Brouckère, although he did not publish much on economics.[4]

The impact of the Saint-Simonian and Fourierist movements on the diffusion of economic ideas in Belgium was considerable. Both the statistician and sociologist Adolphe Quetelet,[5] and the influential Catholic writer and inspector-general of prisons and charity houses, Edouard Ducpétiaux[6] had nourished Saint-Simonian sympathies in their youths (Michotte 1908: 400). Fourier's most important disciple, Victor Considérant, had an extensive circle of friends in Belgium (Discailles 1895) and there were many Fourierist groups.[7] Other important socialist sources of inspiration were Hippolyte de Colins, the Belgian baron who propagated the system of 'rational socialism',[8] and François Huet, the French professor of philosophy in Ghent who developed a form of Christian socialism.[9] In the second half of the nineteenth century the influence of Colins can be traced in the work of César De Paepe and that of Huet even more so in the work of Emile de Laveleye.

2 The period 1845–55

Before 1845 no initiative seems to have been taken to form a group or association of economists. Probably inspired by the work of Richard Cobden and Frédéric Bastiat, the first successful attempt was made by Adolphe Le Hardy de Beaulieu with the help of Victor Faider. In 1846 they succeeded in founding the Association Belge pour la Liberté Commerciale, an organisation designed to condemn protectionism and promote free trade (Michotte 1904: 30). The Association was headed by Charles de Brouckère (President), Giovanni Arrivabene and Fr. Basse (Vice-presidents), Victor Faider and Adolphe Le Hardy de Beaulieu (Secretaries), Frédéric Fortamps (Treasurer) and Michel Corr-Vandermaeren and Van De Vin (ordinary members).

The main accomplishment of the Association was undoubtedly the organisation of the Congrès des Economistes in Brussels, 16th–18th September 1847. Although most of the participants were Belgian economists and businessmen, this was a truly European meeting, perhaps the first of its kind. There was an important delegation from France, including Horace Say, Guillaumin, Garnier and Fonteyraud of the *Journal des économistes*, Blanqui and Wolowski, while Michel Chevalier sent a long letter of support to the organisers (*Congrès des economistes*, 1847: 5–13). But there were also participants from Britain, Germany, Italy, the Netherlands, Denmark, Sweden, Poland, Moldavia, Spain and the United States. The vast majority of the delegates were free-traders, but there were also a few outspoken protectionists, notably Rittinghausen from Cologne and Duchataux from Valenciennes. The list of participants also mentions 'Marx, man of letters and economist, in Brussels' (1847: 7). The main purpose of the Congrès was to advance the cause of 'commercial liberty'. The question was examined from four different points of view (international aspects, industrial aspects, the workers, and public expenses) (1847: 66) and finally agreement was reached on a resolution stressing the many advantages of freedom of trade (1847: 120–1, 178, 182). A committee was charged with the duty to find a time and place for a next conference (1847: 194–5). Apparently, the second meeting was scheduled for Paris in 1848,[10] but the events of that year made it necessary first to postpone it[11] and finally to cancel it. Likewise, the Association Belge pour la Liberté Commerciale, which had taken the initiative for the Congrès, had to be dissolved (Michotte 1904: 33).

3 The foundation and first fourteen years of the Société Belge d'Economie Politique

For a few years the free-traders kept a low profile. In 1855, however, there was a burst of activity, of which one of the results was the creation of a Belgian Political Economy Society. I will begin by saying a few words about the three persons that played a major role in this process: Gustave de Molinari, Charles Le Hardy de Beaulieu and Giovanni Arrivabene.

3.1 The protagonists

Gustave de Molinari was a Belgian economist, born in 1819 in Liège. From 1840 until the *coup d'état* of Napoléon III in December 1851, he lived in France where he became an active member of different *laissez-faire* groups and a frequent contributor to the leading liberal journals of the day.[12] He obtained the membership of the Société d'Economie Politique and wrote for the closely affiliated *Journal des économistes*. In 1849 he published a radically libertarian article in this journal, 'De la production de la sécurité', in which he argued that free competition should also be introduced with respect to provision of public goods such as security. In that same year he expounded similar theses in his book *Les Soirées de la rue Saint-Lazare. Entretiens sur les lois économiques et défense de la propriété*. He continued to defend these radical views for most of his (long) life, making him an early exponent and champion of 'anarcho-capitalism'.[13] After his return to Belgium in 1851, he obtained lecturing positions at the Musée Royal de l'Industrie in Brussels and at the Institut Supérieur de Commerce in Antwerp. He abandoned these positions in 1867, when he again moved to Paris to become a collaborator of *Journal des débats*. In 1881 he succeeded Joseph Garnier as the editor of *Journal des économistes*, a position which he retained until 1909 (he was ninety years old by then!) (see Laurent and Marco 1996). As one of the leading figures of liberalism in the second half of the nineteenth century, he exerted a considerable influence on many economists[14] and on Vilfredo Pareto in particular (see Tommissen 1971: 59–60 and *passim*). He died in De Panne in 1912.

For our purposes it is important to know that de Molinari founded and edited the Brussels-based journal *L'Economiste belge*, the first issue of which was published on 5th January 1855. For the next fourteen years the journal was the voice of the Belgian free-trade and *laissez-faire* movements and also served as the 'organ' of the Belgian Political Economy Society. In its first issue, the journal declared itself in favour of 'the system of cheap government' (*L'Economiste belge*, 1, 1: 3). Despite the success of the free-trade movement, in the very last issue de Molinari had to admit that Belgium had moved further away from this system (*L'Economiste belge*, 14, 26: 301).

Charles Le Hardy de Beaulieu, cousin of the already mentioned Adolphe, was a Belgian economist born in 1816 in Brussels. After his engineering studies in Paris, he spent a few years in Spain. In 1846 he was appointed lecturer in mineralogy, geology and metallurgy at the Ecole spéciale de commerce, d'industrie et des mines [Special school of trade, industry and mines] in Mons; a few years later the course of political economy was added to his academic duties.[15] An active member of many learned societies, he was above all a gifted populariser of science. This is clearly visible in his *Traité élémentaire d'économie politique*, published in 1861. Like de Molinari, he was an ardent defender of the cause of free trade and economic liberalism. Although blind from 1858 onwards, he continued to work and publish his writings; he died in 1871.

Count Giovanni (or Jean) Arrivabene was an Italian/Belgian economist born in 1787 in Mantova. As an exile he wandered around Europe until he settled in Brussels in 1829[16] (he obtained Belgian citizenship in 1841). In 1860, when the Italian king Victor Emmanuel made him a life senator, he returned to Italy but regularly came back to Belgium. He died in 1881. His work as an economist does not seem to have been very original. In collaboration with Ducpétiaux, he did some empirical research on the conditions of the working class and the poor. In his *Considérations sur les principaux moyens d'améliorer le sort des classes laborieuses*, published in 1832, he advocated free trade and education as a means to improve the situation of the working class. As a guest of the Political Economy Club in London, he had met James Mill, McCulloch and Tooke, and he was also on friendly terms with Nassau Senior; in Paris he had followed Jean-Baptiste Say's courses. He translated James Mill's *Elements of Political Economy* into Italian and adapted Senior's *Lectures* for a French edition.

3.2 The foundation

The proposal to create a Belgian Political Economy Society was officially launched in the middle of 1855. To the outside world it seemed as if Charles Le Hardy de Beaulieu was alone in taking the initiative, but it is clear that he acted in close collaboration with de Molinari. The plan was made public in the 20th July 1855 issue of *L'Economiste belge*.[17] It contained a letter by Le Hardy de Beaulieu to de Molinari, dated 1st July 1855, in which Le Hardy de Beaulieu argued that it seemed imperative to back up and amplify de Molinari's efforts in favour of the diffusion of economic ideas in Belgium. Le Hardy de Beaulieu suggested organising regular gatherings of economists in Brussels, which would discuss a range of previously announced economic questions. After each session, de Molinari's journal would publish a summary of the discussions. Le Hardy de Beaulieu explicitly indicated the Société d'Economie Politique of Paris and the Political Economy Club of London as his guiding examples:

> What I am proposing here cannot boast the merit of true innovation; a similar association has been in existence in Paris since 1842, under the name of *Free society of political economy*, which today numbers over sixty members. In London there is an *Economists' Club*, set up in 1821 and now composed of 35 members, among whom are numbered some of England's most eminent publicists. These societies have rendered great service to science by drawing the attention of the public to questions of political economy that arise from events and circumstances, by clarifying them through the insight gained from discussion and by favouring the blossoming of new ideas that would otherwise remain buried within the brain of their authors.
>
> (*L'Economiste belge*, 1, 14: 2)

In his editorial comments on the letter, de Molinari made no secret of his wish to use the Society as a vehicle to spread his liberal ideas. One can certainly say that for him the inclusion of the term 'political' in the expression 'political economy' was wholly appropriate:

> We cannot but approve the excellent suggestion by our contributor and thank him for having taken this initiative. We will add nothing to the arguments he has already so clearly put forward, which demonstrate the usefulness of an association designed to disseminate the economic truths, to remedy the mistakes of protectionism, communism and ultra-governmentalism, and also to act as a focal point in lobbying for economic and administrative reform. Our task is to found a *liberal association* in the real sense of the word, an association that will set itself the aim of ensuring that the principle of freedom and, consequently, that of non-intervention of government, prevails in all spheres of human activity.
>
> (*L'Economiste belge*, 1, 14: 1)

In accordance with his libertarian and anti-government convictions, de Molinari was determined the Society should be a completely private affair. He categorically refused all public support for the Society (*L'Economiste belge*, 1, 14: 3).

In the following issues of *L'Economiste belge*, regular updates were given on the process of foundation. The editor was proud to announce that the Paris Society had taken note of the Belgian initiative,[18] and added:

> The highly successful experience in Paris will naturally serve as our guide, and we hope that by taking its cue from the sound traditions of its elder relation, our association will be able to provide economic science with a propaganda centre, which is – alas! – just as necessary in Belgium as it is in France.
>
> (*L'Economiste belge*, 1, 16: 7)

The preparations came to an end in September, with the announcement of the first session of the Society on Sunday 23rd September 1855, under the presidency of Arrivabene and with two points on the agenda: 'I. Establishment of the society. II. Freedom of exchange and the means for achieving it in Belgium' (*L'Economiste belge*, 1, 18: 3).

3.3 Board and membership

Undoubtedly as a result of his age, fame, experience and diplomatic qualities, Arrivabene was chosen to preside over the session in which the Society was founded. During that same session he was also elected President of the Society, a function he retained at least until 1868. The first board of the Society consisted furthermore of Charles Le Hardy de Beaulieu and François-Henri Matthyssens,[19] Vice-presidents, and Charles de Cocquiel,[20] Secretary.[21] As early as February 1856, however, the *compte-rendu* of the session of the Society was signed by two secretaries, de Cocquiel and Eugène de Molinari, Gustave's brother.[22] In 1860, Arrivabene's return to Italy prompted the Society to opt for a system with two chairmen; it decided to ask Charles de Brouckère, Chairman of the legendary 1847 conference and mayor of Brussels since 1848, to be chairman alongside Arrivabene.[23] The plan failed, however, because de Brouckère died on 20th April of that year. Although Arrivabene spent most of his time in Italy, he managed to preside over many of the Society's sessions in the period 1860–6; occasionally he was replaced as chairman by Lucien Masson and Florent Gouvy, both members of the Chamber of Commerce in Verviers. In January 1865 a new secretarial team was appointed, consisting of Emile Despret, Alfred Geelhand and Léon Estivant.[24] In March 1866 the joint chairmanship idea resurfaced, and the Board of the Society was composed as follows: Arrivabene and Gouvy, Presidents, Ch. Le Hardy de Beaulieu and Masson, Vice-presidents, Mayer-Hartogs (a Brussels industrialist), Treasurer, G. de Molinari, Permanent Secretary, and Geelhand, Estivant, Despret and Ernest Allard, Secretaries.[25]

A full list of members of the Society was produced only for the first session.[26] Twenty-five members were present at the foundation and thirteen others had joined the Society but did not attend the session. The vast majority of those who were present belonged to the liberal and free-trade movements: the leading liberal Belgian economists of the time (Arrivabene, the two de Molinari's, the two Le Hardy de Beaulieu's), the free-trade activist Michel Corr-Vandermaeren, the French liberal economist Pascal Duprat, a considerable number of business men, but also Edouard Ducpétiaux. Among the absent members we find the name of Quetelet; as far as we can see, however, he never played an active role in the Society. Over the years the membership probably increased, but certainly in the first fourteen years no precise accounts were ever given. The Society functioned very much like a relatively open and free debating club, with a minimum of rules and regulations. Sometimes guests were invited to open the discussion while others (often visitors from abroad) could be asked by members to attend the sessions. For instance, in 1858 Kapoustine, a professor at the University of Moscow, was asked to speak on economic reforms in Russia.[27] Distinguished visitors included Hans von Mangoldt from the University of Göttingen (session of 23rd September 1861) and, surprisingly, Pierre-Joseph Proudhon, 'the famous French publicist' (*L'Economiste belge*, 7, 13: 105), who attended the sessions of 24th March 1861 and of 24th March 1862. According to Arrivabene, Proudhon remained very silent during his visits (Arrivabene 1879: 301–2). Arrivabene contrasted this with what happened during the anniversary banquet of 26th September 1857, when the American economist and avowed protectionist Henry Charles Carey clashed verbally with the free-trader Pascal Duprat.[28]

3.4 The activities

The Société d'Economie Politique of Paris, of which de Molinari had been a member since 1847,[29] served as the model for the new Society. Given the more limited pool of Belgian economists and businessmen, the ambition was to organise about four sessions a year in Brussels. As a rule these were held in a restaurant;[30] first the participants dealt with administrative affairs, then they enjoyed dinner, after which they discussed the questions listed on the agenda. The first point on the agenda of the very first session concerned the aim and means of the Society. There was a debate on whether the Society should concentrate exclusively or mainly on the issue of free trade and on whether the question of government interference should be left out of consideration. It was decided that free trade would not be the single issue and that government interference could be a subject for discussion. Agreement was reached on the following definition of the aim and means of the Society:

> Its aim is to spread knowledge of the true principles of economic science throughout our country, in order to achieve harmonisation of our legislation with these principles. The means of action to be adopted by our Society shall consist mainly in the establishment of sub-committees,

which shall be entrusted with active propaganda in different parts of the country and shall communicate to the Board of the Society whatever local information they may consider useful and appropriate for illuminating the debate on the questions placed on the agenda.

(L'Economiste belge, 1, 19: 1)

The proposed decentralised structure never materialised. In Mons a subcommittee was formed under the presidency of Charles Le Hardy de Beaulieu, but in Antwerp and Verviers the attempt apparently failed.

In the period 1855–1869 the Society held thirty-seven sessions in Brussels, which means that on average two or three sessions a year were organised. Free trade, customs and commercial affairs in general were recurrent themes on the agenda, but also questions relating to money. Towards the end of the period more attention was paid to labour issues, such as the employment of children in factories.

3.5 The free-trade campaign

In the first years of its existence the Society instigated and supported a broad campaign in favour of free trade, which was crowned with success when the Belgian government radically changed its trade policy in the years 1860 and 1861. The Society had taken care not to identify itself completely with this campaign. One of its first 'decisions' was to support the creation of a Comité de la Réforme Douanière, an initiative of one of its members, Corr-Vandermaeren.[31] This committee met on 29th November 1855 and decided to transform itself into the Association pour la Réforme Douanière.[32] Soon thereafter a manifesto and by-laws were drafted; when these were published in *L'Economiste belge*, the relationship between the Society and its offshoot was described (undoubtedly by de Molinari) as follows:

The Association for reform of customs barriers is destined to act as a complement to the Society of Political Economy. [...] The aim of the Association for reform of customs barriers is more limited and more immediately practical.

(L'Economiste belge, 1, 24: 1)

The first general assembly of the Association, held in early 1856, designated a board consisting of Corr-Vandermaeren, President, Barbier Hanssens, Vice-president, Keutter, Treasurer, Gustave de Molinari, Archivist and Auguste Couvreur and Hyacinthe Deheselle, Secretaries. The Association immediately launched a campaign to try and win public support. Its preferred means of action was the organisation of 'meetings' and 'grand meetings' in the most important Belgian industrial and commercial cities. Everywhere in Belgium the protagonists of the Association gave speeches to defend the cause of free trade. During one of the Association's meetings in

Antwerp, de Molinari had been so critical of the Belgian government's policy that he was forced to resign from his teaching position at the state-controlled Institut de Commerce Supérieur in February 1859.[33]

Guided by the memory of the successful 1847 Congrès des Economistes, the Association decided in April 1856 that it would organise an international conference on free trade later that year.[34] The Congrès International des Réformes Douanières was held in Brussels, from 22nd to 24th September 1856. It was a big success, both in terms of attendance (more than 650 persons had been registered) and in terms of the boost of confidence it gave to the free-trade movement.[35] To promote the cause of commercial freedom and customs reform in as many countries as possible, the decision was taken to found the Association Internationale pour les Réformes Douanières, with the seat in Brussels. The first board of the International Association was largely Belgian: Corr-Vandermaeren, President, Ch.-Al. Campan, Vice-president, Adolphe Le Hardy de Beaulieu and Auguste Couvreur, Secretaries, Barbier-Hanssens, Gustave de Molinari and Frédéric Fortamps, members.[36] This Association transformed itself in 1863 into the Association Internationale pour la Suppression des Douanes. This probably came about under the influence of the (international) campaign in favour of the abolition of customs launched in early 1861 by Alexis Joffroy of the Antwerp Chamber of Commerce. The Société Belge d'Economie Politique, of which Joffroy was a member, supported his proposals.[37]

3.6 Relationships with other Political Economy Societies

Many of the economists involved in the Société Belge d'Economie Politique, and especially de Molinari and Arrivabene, had good contacts with like-minded colleagues abroad. They were of course interested in what happened elsewhere and *L'Economiste belge* regularly reported on developments in other European political economy societies.

3.6.1 Société d'Economie Politique de Paris

As soon as the group of economists around de Molinari had founded the Brussels Society, they decided to strengthen the ties with their colleagues in Paris. In February 1856 the Society proposed to nominate Dunoyer, Horace Say, Michel Chevalier and Joseph Garnier of the Paris Society as corresponding members.[38] Later that year Chevalier wrote a letter in which he accepted the corresponding membership (*L'Economiste belge*, 2, 15: 5–6). In June 1857 mention was made of the fact that the Paris Society, in its two last sessions, had listened to reports by Adolphe Le Hardy de Beaulieu and Arrivabene on the customs reform movement in Belgium.[39] In September 1858 Garnier and Guillaumin attended the session of the Belgian Society.[40] Of the visitors who went in the opposite direction, mention was made in June 1861 of a session of the Paris Society, attended by Léon Vercken

(Secretary of the Antwerp Chamber of Commerce and member of the Belgian Society) as well as by John Stuart Mill, and in which there was a discussion on the customs abolition proposal launched by Alexis Joffroy.[41] A few years later, in 1865, the Belgian Society inquired whether it would be appropriate to jointly organise a conference of economists; in his answer to de Molinari, Garnier indicated that it would be better to postpone such a conference until 1866.[42] Apparently the project never got off the ground.

3.6.2 Italy

Occasionally *L'Economiste belge* also cited from the *comptes-rendus* of the Paris Society on matters that were not directly related to the Belgian Society or to Belgium in general. This happened for instance in 1855, to draw attention to the suspension of the activities of the Political Economy Society of Turin (*L'Economiste belge*, 1, 16: 6–7). Probably under the influence of Arrivabene, events in Turin were followed with particular interest in Brussels. In 1856 the journal mentioned that the *Giornale delle arti e delle industrie* of Turin had written about the Belgian Society (*L'Economiste belge*, 2, 1: 3). More important was the resurrection of the Italian Political Economy Society in Turin in 1860. Apparently Arrivabene's return to Italy in that same year had created a new dynamic: he actively supported the new foundation and was asked to be its President (a duty which he accepted only after some resistance) (*L'Economiste belge*, 6, 31: 492; see also Carina 1875: 143). This appointment was celebrated in the Belgian Society with a toast to Arrivabene, '"international president" of the political economy societies of Belgium and Turin'.[43] When the Turin Society met on 16th May 1861, Arrivabene returned the compliment by drinking a toast to the Political Economy Societies of Paris, Brussels, Madrid and Holland (*L'Economiste belge*, 7, 21: 170–1). At the next session of the Paris Society, comments were made about the incompleteness of Arrivabene's list: Garnier remarked that the Political Economy Club of London had been in existence for forty years, while Horn pointed out that in Germany different societies were active.[44] Finally, in 1866 the foundation of a Political Economy Society by Scialoja and others in Florence was also reported.[45]

3.6.3 Spain

The contacts with the Spanish Society do not seem to have been very intense. In March 1857 the recently founded Political Economy Society of Madrid wrote a letter in which it expressed its wish to 'enter into relations' with the Belgian Society.[46] Not many traces of cooperation of any kind can be found. In 1865, though, the discussions in the Madrid Society on the abolition of slavery on the Spanish Antilles were extensively reported (*L'Economiste belge*, 11, 20: 216–17; 11, 22: 245–6).

3.6.4 *Russia*

The contacts with Russian economists and societies were mainly the result of de Molinari's efforts. He went on a long journey to Russia in 1860 (February–July) and visited the country again in 1865 and 1867. In 1861 Horn of the Paris Society provided information on a session of the Comité d'Economie Politique de la Société Impériale de Géographie of Saint Petersburg (*L'Economiste belge*, 7, 32: 261–2). In 1865 a report was published on a session of the Société Russe d'Economie Politique held in February and attended by de Molinari (*L'Economiste belge*, 11, 5: 40–1). In January 1867 details were given about a recent session of the Société d'Economie Politique de Saint Pétérsbourg, where de Molinari had been the guest of honour (*L'Economiste belge*, 13, 2: 13–16).

3.6.5 *The Netherlands*

At the end of the session of the Belgian Society held on 24th March 1861, de Molinari announced the foundation of a Political Economy Society in Holland. 'This news was warmly welcomed by the assembly.'[47]

4 The period 1868–1900

What happened with the Société Belge d'Economie Politique in the period 1868–1889 is not completely clear. In 1890 the Antwerp-based *La Revue économique*, edited by Louis Strauss,[48] began to publish the *comptes-rendus* of the Society in more or less the same way as *L'Economiste belge* had done in the period 1855–1868; for the period 1890–1900 we are therefore on somewhat firmer ground.

In 1869 the board of the Society consisted of Arrivabene, Honorary President, Charles Le Hardy de Beaulieu and Corr-Vandermaeren, Presidents, Adolphe de Vergnies, Secretary, and Louis Geelhand, Treasurer (*La Revue économique*, 8, 5: 33). Charles Le Hardy de Beaulieu died on 30th December 1871; Corr-Vandermaeren died in 1878 and at the time of his death he was still described as one of the presidents of the Society.[49] In 1890 the board consisted of Adolphe Le Hardy de Beaulieu, President, Couvreur, Vice-president, Geelhand, Treasurer, and Demeurisse, Secretary. By the end of 1890, the members of the Society numbered 147.[50] A serious blow was dealt to the Society when in 1894 Le Hardy de Beaulieu, Couvreur and Geelhand all died. Gustave de Molinari, Honorary President, came back from Paris in April 1895 to preside over a session in which the Society was relaunched.[51] A new board was appointed with de Vergnies, President, Jottrand and Strauss, Vice-presidents, Julien Weiler, Secretary and Anspach-Puissant, Treasurer. But apparently serious difficulties were experienced in endeavouring to revive the Society; by the time it met in February 1897 there had been a spell of eighteen months without any session.[52]

In the period 1890–1900 the Society regularly discussed the theme to which it never ceased to pay attention: freedom of trade and obstacles to free trade (sessions of 16th February 1890, 28th December 1890, 5th April 1891, 21st February 1892, 14th December 1892 and 28th April 1895). Another typically liberal concern which appeared on the agenda was the tax on immovable property (20th February 1898). But in contrast to the situation in the early years of the Society, the 'labour question' became much more prominent. There were discussions on labour rules and regulations (23rd March 1890, 14th July 1890 and 5th April 1891), trade unions (14th February 1897), 'state socialism and social progress' (9th May 1897) and even one on the effects of 'plutocracy' (3rd July 1898). Although the Society was still predominantly liberal, the two leading Belgian socialist intellectuals of that period, Emile Vandervelde and Hector Denis, were active members.[53]

A remarkable feature in the 1890–1900 period was the brief cooperation between the Société Belge d'Economie Politique and the Société d'Etudes Sociales et Politiques, founded in 1890. In fact the Société d'Etudes Sociales et Politiques had risen from the ashes of the much older but short-lived Association Internationale pour le Progrès des Sciences Sociales.[54] The Secretary-general of both was Auguste Couvreur. His account of the motives for creating the Association ran as follows:

> In 1862, at the behest of Lord Brougham in England, MM. Michel Chevalier and Garnier Pagès in France, a group of Belgians conceived the idea of creating an *International association for the advancement of the social sciences* in Belgium, on the model of a similar, but national, institution existing in the United Kingdom.
>
> (Couvreur 1891: 1)

The association was effectively founded in September 1862, during a four-day international conference in Brussels. Similar conferences were held in Ghent (1863), Amsterdam (1864) and Bern (1865), but those scheduled for Turin (1866) and Paris (1867) had to be cancelled. The association was organised around different 'sections', one of which was that of 'political economy'. Although its official policy was to be neutral,[55] it chose the Association Internationale pour les Réformes Douanières to coordinate the political economy section (*L'Economiste belge*, 8, 12: 138–9). In May 1867 the Association ceased all activity. It was resurrected in 1890, albeit on a Belgian scale only, in the form of the Société d'Etudes Sociales et Politiques. Adolphe Le Hardy de Beaulieu became one of its Vice-presidents, and for a brief time the two societies worked in close collaboration.[56] Yet the 'political and social economy' section of the Société d'Etudes Sociales et Politiques was by no means identical to the Société Belge d'Economie Politique. When Couvreur (and Le Hardy de Beaulieu) died in 1894, the Société d'Etudes

Sociales et Politiques lost its main driving force, and in 1895 its existence ended.

5 Concluding remarks

A few tentative and provisional conclusions may be drawn from this story. Firstly, it is clear that more research is needed; in particular, archival material should be exploited to complement the sources already used. Secondly, the push to create a Political Economy Society did not come from university professors, but from those outside or on the margins of academia. Thirdly, the Society was founded and dominated by liberal economists and businessmen; catholic economists in particular, with the exception of Ducpétiaux, avoided the Society and remained very much within their own sphere.[57] Emile de Laveleye, perhaps the most famous Belgian economist of the nineteenth century, also played only a minor role, if any, in the Society.[58] Fourthly, the formation of the Belgian Political Economy Society was closely linked to, but nevertheless distinct from, the economic policy reform movement in favour of free trade and the abolition of customs. And finally, there was a clear tendency to actively promote international cooperation in the realm of economics, as witnessed by the organisation of several international conferences.

Notes

* I thank Christian Bidard, Wilfried Parys and the participants in the conference 'L'associazionismo economico nell'Italia dell'Ottocento. Della Società economico-agrarie alle Associazioni di Economisti' (Pisa, 14th–16th October 1999) for useful comments. The usual caveat applies.

1 Its official name today is Société Royale d'Economie Politique de Belgique. The secretariat of the Society is assumed by the Cifop (Centre Interuniversitaire de Formation Permanente), Avenue Général Michel 1B, 6000 Charleroi.

2 This chapter is based exclusively on published material. I did not have access to archival sources; if ever these come available, I am certain that I will have to modify my account on several points.

3 Ackersdijck later became professor in Utrecht (see Zuidema 1992: 44–8, for his role in the development of economics in the Netherlands). Arrivabene (1879: 167) had been impressed by Ackersdijck's lectures. When Ackersdijck returned to Belgium to deliver a speech at the 1847 Congrès des Economistes in Brussels, he was interrupted by Charles de Brouckère, the Chairman: 'I apologise for interrupting the speaker, but I must state that all the statesmen who are in office in Belgium were students when he was a professor of political economy at the university of Liège (noisy applause)' (*Congrès des économistes* 1847: 156).

4 De Brouckère was several times minister and from 1848 to 1860 mayor of Brussels; for a somewhat biased assessment of his economic work, see Michotte 1904: 275–87.

5 On Quetelet, see Michotte 1904: 400–51.

6 On Ducpétiaux, see Aubert 1964.

7 For a clear example of Fourierist inspiration, see Cunliffe and Erreygers 2001.

8 On Colins, see Rens 1968.

9 On Huet, see Cunliffe 1997.

10 The following announcement appeared in the 1st September 1848 issue of the organ of the Société d'Economie Politique of Paris: 'At its last meeting, the Society of political economy dealt with the second session of the Congress of Economists. The Society expressed the desire for this session to open on 2nd October and to be held in Paris.' (*Journal des économistes*, 8, 87: 168). Two years earlier, the journal had devoted a long article to the Brussels conference and the banquet following it (*Journal des économistes* 6, 71: 250–76, 305–8).

11 In the 15th September 1848 issue it is said that: 'The Society of political economy, having received a number of observations from some of its foreign correspondents, has judged that it is appropriate to set back by one or two months the projected date for the meeting of the second session of the Congress of economists, previously fixed for 2nd October' (*Journal des économistes*, 7, 88: 224).

12 For more details on de Molinari's life and work, see Hart 1981–2.

13 For this reason he is praised in libertarian and 'Austrian' circles; see, for instance, Rothbard 1995: 453–5.

14 For his influence on French economists, see Breton 1998 and Potier 1998.

15 See Marchant 1890–1 for more details on his life and work.

16 See Carina 1875 and Van Nuffel 1957 and 1964 for more details on his life and work.

17 'Fondation d'une Société Belge d'Economie Politique', *L'Economiste belge*, 1, 14: 1–3.

18 See the *compte-rendu* of the session of 6th August 1855 in *Journal des économistes*, 14, 8: 306.

19 Matthyssens was a member of the Antwerp Chamber of Commerce and lectured at the Institut Supérieur de Commerce d'Anvers; he died in 1870.

20 From 1853 to 1903 de Cocquiel was professor of economics at the Institut Supérieur de Commerce in Antwerp; he died in 1915. Between 1854 and 1866, with an interruption in 1859–1860, de Molinari also taught in this institute (economic geography and general economic history).

21 The absence of de Molinari from the board was not a coincidence. In the *compte-rendu* of the session of 10th October 1855 of the Société d'Economie Politique of Paris the following explanation was given: 'Mr. de Molinari has refused to become a member of the board because he fears that his name may discourage those who complain of the radicalism of the *Economiste Belge* on questions of government intervention from joining the Society, and also because he wishes the journal and the Society to remain independent from each other, although mutually supportive' (*Journal des économistes*, 14, 10: 150).

22 On Eugène de Molinari, see Christophe 1899.

23 See the summary of the session of 5th February 1860 in *L'Economiste belge*, 6, 6: 83.

24 See the *compte-rendu* of the session of 8th January 1865 in *L'Economiste belge*, 11, 1: 7–8.

25 See the *compte-rendu* of the session of 4th March 1866 in *L'Economiste belge*, 12, 5: 49.

26 See the *compte-rendu* of the session of 23rd September 1855 in *L'Economiste belge*, 1, 19, supplement: 1.

27 See the *compte-rendu* of the session of 20th December 1857 in *L'Economiste belge*, 4, 2: 3–4.

28 See the *compte-rendu* of the discussion in *L'Economiste belge*, 3, 30, supplement: 8–11, and Carey's letter of complaint, *L'Economiste belge*, 3, 29: 6.

29 In the session of 5th November 1897 the 50th anniversary of his membership was celebrated; see *Journal des économistes*, 56, 11: 245–53, and *La Revue économique*, 8, 23: 183–6.

30 In the first years the Society always met in the restaurant of *La veuve Dubost, rue de la Putterie*.
31 See the announcement in *L'Economiste belge*, 1, 21: 2–3.
32 See the *compte-rendu* of the session in *L'Economiste belge*, 1, 23: 4–5.
33 He was able to resume teaching in October 1860; see Dubois 1928: 70–1.
34 See the announcement in *L'Economiste belge*, 2, 9: 6–7.
35 See the summary and the report of the results of the conference in *L'Economiste belge*, 2, 19: 1, 2–7.
36 See the announcement in *L'Economiste belge*, 3, 3: 1.
37 See the resolution adopted by the Society in its session of 24th March 1861: 'The Belgian Society of political economy expresses its desire that, in the interests of industry and trade, customs barriers be abolished and, at the same time, in order to safeguard the interests of producers on whom excise duties are imposed, that these taxes be transformed' (*L'Economiste belge*, 7, 13: 105).
38 See the *compte-rendu* of the session of 17th February 1856 in *L'Economiste belge*, 2, 4: 6.
39 See *L'Economiste belge*, 3, 16, supplement: 4; reference is made to the *comptes-rendus* of the sessions of 4th April and 5th May 1857 in *Journal des économistes*, 16, 5: 298–311.
40 See the *compte-rendu* of the session of 26th September 1858 in *L'Economiste belge*, 4, 28: 6.
41 See *L'Economiste belge*, 7, 25: 205; reference is made to the *compte-rendu* of the session of 5th June 1861 in *Journal des économistes*, 20, 6: 481.
42 See the *compte-rendu* of the session of 28th May 1865 in *L'Economiste belge*, 11, 11: 109. Garnier mentioned the proposal in the Paris Society at the session of 5th January 1865; see the *compte-rendu* in *Journal des économistes*, 24, 1: 147.
43 See the *compte-rendu* of the session of 5th August 1860 in *L'Economiste belge*, 6, 32: 508.
44 See *L'Economiste belge*, 7, 25: 205–6; reference is made to the *compte-rendu* of the session of 5th June 1861 in *Journal des économistes*, 20, 6: 484–6.
45 See *L'Economiste belge*, 12, 3: 36. But perhaps the attempt failed. During the session of 5th August 1868 of the Société d'Economie Politique de Paris a letter by Arrivabene was read, in which the foundation of a Political Economy Society in Florence was announced. The board of this Society consisted of Arrivabene, Permanent President, Ferrara, Minghetti and Scialoja, Vice-presidents, Protonari, Permanent Secretary, and G. Corsi, Treasurer (*Journal des économistes*, 27, 8: 283–4).
46 See the *compte-rendu* of the session of 8th March 1857 in *L'Economiste belge*, 3, 9, supplement: 1.
47 See the *compte-rendu* of the session of 24th March 1861 in *L'Economiste belge*, 7, 14: 116.
48 Strauss had been a student of de Molinari at the Institut Supérieur de Commerce, and in the 1890s was president of the Conseil Supérieur de l'Industrie et du Commerce en Belgique.
49 See the announcement of his death in the 6th May 1878 session of the Société d'Economie Politique of Paris; *Journal des économistes*, 37, 5: 298.
50 See the *compte-rendu* of the session of 28th December 1890 in *La Revue économique*, 2, 1: 1.
51 See the *compte-rendu* of the session of 28th April 1895 in *La Revue économique*, 6, 18: 137–41.
52 See the *compte-rendu* of the session of 14th February 1897 in *La Revue économique*, 8, 5: 33–6.
53 On Vandervelde, see Abs 1973; on Denis, see Vandervelde 1938.
54 More information on both associations can be found in Crombois 1994: 16–20.

55 The principle was that 'this enterprise must remain free from any partisan or sectorial spirit or school of thought' (Couvreur 1891: 2).

56 At a certain point there was considerable confusion about the activities of the two; see the *compte-rendu* of the session of 14th July 1890 of the Société Belge d'Economie Politique in *La Revue économique*, 1, 29: 342.

57 For instance, in 1869 they founded their own journal *L'Economie chrétienne*, which was later transformed into *L'Economiste catholique*; in 1881 they also founded an association, the Société d'Economie Sociale. For more details on the Catholic school, see Michotte 1904: 194–231, 329–99.

58 Emile de Laveleye was professor of political economy in Liège. In the session of 21st February 1892 of the Société Belge d'Economie Politique, Adolphe Le Hardy de Beaulieu paid tribute to de Laveleye, 'former member of the Society, whose thought was often evoked during these annual meetings. Everyone admired his talent; people were enthralled by his flowing elegant writing style which, it must however be acknowledged, has not always seemed persuasive to the purists' (*La Revue économique*, 3, 9: 65). With his sympathies for the Historical School and the *Kathedersozialisten*, de Laveleye must have felt somewhat out of place among the *laissez-faire* proponents of the Society. Moreover, as early as 1867 de Laveleye had become a member of the Académie Royale de Belgique, in which he played a very active role (see Goblet d'Alviella 1895: 174–5).

Bibliography

Journals

L'Economiste belge, Brussels, vol. 1, 1855 – vol. 14, 1868.
Journal des économistes, Paris, vol. 1, 1841–2 – vol. 99, 1940.
La Revue économique, Antwerp, vol. 1, 1890 – vol. 15, 1904.

Books and articles

Abs, R. (1973) *Emile Vandervelde*, Bruxelles: Editions Labor.
Arrivabene, G. (1875) *Un' epoca della mia vita*, Mantova: Stab. Tip. Eredi Segna.
—— (1879) *Memorie della mia vita, 1795–1859*, Firenze: G. Barbera.
Aubert, R. (1964) 'Ducpétiaux (Antoine-Edouard)', in *Biographie nationale publiée par l'Académie royale des sciences, des lettres et des beaux-arts de Belgique*, vol. 32, Bruxelles: Emile Bruylant.
Brants, V. (1899) 'Coup d'œil à vol d'oiseau sur les écoles d'économie politique en Belgique', *Revue générale* 70: 145–65.
Breton, Y. (1998) 'French Economists and Marginalism (1871–1918)', in G. Faccarello (ed.) *Studies in the History of French Political Economy. From Bodin to Walras*, London: Routledge.
Carina, D. (1875) [1869] 'Della vita e delle opere del Conte Giovanni Arrivabene', in G. Arrivabene (ed.) *Un'epoca della mia vita*, Mantova: Stab. Tip. Eredi Segna.
Christophe, Ch. (1899) 'Molinari (Eugène-Clément de)', in *Biographie nationale publiée par l'Académie royale des sciences, des lettres et des beaux-arts de Belgique*, vol. 15, Bruxelles: Emile Bruylant.
Congrès des économistes (réuni à Bruxelles par les soins de l'Association belge pour la liberté commerciale. Session de 1847. – Séances des 16, 17 et 18 Septembre) (1847), Bruxelles: Imprimerie de Deltombe.
Couvreur, A. (1891) 'La Société d'études sociales & politiques – son origine – son but', *Revue sociale et politique* 1: 1–9.

Crombois, J.-F. (1994) *L'Univers de la sociologie en Belgique de 1900 à 1940*, Bruxelles: Editions de l'Université de Bruxelles.

Cunliffe, J. (1997) 'The Liberal Case for a Socialist Property Regime: The Contribution of François Huet', *History of Political Thought* 18, 4: 707–29.

Cunliffe, J. and Erreygers, G. (2001) 'The Enigmatic Legacy of Fourier: Joseph Charlier and Basic Income', *History of Political Economy* 33, 3 (Fall): forthcoming.

Discailles, E. (1895) 'Le socialiste français Victor Considérant en Belgique', *Bulletin de l'Académie royale de Belgique* 3rd series, 55, 29: 705–48.

Dubois, E. (1928) *Institut supérieur de commerce d'Anvers*, Anvers: Imprimerie Labor.

Goblet d'Alviella, E. (1895) 'Emile de Laveleye. Sa vie et son œuvre', *Annuaire de l'Académie royale de Belgique* 61: 45–246.

Hart, D.M. (1981–82) 'Gustave de Molinari and the Anti-statist Liberal Tradition', *Journal of Libertarian Studies* part I, 5, 3: 263–90; part II, 5, 4: 399–434; part III, 6, 1: 83–104.

Laurent, E. and Marco, L. (1996) 'Le *Journal des économistes*, ou l'apologie du libéralisme (1841–1940)', in L. Marco (ed.) *Les Revues d'économie en France. Genèse et actualité. 1751–1994*, Paris: L'Harmattan.

Le Hardy de Beaulieu, Ch. (1861) *Traité Elémentaire d'Economie Politique*, Bruxelles: Lacroix & Van Meenen.

Marchant, A. (1890–1) 'Le Hardy de Beaulieu (Jean-Charles-Marie-Joseph)', in *Biographie nationale publiée par l'Académie royale des sciences, des lettres et des beaux-arts de Belgique*, vol. 11, Bruxelles: Emile Bruylant.

Michotte, P. (1904) *Etudes sur les théories économiques qui dominèrent en Belgique de 1830 à 1886*, Louvain: Charles Peeters.

—— (1908) 'Les sciences économiques', in *Le Mouvement scientifique en Belgique. 1830–1905*, vol. 2, Bruxelles: Société Belge de Librairie.

Molinari, G. de (1849a) 'De la production de la sécurité', *Journal des économistes* 8, 95: 277–90.

—— (1849b) *Les Soirées de la rue Saint-Lazare. Entretiens sur les lois économiques et défense de la propriété*, Paris: Guillaumin & Cie.

Potier, J.-P. (1998) 'Léon Walras and Applied Science. The Significance of the Free Competition Principle', in G. Faccarello (ed.) *Studies in the History of French Political Economy. From Bodin to Walras*, London: Routledge.

Rens, I. (1968) *Introduction au socialisme rationnel de Colins*, Bruxelles: Institut belge de science politique; Neuchatel: A la Baconnière.

Rothbard, M.N. (1995) *Classical Economics. (An Austrian Perspective on the History of Economic Thought, Volume II)*, Aldershot: Edward Elgar.

Tommissen, P. (1971) *De Economische Epistemologie van Vilfredo Pareto*, Brussels: Sint-Aloysiushandelshogeschool.

Vandervelde, E. (1938) 'Notice sur Hector Denis', *Annuaire de l'Académie royale de Belgique* 104: 1–32.

Van Nuffel, R. (1957) 'Arrivabene (Jean, comte)', in *Biographie nationale publiée par l'Académie royale des sciences, des lettres et des beaux-arts de Belgique*, vol. 29, Bruxelles: Emile Bruylant.

—— (1964) 'Arrivabene, graaf Giovanni', in *Nationaal Biografisch Woordenboek*, vol. 1, Brussel: Paleis der Academiën.

Zuidema, J.R. (1992) 'Economic Thought in the Netherlands between 1750 and 1870', in J. van Daal and A. Heertje (eds) *Economic Thought in the Netherlands: 1650–1950*, Aldershot: Avebury.

6 Spanish societies, academies and economic debating societies

Salvador Almenar and Vicent Llombart

Scientific associations of economists are a very recent phenomenon in Spain, although there are notable historic precedents. In this chapter we present a panorama of the institutions and organisations that served as a channel for scientific communication and debate within the group of authors and professors of economics from the end of the eighteenth century to 1914. The scarcity of previous studies on these subjects has obliged us to complete the scattered information available with our own inquiries into primary sources.

Section 1 takes a brief look at the role played from 1767 to 1820 by the Reales Sociedades Económicas de Amigos del País as intermediate institutions between traditional academies and organisations that promote economic initiatives. Section 2 analyses the economic debating societies during the period of consolidation of the teaching of political economy in Spanish universities. In 1845 the study of political economy was introduced in the law faculties of ten public universities, giving rise to a stable group of professors that would become the driving force of the Sociedad Libre de Economía Política of Madrid (1856–68). Section 3, devoted to the period between 1875 and 1914, studies the peculiar relations between the institutionalisation of economic studies and the professionalisation of economists in Spain. Section 4 presents a brief synopsis and some remarks on the asymmetry between the institutionalisation of teaching, economic associations and the professionalisation of economists in the case of Spanish.

1 The Royal Economic Societies of friends of the country (1767–1820)[1]

The Reales Sociedades Económicas de Amigos del País (Royal Economic Societies of Friends of the Country) appeared in Spain from 1765 (with the Basque Society) and especially from 1775 until the end of the eighteenth century. They were the first institutions denoted 'economic' and had among their primary goals the diffusion, study and application of economic knowledge. Although they did not belong to the public administration and had no particular competence in economic policy, they also functioned as advisory governmental bodies on such subjects. However, these societies were not exclusively specialised in economic issues; they responded to the spirit of the Enlightenment period and to the pre-institutional stage in the development of economic thought. For these reasons, the economic societies were a venue for conversations and debates and became an intellectually stimulating experience for most Spanish economic writers during the last quarter of the eighteenth century. The activity of the more important Societies continued during the nineteenth century and played a significant role in the early pre-university stage of the teaching of economics in Spain.

The Sociedades had three basic goals: (1) to become advisory bodies and to provide a support for economic and social governmental policy; (2) to study the local economies and to promote their development; (3) to function as centres that cultivated and spread economic, scientific and technical knowledge that could be useful in order to promote production and to struggle against poverty and idleness. Campomanes – their most prominent propagator – defined these societies 'as open schools for the theory and practice of political economy in all the provinces of Spain', arguing that they should become the 'guiding lights of political economy' (Campomanes 1774: 163). In Campomanes' view, these Societies should be intellectual centres for the diffusion of political economy, where its principles would be taught to its members and to a wider public, and serve to encourage the increase of wealth. Many of these Sociedades – especially the Basque, Madrilenian and Aragonese Societies, and those located in Valencia, Santiago, Lugo, Mallorca, Tenerife, Las Palmas, Sevilla, Segovia, Valladolid, etc. (some societies were also established in the colonial territories) – produced a wealth of publications and studies on the economic conditions of several provinces and regions. They sent reports to the government, created libraries, awarded prizes, organised discussions and translated foreign books, paying special attention to economic subjects. The new demand for economic studies that arose from these Societies prompted a remarkable growth of economic literature and translated into an increased supply of economic ideas. This supply amounted to a considerable fraction of the more important economic writings of the second half of the eighteenth century. But the goals of these institutions were even more ambitious: they aspired to become the instruments of general progress through education, the creation of a social environment favourable to economic growth, and scientific and technical experimentation. Nevertheless, the Sociedades were not the only institutions fostering economic studies and technical training in this period. The Junta General de Comercio (General Board of Commerce) and the Consulados de Comercio also contributed, and the Junta de Comercio de Barcelona was especially active in these fields following its re-establishment in 1758.

On 24th October 1784 the Aragonese Economic Society of Friends of the Country opened a chair of civil economy and commerce, modelled on the Neapolitan chair held by Antonio Genovesi. The first appointed professor was Lorenzo Normante, who initially adopted as a textbook Bernardo

Danvila's *Lecciones de economía civil*, replacing it with Genovesi's *Lezioni di commercio* as soon as it was translated into Spanish in 1786. In 1801 the new professor, José Benito de Cistué, added as a textbook a translation of the compendium of Smith's *Wealth of Nations* written by Condorcet (*Compendio de la riqueza de las naciones*) and as reading material the works of the Spanish economists Foronda and Enrique Ramos. In 1807, José Benito de Rivera adopted as a textbook the recent translation of J.-B. Say's *Traité* (*Tratado de economía política*). Teaching was interrupted between 1808 and 1814 due to the War of Independence, but was resumed from 1815 to 1846, when the chair was definitively consolidated in the University of Zaragoza and awarded to Mariano Nougés Secall – who was then professor of the Aragonese Society.

This pioneering initiative in the teaching of economics was intended by the Aragonese Society – in collaboration with Floridablanca – as a pilot experience for other Sociedades, but from the very outset it encountered the strong opposition of various sectors of Spanish society. Between 1786 and 1788 Normante was the object of a preaching campaign stemming from the eloquent Capuchin Brother Diego José de Cádiz, who denounced Normante to the Inquisition, contending that the ideas espoused by the latter on the legality of usury, on the benefits of luxury consumption and on limiting access to the religious profession up to the age of 24 were heretical. All this at the moment in which opposition to the economic reform projects promoted by the Society reached its climax. Opposition was finally silenced by the government, but the experience perhaps limited the possibility of generalising the experience of the teaching of economics to other societies. The only exception known for the eighteenth century – apart from the brief experience of Ramón Salas (who taught political economy in the law school of the University of Salamanca between 1788 and 1792, when teaching was suppressed by the Senate of the University) – was the Academy of Political Economy, created by the Economic Society of Majorca in 1793, whose leading figure, José Antonio Mon Velarde, taught Genovesi's *Lezioni*.

After the failure of various projects and an extenuating discussion, the chair of political economy of the Economic Society of Madrid was established in December 1813 and awarded to Antonio Osteret Narío. The future of the chair appeared somewhat uncertain until the first public selection to fill this post was held in 1819, resulting one year later in the appointment of José Antonio Ponzoa (Say's translator), selected from among six candidates. Eusebio María del Valle carried out the teaching in 1833–4. Another known case is that of the chair of political economy of the Society of Murcia, whose titular professor in 1815 was Felipe de Olive.

2 Economic debating societies (1808–74)[2]

According to the evidence now available, there was little personal interaction among Spanish writers on political economy of the first third of the nineteenth century. No correspondence among them is available, while review articles, debates or mutual commentaries were infrequent. There were also no institutions that could act as a forum for debate, apart from Parliament. Moreover, many economists were in jail or exiled during the periods of absolutist restoration (1814–20, 1823–33). However the main authors of the period were aware of what others wrote. It is even possible to find explicit influences or discrepancies among them, as for example between A. Flórez Estrada, J. Canga Argüelles and E. Jaumeandreu.

During the second third of the century the Athenaeum of Madrid functioned as an intellectual debating society supporting the new liberal order. Two other initiatives undertaken during this period were designed to further the study and free flow of economic ideas: the Sociedad de Hacienda y Crédito Público (Society of Public Finance and Credit) (1841), and the Sociedad Libre de Economía Política de Madrid (1856–63). Some associations favoured the propagation of free-trade ideas in a detached perspective – such as the Asociación para la Reforma de Aranceles de Aduanas (Association for the Reform of Customs Tariffs) (1859–68, 1879–94?) – while other organisations represented specific economic interests in a more direct way – such as the Confederación Mercantil Española (1846), endorsing free-trade opinions, and the Instituto Industrial de Cataluña (1848) and the Fomento del Trabajo Nacional (Promotion of National Labour) (1888), which were the defenders of protectionism. The public activities promoted by the Athenaeum of Madrid and the internal debates in the Royal Academy of Moral and Political Sciences established in 1857 contributed to this debate in a wider intellectual perspective.

2.1 Debates on economics and the teaching of political economy in societies and athenaeums

During the two revolutionary periods of 1808–14 and 1820–3, a host of clubs and 'patriotic societies' favoured the free exchange of political ideas, but these rarely focused their attention on economic problems (Gil Novales 1975). Economic debates in the press became more frequent after 1834, and concerned three strategic subjects: (1) the manner of transferring to private ownership land that still belonged to the church, the state or the municipalities; (2) the new organisation of public finance in a framework of economic and constitutional freedom; and (3) the reform of customs tariffs and the choice of free trade, a question that absorbed the energies of most Spanish writers on economics until the end of the century.

One of the more active centres in this debate was the Ateneo Español of Madrid. The Athenaeum was a cultural and political institution created in 1820 'with a view to exchanging ideas, undertaking the study of the exact, moral and political sciences [...] spreading the light [...] ' (Gil Novales 1975: 137). It soon became an unofficial Academy, where 'in a calm and friendly way' one could 'discuss questions of legislation, politics, economics and, in general, all subjects in which public utility could be recognised'. Debates dealt with the elimination or reduction of tithes, colonial policy, public debt and free trade. The Athenaeum also created a chair of political economy, entrusted to Casimiro Orense and Manuel Flores Calderón (Ruiz Salvador 1971: 22–7).

The Athenaeum was re-launched in 1835 under the name of Ateneo Científico, Literario y Artístico (Scientific, Literary and Artistic Athenaeum) of Madrid. It included a section for moral and political sciences, and was partially intended as an alternative to the Madrid Economic Society. From 1836 to 1843 the new Athenaeum instituted a chair of political economy awarded to Eusebio María del Valle, and from 1836 to 1838 a chair of public finance and credit, conferred on José Antonio Ponzoa. Lastly, in 1839–40, a chair of social economy was entrusted to Ramón de La Sagra. The debates organised in the section of moral and political sciences dealt with topics concerning public finance, agriculture and the main economic institutions. Among the economic subjects examined in the courses on political economy, one should mention the reform or suppression of tithes and the 'extinction of the public debt in Spain' (1836–7), 'the best means of promoting the spirit of industrial and mercantile association in Spain' and 'the need for a law on the enclosure of lands that reconciles the interests of Agriculture and Livestock' (1837–8). The 1841–2 course debated the issue of the role and scientific status of political economy and the effects of 'free competition' on industry, and more specifically of 'free trade' on the economic condition of Spain. Another topic examined during this year was the comparative study of 'socialism and individualism' and the possibility of 'combining them' (Ruiz Salvador 1971: 20–72).

The Reales Sociedades Económicas de Amigos del País conserved their original institutional formula until 1834, a mixture of autonomous functioning and limited financial resources. During the 1823–33 backlash, even their ordinary sessions were banned. Subsequently, a chair of political economy still functioned in some economic societies between 1835 and 1845. However, the appearance of institutions such as the Athenaeums and, more generally, the strengthening of constitutional monarchy between 1837 and 1844, determined the progressive loss of the functions formerly exerted by these Societies.

In 1845 the government decided to include political economy in the syllabi of the Bachelors' degrees in philosophy and law and to create a chair in the same field in the ten public universities then existing in Spain. In many cases the newly appointed professors were the same persons who had taught in the economic Societies and Athenaeums. The importance of political economy further increased in 1857, when it was also included among the courses in the new schools of commerce (Martín Rodríguez 1989). The result of this growth was the rise of a wider and more stable group of professors of economics.

Another result of the institutionalisation of political economy in universities and schools of commerce was that the courses promoted by the economic societies disappeared within a few years. During the so-called 'moderate decade' (1843–53), the Athenaeum of Madrid lost its vitality as an arena of economic debate, while its courses and chairs lost their continuity. There were however some isolated lectures on political economy (E.M. Valle), industrial economy (J. García Barzanallana), advanced political economy (A. Borrego) and public finance (M. Capalleja) (Ruiz Salvador 1971: 75–92).

2.2 The failure of the Society of Public Finance and Credit (1841–3)

In January 1841 the financier and economist Pablo Pebrer first proposed the creation of a forum for the study and discussion of the problems concerning 'public finance and credit', the Sociedad de Hacienda y Crédito Público. Pebrer had been living in England for many years, and while there had published an extensive statistical work on the British system of public finance; he was also known as the author of a tract on free trade published in 1837. His model was probably the London Political Economy Club, since the Paris Société des Economistes was still to be established. The project was immediately taken up by the Madrid Economic Society, which promoted a meeting in its head office on 14th March. Fifty persons attended, plus the thirty-three members of the Economic Society.[3]

On 11th April 1841 the by-laws were passed. On 22nd April the first board of directors was formed, including José Canga Argüelles as President, two Vice-presidents (Eusebio María del Valle and Diego Alvear), two Deputy-secretaries (Juan Miguel de los Ríos and Ruperto Navarro), a Treasurer (Vicente Beltrán de Lis) and an accountant (José Antonio Ponzoa). Two professional profiles can clearly be distinguished in this board: on the one hand, the writers or teachers of political economy and public finance such as Valle, Pebrer, Ponzoa, Flórez and Canga – the latter two with remarkable political experience; on the other hand, a heterogeneous majority of experts, financiers, politicians and journalists, which was more representative of the initial composition of the Society. The simultaneous presence of Canga and Valle suggests that an equilibrium between free-traders and protectionists was cautiously maintained and that the Society had been projected as an universal forum for economic discussion.

In accordance with new administrative regulations, in 1842 the government was asked to give official recognition to the by-laws of the Society. In January 1843 a decision was finally taken; the government required substantive changes in the by-laws, which restricted the territorial span of the Society to Madrid, transformed it into an Academy and imposed that its sessions should be open to the public.

According to available information, the Sociedad de Hacienda remained at the stage of a project. However, its failure cannot be exclusively attributed to political or bureaucratic difficulties. Two key figures disappeared during the crucial period in which the government was evaluating the request for official recognition of the society: its president Canga Argüelles died in December 1842, while Pebrer had died in June 1841.

2.3 The Free Society of Political Economy of Madrid (1856– 64): the 'Economists' School'

The period between 1834 and 1854 was a period of change: the 'authority' in the field of economics shifted from Say to Bastiat, the institutionalisation of political economy in universities was reinforced, and a new division within the political élite between 'moderates', 'progressists' and 'democrats' arose. In this period a deep disagreement on the reform of custom tariffs and public finance also divided the community of Spanish economists.

The echo of English tariff reform was amplified in Spain by Richard Cobden's visit in 1846, and through the increasing popularity enjoyed by Frédéric Bastiat's works and by the group of the *Journal des économistes*. The foundation of some economic journals was an outcome of this new climate. Another event in this period was the rise of the first business organisation with a free-trade orientation, the Sociedad Mercantil Matritense (1844). This led two years later to the creation of the Confederación Mercantil Española, which recruited a significant number of associates in Madrid and in some cities of Andalucia.[4]

The main opposition to free-trade opinions came from Catalonia. Before the 1840s, two institutions located in Barcelona, the Junta de Comercio (Board of Commerce) and the Comisión de Fábricas (Factory Commission), had advocated bans on the importing of manufactured products as a means to encourage industrial development. The Instituto Industrial de Cataluña, founded in 1848 – which represented a strong network of factories – replaced this old fashioned defence of import bans with a protectionist strategy based on the 'infant industry argument'. Its principal activities consisted of the publication of reports and petitions, of support given to newspapers and journals, and political lobbying addressed to the government and MPs. All these 'prohibitionist' or protectionist organisations systematically sought the collaboration, either voluntary or by contract, of renowned professors and experts of economics like E. Jaumeandreu, M.M. Gutiérrez, E.M. del Valle, P. Madoz and A. Borrego (Solá 1997).

Some ephemeral free-trade initiatives were promoted by the economists influenced by mainstream English and French classical economics, such as A. Flórez Estrada, P. Pebrer, J.J. de Mora, M. Marliani and J.M. Vadillo. However, during the second half of the 1840s, some professors of political economy – like L. Figuerola, M. Colmeiro and the disciples of E.M. del Valle who animated the *Revista económica de Madrid* – modified their protectionist doctrines in favour of free trade. As a result, the 1850s saw the triumph of free-trade doctrines among the majority of academic economists (Lluch and

Almenar 1992). The foundation of the Sociedad Libre de Economía Política in 1856 was evidence of this turn in economic thought and economic institutions.

The initial drive to create this Society came from the Congrès International des Réformes Douanières held in Brussels in September 1856, which was attended by L. Figuerola, M. Colmeiro and G. Rodríguez. These economists were also the promoters of the Sociedad (Cabrillo 1991: xx). The latter was founded in Madrid in December 1856 and its activities continued smoothly for almost seven years. The explicit reference model was the Paris Société d'Economie Politique, both as regards the doctrinal orientation of its members and the organisation structure based on monthly discussions.[5] A minor difference was that at the end of each session the Society of Madrid deliberated on the subject of the following session. The minutes or summaries of the meetings were published in *El economista* (1856–7), *La tribuna del economista* (1857–8) and the *Gaceta economista. Revista económico-política* (1861–3). These new periodicals – whose intellectual style endeavoured to imitate that of the *Journal des économistes* – predominantly hosted contributions by Society members (Almenar 1996).

At the beginning, the Society had fifty-four members, and thirty-eight attended the first ordinary session on 2nd January 1857. Over the years the Society experienced a gradual transformation. Many affiliates ceased to attend meetings, while others who were admitted later revealed uneven levels of commitment. The number of people present at meetings varied from eighteen to twenty-four during the first years, although only five to ten members spoke in each session. The most active members were the professors and writers of texts on political economy, but a variable group of civil servants, politicians, jurists, businessmen and popularisers was also present. Nominally, the Society was open to any economic and political persuasion, although a vast majority of members shared a set of opinions directly taken from French economic literature. This explains why the Sociedad Libre de Economía Política was labelled a product of the 'Economists' School' or 'Economists' group'. It is important to underline the role played by professors and writers of political economy in the foundation and management of the Society, in the organisation and content of debates. The most outstanding members were L. Figuerola, M. Colmeiro, G. Rodríguez, L.M. Pastor, B. Carballo, F. de Bona, S. Moret, J.M. Sanromá, S.D. Madrazo and M. Carreras. All of them were professors of political economy or law, except two – Bona and Pastor – who were financiers (the latter was the author of some works on money and taxation).

The subjects chosen for debates within the Sociedad were heterogeneous. A common feature was that discussions almost always focused on the ways of *applying* to Spanish circumstances the economic principles implicitly accepted by the majority of members. Strictly theoretical issues were normally left aside, with some exceptions such as wage theory or economic relations between individuals and the state. The two main areas of debate were:

1 the economic problems of Spain: obstacles to the introduction of machinery into agriculture, the consequences of the construction of railways, the effects of wage labour on the condition of women;
2 economic policy in general, and the reform of customs in particular (this subject occupied a large number of sessions). Some typical topics examined were the limits of state intervention in the economy, the regulation of urban expansion, compulsory teaching, the regulation of financial markets, the 'new' colonial policy, the utility of universal exhibitions, etc.

The basic economic arguments employed by the supporters of free-trade policies were similar to those embraced by the editors of the *Journal des économistes*: (1) the absolute advantage of foreign trade both from a static and a dynamic point of view; (2) an implicitly utilitarian welfare criterion that implied an opposition between the interest of the *majority* of consumers and that of a *minority* involved in the protected sectors; (3) the positive effect of low customs tariffs on the increase of public revenue; and (4) Say's (and Bastiat's) 'law of markets', etc.

The members of the Sociedad agreed on the general theoretical principles and on the criteria of economic policy, including the sanctity of private property and of minimum state intervention.[6] The apparent homogeneity within the 'Economists' School' was based on the similarity between the arguments displayed in the textbooks of political economy published by its leaders and those presented by the members of the Society in its internal debates. However, a detailed study of deliberations reveals that this homogeneity was more controversial when practical problems were at stake. Disagreement could be classified into three main categories. Firstly, theoretical disagreement (eg. banking school vs. currency school); this kind of contrast was relatively rare. Secondly, different methods of evaluating the economic condition of Spain. The minutes of meetings report very synthetic judgements, usually in the form of occasional and subjective evaluations; conversely, these judgements were rarely based on exact statistical data. Some members were purposely adverse to the use of statistics, since they thought that this use was associated with an empiricist and gradualist approach to economic policy that was inconsistent with the universal principles of political economy.

The third source of disagreement consisted of two divergent systems of social choice. No contrast emerged concerning the principle that custom tariffs should be exclusively a source of fiscal revenue, not an instrument of protection. Conversely, consensus was less pronounced on the schedule for reform (i.e. on consideration of the effects the latter would have on formerly protected sectors), while some participants in the debate emphasised that any attempt at reform should necessarily seek to build up support among public opinion. The discussions implicitly revealed the opposition between the two rival groups: on the one hand, the pure 'liberals', who advocated immediate and unconditional suppression of protection and distrusted any majority rule; on the other hand, the 'democrats' and 'moderates', who defended majority rule and argued in favour of gradual reform, to be preceded by a campaign of persuasion addressed to public opinion. The Asociación para la Reforma de Aranceles de Aduanas, created by some members of the Society in 1859, was directed to this function of propaganda *vis-à-vis* public opinion.

No full information on the discussions at the meetings of the Sociedad is available, since the summaries published in the press are brief and without detail. We do know, however, that the Madrid Society had frequent exchanges of information and publications with parallel societies in other European countries, especially the societies of political economy located in Paris, Brussels, St Petersburg and Turin, and the Greek Society for the Freedom of Trade. However, a close relationship existed above all with the Society of Paris, both through the model represented by the *Journal des économistes* and thanks to the personal contact assured by the Spanish financier Manuel García Quijano, who was a member and treasurer of the Parisian society. During the first years of the Sociedad, these relationships were attested to by the publication of informative notes and summaries concerning the meetings of the aforementioned societies in *El economista*, *La tribuna de los economistas* and *Gaceta economista*. In addition to these institutional relationships, there were also personal exchanges between single economists of different nations; a case in point is that of the commentary on the book by the Spanish economist Mariano Carreras, *Filosofía del interés personal*, published in 1862 by Charles Le Hardy de Beaulieu in *L'Economiste belge*.[7]

From 1864 onwards, with the virtual disappearance of the journals that had formerly published the summaries of meetings, no evidence of the Sociedad de Economía Política is available to our knowledge, although according to G. Rodríguez, it survived until 1868. However, the restrictions imposed by the government on the right of assembly between 1864 and 1868 may have contributed to less intense activity.

Lastly, there is an isolated testimony on the existence of another Sociedad de Economía Política in Murcia.[8] Among its members one should mention Juan López Somalo, who was later professor of political economy and the author of *Lecciones elementales de economía política y estadística*, published in 1871.

2.4 Forums of persuasion and politico-economic influence (1848–74)

From 1848, the diffusion of protectionist arguments was encouraged by the Instituto Industrial de Cataluña with the collaboration of some economists, among whom one should mention José Illas, Juan Güell and Ramón Anglasell, the latter professor of political economy of the University of Barcelona (1846–63). The 'infant industry argument' they advanced, based on the works of List and Carey, was often reinforced by a mass of statistical documentation on the significant industrial development of Catalonia (Artal 1991). The Institute supported the publication of periodicals that endorsed its views and solicited the collaboration of protectionist writers, in particular those from Madrid. During the 1850s the protectionist view was propagated by the *Revista industrial*, edited by Matías Gómez de Villaboa, who had attended the Congrès International des Réformes Douanières in 1856. In Madrid agrarian protectionism was defended by a group led by Genaro Morquecho, who was a professor at the School of Agriculture and whose economic approach was based on a theory of economic stages and on a broad historicist perspective.

As we have pointed out, the question of free trade was the focus of the debates held at the Sociedad de Economía Política of Madrid. The most active group within the Society founded the Asociación para la Reforma de Aranceles de Aduanas on 25th April 1859, which was intended to highlight the benefits of a reform that would transform the customs tariffs 'into purely fiscal tariffs'.[9] The members of the Sociedad and those of the Asociación almost entirely overlapped, and the managing nucleus was practically the same: Luis M. Pastor was elected President in the opening assembly and G. Rodríguez was the appointed Secretary. The basic activity of the Association consisted of conferences, debates and manifestos, generally addressed to the Stock Exchange or the Athenaeum of Madrid. The passing of the Cobden–Chevalier treaty in 1860 and the revision of customs tariffs in Spain in 1862 undoubtedly acted as a catalyst for some special initiatives such as the *Free-trade Lectures* organised by the Association in 1862–3 inside the Athenaeum.[10] There were attempts to spread the Association outside Madrid, but only one 'delegation' in Zaragoza was founded, thanks to the collaboration of Mariano Carreras, then professor of political economy.[11]

The history of the Asociación can be divided into two stages. The first stage, between 1859 and 1868, was followed by a period of implicit dissolution at the outbreak of the 1868–9 revolution, since many of its members were appointed to the government. This was particularly the case of Laureano Figuerola, the Treasury Minister who in 1869 actively promoted a reform suppressing import bans and establishing tax differentials, and fixed a schedule of gradual reductions of customs duties, which is considered the most systematic programme of liberalisation concerning foreign trade in nineteenth-century Spain (Costas 1988). As we will see later on, the second stage of the Asociación began in 1879.

The intellectual debate on customs tariffs reform evolved into a battle between two irreconcilable fronts, which did not communicate with one another and were unable to find a common ground for discussion. Even the Athenaeum of Madrid could not fulfil this function between 1853 and

1874, since it was dominated by the partisans of free trade (Rodríguez, Figuerola, Moret), while the supporters of protectionist policies were virtually absent from debates. The Royal Academy of Moral and Political Sciences – created in 1857 to imitate the French model – likewise included among its members the principal representatives of free-trade economists (Figuerola, Colmeiro, Pastor).

3 Academic institutionalisation without associations: the stagnation of professionalisation (1875–1914)

After the revolutionary period of 1868–74, there began in Spain a long period of institutional stability known as the Restoration (1875–1923). It was also a period of stabilisation and consolidation of the teaching of political economy and public finance. During this period, however, no professional forums for economic debate were created; neither were there any of the short-lived organisations fostering economic reform that had been frequent in the previous period. Nor was any initiative taken in the parallel field of the economics journals, outside the weekly publications specialising in financial subjects. This relation between the institutionalisation of political economy, the professionalisation of economists and the absence of associations requires a detailed explanation.

Firstly, the loss of influence of the 'Economists' School' was a gradual process due to the disappearance of its most prominent members and to the change of attitude towards free trade in the leading political milieu. During the 1870s, Figuerola's reform was first suspended, then definitively repealed in 1891. In order to counteract this protectionist turnabout, the Asociación para la Reforma de los Aranceles de Aduanas began in 1879 a second period of activities, mainly consisting of meetings at the Ateneo de Madrid, articles in the press, and reports to the government and parliament. But these activities soon languished, until the practical disappearance of Association by 1894 (Serrano Sanz 1987). Even before 1879 some internal disagreements had already appeared in the 'Economists' School' (Serrano Sanz 1997). Until 1874, the leading members of the School assumed that Bastiat's notion of economic harmony was perfectly compatible with the philosophy of social harmony expounded by Karl Krause, propagated by Heinrich Ahrens and transformed in Spain into a formal philosophical group known as 'Krausist'. The identity of principles between 'Economists' and 'Krausists' was absolute (Malo Guillén 1998). After the revolutionary period (1868–74), a small group of authors interested in economics (G. de Azcárate, J.M. Piernas Hurtado, A. Alvarez Buylla) emerged from the Krausist group, arguing that the urgency of the 'social problem' required that the individualist assumptions contained in political economy be complemented with the principle of state subsidiarity.

However the revision they advocated was more nominal than real. The proposals for epistemological renewal put forward by J.M. Piernas Hurtado provoked a dispute between himself and G. Rodríguez in the Athenaeum of Madrid, but the approach adopted by the profession as a whole was not substantially modified. Azcárate's critique of individualism was based on Cairnes and Laveleye (Azcárate 1876), but this criticism did not imply the defence of a new economic role for the state, nor a loss of confidence in the natural laws of political economy. The progress of alternative approaches among professors of political economy was marginal, gradual and had no 'revolutionary' character. The influence of the 'Historical School' or 'chair socialist' was quite weak, but the Christian social doctrine and the cooperative movement obtained some support among some professors of political economy, such as A.J. Pou Ordinas and A. Brañas.

The intended Krausist revision of the principles of political economy did not threaten the intellectual hegemony of the 'Economists' School' in the economic debates of the Royal Academy of Moral and Political Sciences (Malo 1999). However these debates, as well as the general political debate, revealed the increasing prestige of some outstanding writers who had undergone prolonged training in the civil service or in other institutions. Their technical superiority became manifest in the extended debate on the reasons why Spain did not belong to the gold standard system.

A second important characteristic of the state of economics in Spain at the end of the nineteenth century was the fact that academic economists very often confined themselves to teaching activities. An analysis of the writings produced by the group of professors of political economy during the period 1874–1914 reveals three fundamental features: (1) the scanty degree of innovation contained in their work, (2) the virtual absence of any influence of marginalist (or neo-classical) economics, and (3) the lack of specialisation in the content of their works (with a full range of economic, political and juridical subjects). The latter aspect, which reveals the multiplicity of engagements and occupations in which economists were often compelled to engage and their low degree of specialisation, ran in parallel with the complementary nature of the teaching of political economy in law faculties and higher schools (Almenar 2000).

Thirdly, the absence of an association of Spanish economists may have been the result of the reduced 'critical mass' of professionals, as a contemporary observer had already pointed out (Olascoaga 1896). The increasing epistemological and doctrinal divergence among economists may also have played a role. But when observed in detail, the absence of a scientific association among economists seems to be the result – rather than the cause – of the low profile of their professionalisation, with routine activity and limited specialisation as its main characteristics.

Only at the end of this period, at the turn of the twentieth century, was a redefinition of the professional activity of economists attempted, following the model of the seminars instituted in German universities. During the early decades of the century, the seminar held by A. Flores de Lemus gave priority to doctoral studies in foreign universities as an indispensable prerequisite for the renewal of the economist's profession.

4 Concluding remarks

The history of the role played by associations in the professionalisation of the economist in Spain, in the period between 1770 and 1914, can be divided into three stages. The first stage (1770s–1820s) was occupied by the Reales Sociedades Económicas de Amigos del País, which played an important role both in institutionalising communication among those interested in economic subjects and in the pioneering initiatives taken for the teaching of political economy up to the 1830s.

The second stage (1820–74) corresponded to the period of expansion and consolidation of political economy as a compulsory subject in university teaching and in some special schools. The early professionalisation of Spanish economists was connected to the practical character of political economy, considered by its practitioners as an instrument of economic reform (in a free-trade sense), rather than as a means to develop scientific speculation. This circumstance, which was partially common to other European countries, favoured the internal coherence and the capacity for intellectual expansion of the Spanish 'Economists' School', and indirectly helps us to improve our understanding of the practical significance of the debates within the Sociedad Libre de Economía Política in Madrid and – at a more general level – the 'style' of economic thought at that time.

The third stage (1875–1914) represented the gradual loss of hegemony of the 'Economists' School', at the very moment at which the teaching of political economy reached an important degree of diffusion and consolidation. In the Spanish case, a well-developed institutional organisation of economic studies (even more extensive than in France or in Portugal) coexisted with a stagnation in the professional specialisation of professors of political economy, a strong resistance to doctrinal innovation, absence of associations among economists and with specialised journals.

After 1914, a progressive transformation of the role of political economy was undertaken, imitating the model of the seminars in German universities. During the 1930s almost 80 per cent of the professors of political economy had as part of their educational background a course of postgraduate studies in foreign universities, preferably in Germany. But the creation of curricula of economics in universities was delayed until the foundation of the Faculty of Political and Economic Sciences at the University of Madrid in 1943. After the 1960s, there was an expansion of faculties and teaching positions in universities, so that there are currently more than sixty university centres of economics and business administration. Moreover, in the 1980s an Association of Regional Science and the Economic History Association were created, but the ordinary method of organisation of the economist's profession still remains that of 'permanent seminars' with lean institutional structures (Economic Analysis, Public Economics, Spanish Economy, Industrial Economics, Economics of Education, Health, etc.). The absence of a general scientific association among economists until the 1980s can be explained by three circumstances: (1) the late creation (1943) of economic curricula in Spanish universities; (2) the political restrictions on the right of association during the dictatorship of General Franco (1939–75); and (3) the existence since 1947 of a professional organisation of a corporatist and exclusive nature (the Colegio de Economistas).

Notes

1 For an overview of the economic thought in this period see Llombart 2000. Within the abundant literature on economic societies mention should be made of Shafer 1958; Demerson, Demerson and Aguilar 1974; Anes 1986; Martín Rodríguez 1989; Llombart and Astigarraga 2000.

2 For an overview of economic thought in Spain during this period see Almenar 2000.

3 During this first meeting a provisional Board of Directors was appointed, composed of Álvaro Flórez Estrada (President), Diego Alvear (Secretary), and those who were entrusted with drawing up the by-laws: José Canga Argüelles, Eusebio María del Valle, Pablo Pebrer, Juan Antonio Seoane and Sebastián Eusebio Vela. The primary information on the Sociedad de Hacienda y Crédito Público was published in the journal of the Madrid Economic Society *El Amigo del País*, 1843, vol. 1, n. 4, 15th April, pp. 108–12.

4 See Lluch 1973; Bahamonde and Toro 1976; Almenar and Velasco 1987; Lluch 1988; Velasco 1990.

5 *El economista*, 1857, vol. 2, pp. 17–21.

6 After writing the preliminary draft of this paper for the meeting at the University of Pisa (October 1999), we had the opportunity to read the paper by Rocío Román, 'La Escuela Economista española en la segunda mitad del siglo XIX', presented at the Primera Reunión de la Asociación Ibérica de Historia del Pensamiento Económico, Universidad de Barcelona, December 1999. The author, who is completing a Ph.D. thesis on the Spanish 'Economists' School', underlines the common doctrinal features of the School and the importance of the organisational function carried out by L.M. Pastor.

7 The third edition of this work includes the text of Le Hardy de Beaulieu's critique and his private correspondence with Carreras, focusing on the theory of rent. See Carreras González 1881.

8 Juan López Somalo, 'Sociedad de economía política en Murcia', *El economista*, 1857, vol. 4, p. 75.

9 *Asociación para la reforma de los aranceles de aduanas. Noticia de su origen y planteamento, acta de la sesión inuagural y juicio formado por la prensa*, Madrid, Imp. de La España Mercantil, 1859.

10 *Conferencias libre-cambistas. Discursos pronunciados en el Ateneo {...} por varios individuos de la Asociación {...}*, Madrid, Imp. de M. Galiano, 1863.

11 See *Gaceta economista*, 1862, vol. 2, pp. 137–9.

References

Almenar, S. (1996) 'Economic Thought in Spanish Periodical Publications of the Eighteenth and Nineteenth Centuries: An Introduction', *History of Economic Ideas* 4, 3: 119–47.

—— (2000) 'El desarrollo del pensamiento económico clásico en España', in E. Fuentes Quintana (ed.) *Economía y economistas españoles*, vol. 4, *La economía clásica*, Barcelona: Galaxia-Gutenberg – Círculo de Lectores.

Almenar, S. and Velasco, R. (1987) 'Una etapa en la consolidación del librecambio en España: el viaje de Richard Cobden por Andalucía', in G. Ruiz (ed.) *Andalucía en el pensamiento económico*, Prol. de E. Lluch., Málaga: Ed. Arguval.

Anes, G. (1986) 'Los Amigos del País y las enseñanzas de economía', in *Homenaje a Pedro Sainz Rodríguez*, vol. 4, Madrid: Fundación Universitaria Española.

Artal, F. (1991) *Pensament econòmic català 1840–1898: del proteccionisme al regionalisme econòmic*, unpublished Ph.D. Thesis, Universidad de Barcelona.

Azcárate, G. de (1876) 'Estudio sobre las obras del economista inglés Mr. Cairnes', in *Estudios económicos y sociales*, Madrid: Librería de Victoriano Suárez.

Bahamonde, A. and Toro, J. (1976) 'Los orígenes de la Sociedad Mercantil Matritense: estudio de un grupo de presión librecambista (1842–1846)', *Anales del Instituto de Estudios Madrileños* 12: 239–53.

Cabrillo, F. (1991) 'El pensamiento económico de Laureano Figuerola', in L. Figuerola (ed.) *Escritos económicos*, Madrid: Instituto de Estudios Fiscales.

Campomanes, P.R. (1774) *Discurso sobre el fomento de la industria popular*, Madrid: Antonio Sancha.

Carreras González, M. (1881) *Filosofía del interés personal. Tratado didáctico de economía política*, Madrid: Librería de Miguel Guijarro.

Costas, A. (1988) *Apogeo del liberalismo en 'La Gloriosa'. La reforma económica en el Sexenio liberal (1868–1874)*, Madrid: Ed. Siglo XXI.

Demerson, P. de, Demerson, J. and Aguilar Piñal, F. (1974) *Las Sociedades Económicas de Amigos del País. Guía del investigador*, San Sebastián: Patonato J.M. Cuadrado.

Gil Novales, A. (1975) *Las Sociedades Patrióticas (1820–1823). La libertades de expresión y de reunión en el orígen de los partidos políticos*, Madrid: Ed. Tecnos.

Llombart, V. (2000) 'El pensamiento económico de la Ilustración en España (1760–1812)', in E. Fuentes Quintana (ed.) *Economía y economistas españoles*, vol. 3, *La Ilustración*, Barcelona: Galaxia-Gutenberg – Círculo de Lectores.

Llombart, V. and Astigarraga, J. (2000) 'Las primeras "antorchas de la economía": las Sociedades Económicas de Amigos del País en el siglo XVIII', in E. Fuentes Quintana (ed.) *Economía y economistas españoles*, vol. 3, *La Ilustración*, Barcelona: Galaxia-Gutenberg – Círculo de Lectores.

Lluch, E. (1973) *El pensament econòmic a Catalunya (1760–1840). Els orígens ideològics del proteccionisme i la pressa de consciència de la burgesía catalana*, Barcelona: Edicions 62.

—— (1988) 'La "gira trionfal" de Cobden per Espanya (1846)', *Recerques* 21: 71–90.

Lluch, E. and Almenar, S. (1992) 'Difusión e influencia de los economistas clásicos en España', in J.L. Cardoso and A. Almodovar (eds) *Actas do Encontro Ibérico sobre História do Pensamento Económico*, Lisboa: Cisep.

Malo Guillén, J.L. (1998) 'El concepto de Sociedad y Estado en el pensamiento económico español 1839–1868: la conexión entre filosofía krausista y liberalismo', *Cuadernos Aragoneses de Economía* 8, 1: 205–14.

—— (1999) 'El Krausismo en la Real Academia de Ciencias Morales y Políticas', *Papeles y Memorias de las Real Academia de Ciencias Morales y Políticas* 6: 193–215.

Martín Rodríguez, M. (1989) 'La institucionalización de los Estudios de Economía Política en la Universidad Española (1784–1857)', in M. de Valle Santoro,

Elementos de economía política, con aplicación particular a España, Madrid: Instituto de Estudios Fiscales.

Olascoaga, R. de (1896) *Estado actual de los estudios económicos en España*, Madrid: L. V. Suárez.

Ruiz Salvador, A. (1971) *El Ateneo científico, literario y artístico de Madrid (1835–1885)*, London: Tamesis Books.

Serrano Sanz, J.M. (1987) *El viraje proteccionista en la Restauración. La política comercial española, 1875–1895*, Madrid: Ed. Siglo XXI.

—— (1997) 'Los estudios económicos en España a finales del siglo XIX: historia de un estancamiento', in G. Bel and A. Estruch (eds) *Industrialización en España: Entusiasmos, desencantos y rechazos. Ensayos en homenaje al profesor Fabián Estapé*, Madrid: Ed. Civitas.

Shafer, R.J. (1958) *The Economic Societies in the Spanish World (1763–1821)*, New York: Syracuse University Press.

Solá, R. (1997) *L'Institut Industrial de Catalunya i l'associacionisme industrial des de 1820 a 1854*, Barcelona: Publicacions de l'Abadía de Montserrat.

Velasco, R. (1990) *Pensamiento económico en Andalucía (1800–1850). Economía política, librecambio y proteccionismo*, Prol. de E. Lluch., Málaga: Ed. Agora.

7 From learned societies to professional associations

The establishment of the economist profession in Portugal

António Almodovar and José Luís Cardoso

The emergence of economists in a strictly professional sense in Portugal is a twentieth century phenomenon, directly related to the actions and efforts of a handful of men who, during the late 1940s, accomplished the transformation of the Instituto Superior de Ciências Económicas e Financeiras (Institute of Economics and Finance; hereafter: ISCEF) into a fully fledged modern school of economics. Therefore, the whole nineteenth century stands for little else than the unchallenged predominance of laymen with some more or less trivial notions of political economy, together with a few exceptional individuals with a more serious interest in the theoretical elaboration of economic discourse.

This state of affairs is quite understandable in the light of the low level of economic and social development Portugal experienced throughout the nineteenth century. The number of illiterates was immense; the population sparse and scattered over a poorly urbanised territory, with very few means of communication. Agriculture was still the main occupation, while trade and manufacturing encountered serious difficulties on account of a small internal market and an adverse foreign market. In addition, there was an insufficient amount of capital available for business investment, partly on account of a widespread attitude in favour of financial speculation.

Faced with such conditions, it was only natural that the overall demand for modern professions – such as engineers and economists – was extremely weak. Nevertheless, the supply side was somewhat more active. From the late eighteenth century onwards, the Portuguese political élite was deeply committed to the task of promoting the development and modernisation of the country from above, by means of a series of administrative and political actions and regulations. The first measures concerning the supply of accountants were undertaken in the late eighteenth century, to be followed only in the 1820s by an attempt to establish the formal study of political economy at university level. After some twenty years of social and political unrest, a stabilised liberal regime was finally secured, and political economy became part of the curricula of Law Studies in the University of Coimbra – the sole existing Portuguese University up to the twentieth century. As a direct consequence of this arrangement, the study of economics as a scientific field of enquiry became unquestionably conditioned by its subordinate function in the education of lawyers, high administrators and civil servants. It goes without saying that the immediate endeavours to promote the autonomy of economic studies would be faced with an arduous task.

In this chapter an attempt is made to give an account of the lengthy and difficult process of professional certification in Portugal, from the first learned societies of the late eighteenth century right up to the twentieth-century phenomena involving the emergence of professional associations among specialised economists.

In the first section we will bring to light the rudimentary but nevertheless meaningful role played by 'economists' and political economy within Ancien Régime learned societies. In the second section, we will follow the different aspects of the process of institutionalisation of political economy throughout the nineteenth century. Finally, we will look with some detail at the rise and early development of professional associations among graduate economists in the early decades of the twentieth century, highlighting the different, although complementary strategies undertaken by economists in order to substantiate their position in the academic, social and political milieu.

1 Political economy within the Ancien Régime learned societies

In the late eighteenth century the followers of Pombal's enlightened policies were deeply concerned with issues relating to the promotion of social and economic improvement. In 1770 the Aula de Comércio (School of Commerce) was established for the educational training of accountants. Two years later, in 1772, the by-laws of the University of Coimbra were amended in order to update both the subjects and the methods traditionally employed, so that Portugal could harmonise with the rest of Europe. Some teachers came from abroad (in particular the Italian Domenico Vandelli), and their action soon spilled over into other cultural circles, for they were also present in the establishment of other important learned institutions such as the Royal Academy of Sciences of Lisbon. Established in 1779, this organisation soon became a quasi-official forum for the spread of scientific ideas. Although mainly with backgrounds in literature, history and the natural sciences, the members of this learned society were nevertheless sympathetic to other types of knowledge, including law, philosophy and political economy.

Owing to the distinctive attributes of an institution designed in accordance with the spirit of the Enlightenment, it is illogical to attempt to introduce modern boundaries into what was intended as a unified approach to the knowledge of man within society. In spite of the existence of certain natural individual proclivities, the infancy of some of the emerging sciences as well as the prevalence of an overall enlightened attitude preclude any attempt to classify those eighteenth century scholars as specialists (or even professionals) in any modern sense of the word. Clearly, the Academy of Sciences must be regarded as a loose scientific forum where representatives of different traditional branches of knowledge (humanities and natural sciences, not autonomous specialised disciplines) would meet to exchange views over the prospects science could offer to mankind.

To record and describe, but also to prescribe, to seek the best path to the general betterment of society, to help the process of political decision making – these were the shared aims of the members of the Academy of Sciences. Their work – either in the shape of 'philosophical' journeys in the mainland and in the colonies, or in that of seemingly more theoretical 'memoirs' – is connoted by a focus on practical aspects, a quasi-impulsive disposition toward economic issues, among which agriculture clearly prevails. Therefore the increase in the number of members – even as mere local correspondents – fostered the influence and the importance of an institution in which a civilised dialogue between different views and interests could take place and look for political support.

Political and economic motivations had been present among Academy members since the beginning. But they acquired a crucial role from 1789 onwards, together with the establishment of a new series of publications entitled *Memórias económicas*. Many of these publications resulted from memoirs annually judged as the best study on economic subjects (generally they were economic descriptions of a province or a region), while others were the outcome of systematic inquiries on the technical and productive aspects of agricultural practices. All in all, they allowed the Academy to act as a kind of invisible network between men of science and those economic agents capable of promoting social and economic betterment. Accordingly, the Royal Academy of Sciences of Lisbon may be depicted not only as a pioneering institution associating individuals with a common shared interest in the advancement of useful scientific knowledge, but also as the institutional model to be followed by those interested in developing an economic approach to the problems of the Portuguese Ancien Régime society (Cardoso 1989; Almodovar and Cardoso 1998; Pereira 1984).

Following the example of Spain, where several societies were conceived or established in the late eighteenth century, the Portuguese made an effort to set up Sociedades Económicas de Amigos do País. The aims of these territorial societies included the organisation of local claims, as well as the advancement of arts and manufactures within rural areas and the spread of new agricultural techniques. However, most of these attempts were quite unsuccessful.

One of the few successful economic societies was the Sociedade Económica dos Bons Compatriotas, Amigos do Bem Público (Economic Society of the Good Patriots and Friends of the Common Good), established in Ponte de Lima (northwestern Portugal) in 1780. The evidence available suggests that practical pedagogical action concerning agricultural techniques and the economy of the household was undertaken by this economic society (Amzalak 1950). It is also likely that this society may have acted as an organisation for raising funds to promote investment in local agriculture. However, one of its most interesting attributes was the fact that it gathered together a number of different social and economic agents in a common project aiming at the economic development of their region. More generally, this type of economic association, bringing together 'patriots' and 'friends of the common good', was in fact an exercise in citizenship directed towards the fulfilment of certain common goals. The zeal for public betterment was the essence of each and every associative experience, even when professional and organic interests were poorly represented.

The Sociedade Real Marítima, Militar e Geográfica, founded in 1798, and the ephemeral activity of the Tipografia Calcográfica e Literária do Arco do Cego (Literary Printing House of Arco do Cego), established in 1799 and closed in 1801, represent two other types of late eighteenth-century organisations of broad-ranging economic interests. Both institutions were established under the direct initiative of Rodrigo de Souza Coutinho, one of the most important enlightened statesmen of this period. The main purpose of the Geographical Society was the development of cartography, while the Printing House aimed at the diffusion of scientific works (on agriculture, botany and the natural sciences) in Brazil. Notwithstanding these specific statutory aims, they also acted as organisations eliciting professional vocations like those promoted by the Royal Academy of Sciences of Lisbon, not only because they encouraged a scholarly attitude, but especially because they favoured the spread of practical knowledge within the Portuguese colonies.

It seems clear that all these institutions shared a common feature, for they all were embryonic associative projects endeavouring to merge different individual prospects and capacities into a common clear design, usually of an economic nature. One may therefore conclude that individuals could attain their goals only through the social visibility and recognition ascribed by established institutions. In other words, through an institutional setting, individual interests could turn into common goals.

This pattern of activity would survive throughout the nineteenth century, either through the action of some of these societies which succeeded in surviving, or via the action of other newly founded associations. Yet this type of association was soon to endure the competition of other associative models, somewhat more effective in their ability to support specific economic interests by means of judicious application of the principles of political economy.

During this period, however, there were few scholars with a solid background of learning in economic matters, and as a rule they published their works independently of the editions sponsored by the Academy of Sciences. This was the case of Acúrsio das Neves, Silva Lisboa and, to a lesser extent,

Rodrigo de Souza Coutinho. These authors studied the Portuguese economy in their reports, books and pamphlets and shared a strong commitment to the spread of both Adam Smith's and Jean-Baptiste Say's ideas. As such, they were not only responsible for the early diffusion of modern political economy, but they also paved the way for the later establishment of its teaching on a regular basis.

2   The institutionalisation of political economy

Portuguese society faced another burst of modernisation in the first decades of the nineteenth century. Now it was the liberal creed that formed the backbone of the will to change, inspiring a political élite chiefly composed of lawyers toward a series of legal reforms. In the 1820s, a parliament was established, and the new regime embarked on a massive inquiry into the causes of the economic and social backwardness of Portugal. Several different committees were set up in order to examine in detail the major obstacles to the development of agricultural, industrial and commercial activities, so that the impediments could be overcome and the country thereby allowed to prosper. Among the conclusions reached by these committees, there was unanimous judgement concerning the need for widespread education of citizens, especially in matters concerning political economy (Almodovar 1995). Both the political and business élite agreed that the contemporary world required more than the skills involved in ordinary practical craftsmanship or even traditional academic knowledge. The humanities, they argued, and especially conventional Law Studies, were no longer sufficient in order to deal appropriately with both the practical and intellectual challenges of the 'modern' world. Therefore, they manifested their conviction that any prospect for development was necessarily dependent on the ability to catch up with the latest technical discoveries, although it was imperative that innovations should follow the recommendations laid down by the new science of political economy. In this context, special attention should be paid to Francisco Solano Constâncio and to the journals he edited in Paris in the 1820s and 1830s, where both the scientific and technical innovations of the time and the intellectual achievements of political economy as an autonomous field of study were carefully described (Cardoso 1999).

However, prior to the adoption of any specific measures concerning the diffusion of economic ideas, an intricate problem had to be addressed. Insofar as political economy was not only a very recent science, but also scattered between different and conflicting schools of thought with opposite views on significant points, it was necessary to exercise great caution in prescribing the authors and texts to be read and circulated among laymen. As the parliament itself was strongly conscious of this problem, its support for the spread of economic ideas was somewhat circumspect. Accordingly, it notified all those who were interested in establishing private classes on political economy that they should adopt the works of Jean-Baptiste Say (particularly the *Catéchisme* and the *Traité d'économie politique*) as a primary source of inspiration for the writing of a 'Portuguese' textbook on political economy.

The political contingencies of the 1820s postponed these intentions. Only in the 1830s were the liberals able to overcome the resistance of the Ancien Régime to social and economic change; but even then most of the population was poorly motivated and ill-prepared for the changes the liberals wished to introduce. This proved to be a major obstacle, since the immense gap between the élite and the great mass of the population could not be bridged without a serious and systematic educational effort. The real dimension of this problem can readily be understood by considering the obstacles that confronted the commercial associations of Lisbon and Porto (the Associação Mercantil Lisbonense and the Associação Comercial do Porto) and the parliament when both undertook the first positive measures to promote the teaching of political economy.

Part and parcel of the liberal regime, these commercial associations were devised as an important intermediary between the official institutions (particularly the parliament and the government) and the local economic and social élite. Through them, the liberals could establish an institutional channel of communication with those who were expected to act as the agents of modernisation, while the local powers could declare and advocate their own interests in an orderly manner. Therefore, both the parliament and the two major commercial associations agreed to embark on a united effort to establish classes of political economy for the benefit of younger generations. Parliament acted upon the public educational system, establishing classes of political economy at the University of Coimbra and in some of the new institutions set up in 1836 – namely the Liceu and the Academia Politécnica – while the commercial associations provided a series of less formal educational occasions open to the general public.[1]

These good intentions notwithstanding, within less than a year the situation proved to be disastrous. With the exception of the University of Coimbra, where the teaching of political economy was effective and compulsory, all other classes were either abolished due to the shortage of students or experienced serious difficulties.

This failure had serious consequences for the spread of economic ideas. In face of these fruitless attempts to create a wider audience for the messages conveyed by political economy, the liberal élite was forced to favour a less challenging strategy to overcome the pressing educational needs of the country. The next move was therefore an effort to improve the literacy and skill of existing economic agents by establishing classes on business correspondence in Portuguese, English and French, elementary arithmetic, basic notions of geography and accountancy.[2] The study of more demanding theoretical subjects – such as political economy – was left either to law students or to gifted amateurs.

In consequence the evolution of both the proficiency and the number of potential 'economists' was quite slow, thus limiting the chances for the emergence of a new type of learned professional.

The existing 'economists' were consequently naturally led to develop their activities within several different institutional settings, mainly as counsellors and consultants of the more powerful economic lobbies or as supposedly independent pedagogues and opinion-makers. One may also note their presence in several non-specific associations, like the Sociedade Literária Patriótica de Lisboa[3] or the Sociedade Promotora da Indústria Nacional. According to its by-laws, the former aimed 'to guide public opinion, in agreement with the constitutional system, by means of writings, serving as a school for the duty of speaking in public with accuracy and thoughtfulness' (Ribeiro 1874: 128). In spite of this broad educational, political and civic motivation, which was particularly concerned with the setting up of the new liberal regime, the journal of this Society also set itself the goal of 'the diffusion of learning and the spreading of useful knowledge, in order to fight against the errors, prevarication and abuses of the public administration'. Topics concerning political economy were of course on the agenda of this Society, namely those concerned with analysis of the public debt and the appropriateness of subscribing to new loans. The latter subject was discussed in various meetings of the Society, which were attended by two of the most important contemporary Portuguese economists – Mouzinho da Silveira and Carlos Morato Roma.

The object of the Sociedade Promotora da Indústria Nacional was self-evident. In order to encourage the development of the Portuguese economy, the Society established prizes, awards and other kinds of incentives intended to promote the quality and excellence of all industrial ventures. The Society also stimulated the introduction of new industrial processes (instruments, machines and inventions) designed to increase industrial productivity and efficiency. Finally, its promoters did not overlook the need to disseminate the technical and professional knowledge that was required to bring forth a qualified labour force. Through the publication of its own journal (the *Anais da Sociedade Promotora da Indústria Nacional*), this Society fostered the spread of useful knowledge, thus proving its importance as a forum of discussion on applied economic matters.[4]

The political appeasement which Portugal enjoyed from the 1850s up to the mid-1870s only came to reinforce this desolate situation in which political economists were to develop their activities. Throughout this period, Portuguese society shared a widespread belief with regard to the path to progress and wealth advocated by the *laissez-faire* doctrine, embracing both the workings of competition and free trade, and of a state willing to provide for the basic economic infrastructures such as railroads and the telegraph. But ironically, this consensus did not led to any perceptible increase in the number (or quality) of political economists, probably for the very reason that the *laissez-faire* orientation of politics and public opinion was considered a settled matter.

However, the manifest financial failure of this model of development by the end of the century, together with the decline of the so-called French liberal school, helped to revive widespread critical attention to the contents and form of the economic discourse. As the supporters of socialism (namely those inspired by Fourier and Proudhon) acquired some notoriety in Portugal thanks to their merciless attacks on the deeds and thoughts of political economists, the latter felt compelled to gather their strength and try to fight back. Few and unorganised as they were, their power to counteract a fashionable tide[5] of this kind was feeble, especially because precisely the same trend had found its way into the University of Coimbra, where political economy was under assault both from the sympathisers of the socialists and the followers of Comte's views on social science.

As a consequence, after a brief period characterised by open resistance to their opponents, some Portuguese 'economists' sought to take a step further in the direction of their theoretical and (especially) doctrinal improvement. Unable to answer back with their traditional arguments, they engaged in an effort to draw inspiration from the contemporary economic literature of France, Italy, Germany, and to a lesser extent, England. This attitude, which gave rise to a significant introduction of new ideas, would clearly require time in order to select, digest and put to use the new concepts and doctrines, thus giving new life both to economics and to its practitioners, the economists.

3 The rise and early development of economics

It was only in the early decades of the twentieth century that a brilliant young law teacher (Marnoco e Sousa) managed to restore the prestige of political economy at the University of Coimbra. Although having a preference for the 'younger' German Historical School, Marnoco e Sousa paid due attention to each contemporary school of thought, scrupulously summarising the main tenets and major works of each, and thus paving the way for future progress.[6]

When the political regime changed again in 1910, replacing the monarchy with a republic, a third cycle of enthusiastic betterment began. The partisans of the new regime had immense faith in the redemptive properties of education, be it civic, scientific or simply technical. By the same token, they believed in the virtues of sociability, when expressed by means of free associations. These two broad characteristics of the republican worldview (Catroga 1991) led to a reform of all educational institutions, and to the founding of several civic, scientific and professional associations – such as the 1913 Associação dos Comercialistas Portugueses (Association of the Portuguese Commerce Professionals) or the 1926 Associação dos Comercialistas do Norte de Portugal. Furthermore, as the country had progressed during the nineteenth century, there was by now a reasonably large demand in trade and industry for some specialised professionals such as engineers, accountants and even managers.

But not yet for economists. These had still to wait for the time to come when they would be recognised as a socially relevant specialised group. At that moment, economists were considered either as a kind of overeducated accountant (whenever they came out of commercial schools), or as just one more of those lawyers replete with abstract (i.e. useless) explanations and concepts. Moreover, economists had also to endure the claims – and the fierce competition – of those engineers who thought of themselves as the obvious industrial leaders of the future. These engineers, nurtured by an earlier process of academic institutionalisation that allowed them to threaten the traditional importance of lawyers, were enthusiastic about the prospect of including economics within their own curricula as a normal sequel to their professional development. It was only in the late 1940s that these significant obstacles to the professionalisation of economists were removed, granting recognised social, academic and professional status to Portuguese economists.

The major steps towards this fully fledged specialisation were basically three. In 1913 the Instituto Superior de Comércio and its allied lobby, the Associação dos Comercialistas Portugueses, were established in Lisbon; in 1931, this school gave way to the ISCEF, formally placing the specialised study of economics at university level. Finally the advent in 1941 of a new association, the Sociedade de Ciências Económicas paved the way for a decisive curricular reform of the ISCEF in 1949. From then on, Portuguese economists were endowed not only with their own first modern school, but also with one firmly rooted at the élite university level.

The establishment of associations for protection of the professional interests of the graduates of the Institutos Superiores de Comércio marked the inaugural moment of the economist's occupational recognition. The growing importance granted to high-level commercial studies caused a significant expansion in the number of professionals holding a higher education or university-level qualification and working in the civil service. In spite of their scanty knowledge of economic theory, they had a considerable background in practical disciplines such as business correspondence, commercial techniques and, especially, accounting. As their social prestige remained quite poor – not to mention their inferior status in face of the overwhelming political influence of lawyers and engineers – it is no surprise that they fought for the establishment of a professional association. As we have mentioned, the first was founded in 1913, to be followed some years later (1926) by the Associação dos Comercialistas do Norte de Portugal established in Porto. These two associations merged in 1935, giving rise to the Sindicato Nacional dos Comercialistas. However, the severe control exercised by the Portuguese state over all corporations of this kind turned out to be a definite obstacle to the fulfilment of the primary mission of professional, scientific and cultural advancement of their affiliates. These impediments contribute to an understanding of the expectation aroused by the establishment of the Sociedade de Ciências Económicas in 1941. In spite of its ephemeral life, this Society managed to gather a significant number of associates, in particular some of the most prominent teachers from the ISCEF. As the main activity of this Society was the organisation of high-level conferences, it comes as no surprise that some of the papers submitted turned out to be seminal contributions to the modernisation of teaching practices within the ISCEF.

As we have already mentioned, the decisive step towards the academic and professional recognition of economists was reserved for the ISCEF (Portela 1969; Gonçalves 1998; Bastien and Cardoso 1999). This school effectively acted as an institutional umbrella for all those professionally involved either in private or public accounting, management or economics; it sought unceasingly to promote the enrolment of 'modern' economists both in government and in various institutions of national and international economic coordination. And now that this lobbying activity was carried out by a school established at university level, it finally succeeded in enhancing the social and academic status of economists. After a long and winding road, the profession was secure at last.

4 Concluding remarks

As shown in the previous section, economic associations are, in Portugal, a twentieth-century phenomenon. Their development is closely related to the increasing impact of commercial, accounting and economic studies at university level. The demand for such studies may in turn be explained by the very process of economic development which, to a certain extent, led to the institutionalisation and growing relevance of the technical and political role of economists themselves. In this sense, the Portuguese case clearly shows that economic associations and societies are a natural result of the development of practical needs, professional skills and ethical concerns, which represent the main source of the sociability links fostered by their individual members.

Though it is difficult to find any trace of genuine economic societies or associations during the nineteenth century – as we have tried to explain in §2 – the Portuguese experience also highlights the role displayed by different, alternative organisations and professional groups, clubs or societies. These alternative models of association also proved capable of bringing together individual members who were particularly eager to campaign for social and economic betterment. Although the type of commitment underlying these associations was certainly varied, almost all of them display problems characteristic of the coexistence of a twofold purpose – contributing to the defence of particular economic interests and providing a forum for wider discussion of the ideal conditions and instruments for a sustained process of development. Consequently, the acquaintance with, and utilisation of, political economy proved to be a key factor in strengthening doctrinal and theoretical arguments for economic and political change. Could the impact of political economy on nineteenth-century Portuguese society have gone significantly beyond this important argumentative role? Could 'economists' have then emerged, with economics becoming an acknowledged profession? In face of available evidence concerning the level of economic and social development, it seems quite clear that besides this doctrinal function, there was at that time no other realistic use for political economy.

Notes

1   Although mainly designed for use by the members of the associations, these classes were nevertheless open to all those wishing to attend.
2   Some other occupations had their own specific elementary training. Here we refer mainly to the training of clerks, accountants and entrepreneurs.
3   Several other societies of this sort were established in Portugal (Porto, Funchal, Alfandega da Fé and Covilhã). They all supported the constitutional system.
4   Several societies of this kind were established (and also disappeared) throughout the first half of the nineteenth century. Their brief lives help us to understand the fragile and erratic character of those societies set up for the fostering of economic interests.
5   It is worth mentioning that during this period both political economy and economists were also mentioned for the first time in some Portuguese novels. They were, of course, depicted as selfish materialistic supporters of an archaic science.
6   For a general account of the work of Marnoco e Sousa, see the introductory essay by Maria de Fátima Brandão to Sousa 1996 (1910).

References

Almodovar, A. (1995) *A Institucionalização da Economia Política Clássica em Portugal*, Porto: Edições Afrontamento.
Almodovar, A. and Cardoso, J.L. (1998) *A History of Portuguese Economic Thought*, London and New York: Routledge.
Amzalak, M.B. (1950) *A Sociedade Económica de Ponte de Lima (Século XVIII). Apontamentos para a sua História*, Lisboa: pub. by the author.
Bastien, C. and Cardoso, J.L. (1999) 'Antecedentes, Significado e Consequências da Reforma do ISCEF de 1949', unpublished paper.
Cardoso, J.L. (1989) *O Pensamento Económico em Portugal nos Finais do Século XVIII (1780–1808)*, Lisboa: Estampa.
—— (1999) 'The Road to Heterodoxy: F. S. Constâncio and the Critical Acceptance of Classical Political Economy', *History of Political Economy* 31, 3: 473–92.
Catroga, F. (1991) *O Republicanismo em Portugal. Da formação ao 5 de Outubro de 1910*, Coimbra: Faculdade de Letras.
Gonçalves, C.M. da Silva (1998) *Emergência e Consolidação dos Economistas em Portugal*, unpublished Ph.D. Thesis, Porto: Faculdade de Letras.
Pereira, J.E. (1984) 'Economia em Portugal no Século XVIII. Aspectos de Mentalidade', *Prelo* 2: 25–40.

Portela, A.F. (1969) 'A evolução histórica do ensino das Ciências Económicas em Portugal', *Colecção Análise Social* 1, 2: 311–65.

Ribeiro, J.S. (1874). *História dos Estabelecimentos Científicos, Literários e Artísticos de Portugal*, vol. 4, Lisboa: Tipografia da Academia das Ciências.

Sousa, J.F. Marnoco (1996) (1910) *Ciência Económica*, edited with an introduction by Maria de Fátima Brandão, Lisboa: Banco de Portugal.

8 Patriots, the poor and economic progress

Economic societies in the Netherlands

*Evert Schoorl**

The first economic society in the Netherlands was formed in the late eighteenth century by the so-called 'Economic Patriots'. In 1777 they founded the Oeconomical Branch of the Dutch Society of Sciences. Its successor still lives on under the name of Nederlandse Maatschappij voor Nijverheid en Handel (Dutch Society for Industry and Trade). After the revolution of 1795, the Oeconomical Branch became an independent advisory body of the new republican government.

In the first section of this chapter, a brief glance is taken at the economic ideas of the Patriots. Then the ideas and associations of their nineteenth-century successors in societies and journals where the 'Poor Question' was the central issue are examined. While the focus is on economic associations proper, it cannot be denied that economic – and sometimes even non-economic – journals had an equally important role as forums of economic discourse in an age in which economics was still predominantly political economy. Also, the early academic institutionalisation of the new discipline is mentioned briefly. In §2, the founding and further development of the Statistical and Economic Association is described. Still flourishing under the name of Koninklijke Vereniging voor Staathuishoudkunde (Royal Economic Society), it claims to be the oldest economic society in continuous existence in the world. In §3, economic discourse in the literary journal *De Gids*, founded in 1837, is summarised in order to show that such a journal could be an equally influential forum for economists, politicians and men of letters to discuss the issues of the day as a learned society. In §4, some conclusions are drawn about the acceptance of the economists' contribution to economic policy formation and about the specific role of economic associations. It will be argued that in the Netherlands there is a long-standing tradition of political-economic discussions and academic economic debates running parallel, with to a large extent the same actors taking part in both.

1 Early economic associations and the Poor Question

In recent historiography – with Simon Schama's *Patriots and Liberators* (1977) as an outstanding example – the Dutch late eighteenth century or

Age of the Patriots has been rehabilitated. The cartoons of the day had succeeded in establishing an image of provincial quarrels between comical Orangemen, with the fat Stadtholder William V on one side, and the equally ridiculous Patriots or *Kezen* (street dogs) who unsuccessfully tried to practice military drill on the other, as gratifying subjects. The modern picture looks more like a grand rehearsal for the French Revolution, enacted in the Low Countries.

The Dutch Republic was no longer a Great Power, as compared to France and England. But it was only relatively in decline. However the number of urban poor grew in a period of dearth, and it probably came to include impoverished former members of the middle class. As a consequence of the spread of Enlightenment ideas, visible poverty was considered to be less and less tolerable. In the Netherlands the Patriots' movement was aiming at political reform. The group of so-called 'Economic Patriots' tried to reduce poverty by stimulating economic activity, for example by means of putting premiums on entrepreneurship and organising essay competitions.

The social and economic ideas of the Economic Patriots had an egalitarian and, to the modern observer, a somewhat 'green' flavour. In their 'oeconomical shops' only Dutch products were sold. Not the total wealth of the nation, but the relative position of the poor, was their measure of national welfare – long before John Rawls (Boschloo 1989: ch. 3).

The Oeconomical Branch of the Hollandsche Maatschappij der Wetenschappen (Dutch Academy of Sciences) (founded in 1777) was organised in many local societies or departments, all of which sent representatives to the General Assembly. In spite of its limited economic objective, it attracted enormous attention because it managed to set up a national democratic organisation amidst political and regional division. Accordingly this parliamentary testing-plot was regarded with suspicion by the authorities. At the first General Assembly no less than 85 deputies were present, representing 2,625 members from 55 departments. After a few years this large interest dwindled, but the Oeconomical Branch continued to exist. With a number of changes in its name and objectives, it lives on in the twenty-first century as the Dutch Society for Industry and Trade.

In many respects, the activities of the Economic Patriots were typical of the Enlightenment. They wanted to educate the poor in order to enable them to support themselves. In practice, even employment projects and workshops were organised for the poor, with varying success. After the revolt of 1795, the new National Assembly made the Branch into an independent advisory board for the government, under the name of the Netherlands' National Household Society. The constitution of 1798, the first of its kind, made the state responsible for employment and poor relief:

> Society as a whole, in every respect aiming at the welfare of all its Members, procures labour to the active, support to the Needy. Deliberate

idlers cannot claim support. Society requires the complete suppression of begging.

Note two things. Firstly, the use of 'society' as synonymous with state. Secondly, the right of the state to forbid begging only when offering employment at the same time.

After the establishment of the new Kingdom of the Netherlands in 1815, the discussion on economic stagnation and the Poor Question continued to dominate the economic debate. Wishful predictions from the proclamation with which the liberation from the French and the return of Prince William (King William I) were hailed claimed that 'The old times will come back'. But they did not return, for the content and the routes of trade and capital had changed as a consequence of the Napoleonic wars and the Industrial Revolution. It did not take long before even the municipal government of Amsterdam wrote to the sovereign that it would accept that, like Hoorn and Enkhuizen, it would become one of the Dead Cities along the coast of the large inland sea, the Zuiderzee (now IJsselmeer).

King William did his best to foster economic revival by founding new companies (De Nederlandsche Handel-Maatschappij or Colonial Trading Company being one of them), but his efforts did not show immediate results. Unlike in some other European countries, where liberal economics was associated with politically subversive liberal ideas, there was no mistrust of the new discipline of economics. Academic teaching of the subject was encouraged by the government. Around 1800, the first course of economics – as distinct from statistics – had been taught at the University of Leyden. The first professors who took up the subject taught it as a second course, next to the one for which they had been appointed. But from the late 1820s on, many chairs of economics were instituted in the law faculties.

Hans Boschloo has convincingly shown that the backward image drawn by Irene Hasenberg Butter in her dissertation *Academic Economics in Holland, 1800–1870* is a caricature of Dutch economics, based upon reading laws and regulations without paying attention to what happened in practice. Unhampered by the official requirement of Latin, economics courses were taught in Dutch. Many dissertations in law were in fact economic treatises and economics was not at all an alien subject in the law faculties where many civil servants were trained. Thus the three basic arguments of Irene Hasenberg Butter to demonstrate the backwardness of Dutch economics before 1870 have been exposed by Boschloo (1989: ch. 1).

An extra stimulus to offering economic courses was the regulation which made the subject compulsory for law students aiming at a career in the civil service, as the students' fees were a substantial augmentation of the professorial incomes. These students did not have to take examinations in the subject, but only needed a testimonial of attendance.

The Poor Question continued to be a rallying issue for economists. Poor relief was a matter for churches and municipalities, and the number of receiving paupers continued to grow slowly from 1815 onwards, while the means of the parochial and municipal relief boards suffered from stagnation. H.W. Tydeman, the first full professor of economics in the Netherlands, who taught the subject in Leyden for thirty years from 1817 on, published his *Magazijn voor het armen-wezen in het koninkrijk der Nederlanden* (Magazine for Poor Relief) in five volumes between 1817 and 1822 (nothing came of the plan he announced in the first volume, to publish a journal of 'Contributions to the Statistics and Economics, in particular those of the Kingdom of the Netherlands'). Tydeman received little support from his *laissez-faire* contemporaries as they identified his ideas with King William's neo-mercantilist policies. Leyden was always considered a royalist university and Tydeman was one of the private teachers of the princes of Orange, while his colleagues de Brueys and Ackersdijk from Utrecht were officially rebuked for voicing criticism of the Dutch Corn Laws in 1835.

In 1825 Tydeman published a Dutch translation of Mrs Marcet's popular economic textbook. His friend and colleague in Leyden (between 1822 and 1838) G. Wttewaal, who taught agricultural economics, was the first to publish an economic journal in the Netherlands in 1836 under the title announced earlier by Tydeman, *Bijdragen tot de staathuishoudkunde en statistiek*. This was discontinued when he died after publishing the second volume in 1838 (Mooij 1994: 45).

In 1848 only a soft revolution was necessary to realise constitutional reform in the Netherlands. King William II 'turned into a liberal overnight' and the great liberal reformer Thorbecke designed a new constitution in which parliamentary democracy and civil rights were guaranteed. As a professor of economics and law in Ghent before the Belgian uprising, Thorbecke had shown an amazing insight into the development of industrial society and the social divide it engendered. As prime minister in 1848, he initiated an ambitious programme of legislation, in which a new Poor Law was a centrepiece.

The legislative agenda boosted public discussion on the subject. Tydeman, as an interventionist, published his own ideas for a new law in 1850. Three years later he had a translation published of parts of A. & P.W. Alison's writings under the title *De staatsarmenzorg verdedigd en aangeprezen* (In Defense and Praise of State Poor Relief) (Boschloo 1989: 83).

Freedom of association and liberty of the press were more firmly established under the new constitution. This combination occasioned the founding of many societies and journals. In 1850, the Algemeene Vereeniging tegen het Pauperisme (General Association against Pauperism) had been founded in Groningen, primarily as a regional association. Despite its name, its orientation was largely non-interventionist and *laissez-faire*. It aimed at uniting 'all persons and associations intending to promote the moral elevation and economic welfare of the lower classes'.

The fall of Thorbecke's government in 1853 and the parliamentary approval of a new Poor Law in 1854 did not bring an end to the discussion on the subject. The Association against Pauperism held two conferences in 1854 and 1856, where the split between the non-interventionism of the pure liberals and the utilitarianism of the heirs of the Economic Patriots became apparent. The conferences must have offered an amazing spectacle, with the attendance of reverends, medics and economists, do-gooders, temperance advocates and Malthusians. But it is equally remarkable that many influential professors and politicians were present.

The reverend Blaupot ten Cate, one of the founders of the Association, spoke at the 1854 conference. He mentioned the four causes of pauperism which had been put on the conference agenda, to wit alcohol abuse, irresponsible marriages, lack of thrift and lack of work, and added low wages as a fifth one. Immediately Ackersdijk challenged him with the argument that wages reflected productivity and that Blaupot's complaint could be countered with the argument that low wages could only reflect a lack of effort and quality in the worker.

The issue of saving money was discussed only superficially at the first conference. However, in 1856, specific measures to stimulate thrift were raised. Savings desks – not savings banks, but cooperative initiatives for common purchasing of food or combustibles for the winter – were proposed. Ackersdijk opposed this initiative with paternalistic arguments:

> In this way a poor family acquires a rich stock for the winter. That is an abnormal situation. A poor family should not possess any stock of goods. It would not know how to preserve it, just as it does not know how to save money. It does not know how to use it up slowly, or spread it over any amount of time.
>
> (Boschloo 1989: 126)

But on the other hand he held a plea for one-year contracts for workers and for paying salaries weekly or monthly. As to the total amount of work available, he clearly was a believer in Say's Law:

> The general cause of what is commonly called a lack of work, is that many people produce less than they consume. The solution is an augmentation of total output.
>
> (Boschloo 1989: 127)

Neither of the two conferences resulted in a general approval of concrete initiatives. Neither regulation of the sale of alcohol, nor the introduction of excises was recommended by a majority. Extension of compulsory education met with the same fate. There was a general agreement on the necessity of raising the moral and intellectual level of the poor, but the state should not expand its role in these matters (Boschloo 1989: ch. 4).

The role of the Amsterdam professor Jeronimo de Bosch Kemper in the founding of the Statistical (and Economic) Association will be discussed in section 2. But he deserves to be mentioned as a passionate activist and writer on the issue of poverty. Together with the later central bank president W.C. Mees, who published a treatise against workhouses for the poor in 1844, he is considered one of the foremost anti-interventionists with regard to the 'Poor Question'. Yet he is difficult to classify. Boschloo calls him a *laissez-faire* man from the French school, who nevertheless occupies a special position by his social concern and scientific scepticism (Boschloo 1989: 89). In 1851 he published a historical account of poverty in the Netherlands. Already in his review of Mees, De Bosch Kemper had also shown himself to be an advocate of Say's Law:

> When everyone would participate in labouring; when everyone would help in satisfying needs which are still unfulfilled, thereby they would equally supply the means to satisfy their own wants.
>
> (Boschloo 1989: 87)

In the short term, he believed that total savings and capital formation were insufficient to exclude poverty altogether. In the long run he believed in the moral elevation of the lower classes and in teaching them thrift and a working ethic. His Leyden colleague Tydeman, who was practically the single remaining interventionist in these matters, wrote a critical review of De Bosch Kemper's historical account:

> It is a sad, harsh and inhumane doctrine which prescribes low wages and high taxes also for the common man, out of fear that through high wages he will be wanton and debauched, marry too easily, etc. Better grounded is the contrary remark that a certain ease and zest for living are required for someone from the lower classes to practice hygiene and thrift, and a careful education of one's children.
>
> (Boschloo 1989: 89)

But De Bosch Kemper was not just a cold prescriber of harsh recipes. He also was a socially engaged reformer and an indefatigable organiser. In the 1840s, his journal *De Tijdgenoot* (The Contemporary) had been actively propagating constitutional reform. In the next two decades he started his foundation De Vriend van Armen en Rijken (The Friend of the Rich and the Poor) and several periodicals to raise the educational level of the working classes. It goes perhaps too far to count this foundation among the economic societies, but one of its 10 cents booklets was a *Principles of Economics*, and at the foundation's office in Amsterdam people could ask for various kinds of advice. It also tried to act as a kind of labour office and savings advisory desk. His communal sense distinguished De Bosch Kemper from most of his liberal colleagues, who still believed in some kind of invisible hand. His concern with poverty was deeply ethical:

Where ethical and religious principles drive people to labour, we can do without coercion or the fear of hunger and poverty as an incentive to work.

One of his former students wrote of De Bosch Kemper that he was 'overflowing with the milk of human kindness'. On the other hand he did not hesitate to call Thorbecke, the great liberal reformer and the author of the new constitution of 1848, a 'pseudo-liberal'. Thorbecke's Poor Bill never got to the status of an Act; in the bill he defended the view that poor relief should be the task of the government when otherwise support by the church would only be 'the price and premium of religious submission'.

Whatever their attitude was with regard to the task of government, most economists, agriculturalists, medics and politicians did agree on the necessity of good statistics as an instrument for analysis and policy. The modernisation of agriculture was an issue which also gave rise to a number of conferences and societies – sometimes with the same people attending as for the economic and statistical ones. A brief glance is taken at these meetings and organisations.

The influence of Cameralism in the Netherlands was big enough to lead to the institution of several chairs in agricultural techniques and economics ('landhuishoudkunde') after 1815. It has been documented that there was a personal commitment of King William I in this matter (Veldink 1970: 85–6). The management of his German estates during his exile had taught him the importance of theoretical agronomic knowledge. What better way was there to instruct the farmers than by having this knowledge taught to the future country parsons? Accordingly the chairs were instituted in the theological faculties.

Other means of raising the level of agriculture were the newly founded provincial Agricultural Societies, which can be classified among the economic societies in the broad sense, and the Congres(sen) van Vaderland-sche Landhuishoudkundigen (National Conferences of Agriculturalists), both initiated in the 1840s. Baron Sloet tot Oldhuis took the initiative for the first National Conference in 1846, in his capacity of President of the Overijssel Society for Development of Provincial Welfare. Sloet was the staunchest of advocates of government abstinence, whether with regard to poverty regulation, the construction of railways or any other economic problem. In 1841 he asked for just one Royal Decree (*Koninklijk Besluit*) to abolish all previous poverty legislation. He was a member of the Double Chamber in 1848 and, although critical of Thorbecke, supported him in the ministerial crisis of 1853 out of fear of reactionary tendencies. By modern standards he should probably be classified as a libertarian. As a country aristocrat from the eastern Netherlands he never taught economics, but he was influential as the editor of the *Tijdschrift voor Staathuishoudkunde en Statistiek* (Journal of Economics and Statistics) from 1841 till 1875, also known as 'Sloet's journal' (Boschloo 1989: ch. 4; Mooij 1994: 45).

The 1846 conference of agriculturalists wanted to disseminate the advanced scientific knowledge in chemistry, physics, engineering and geology to the agricultural sector. Sloet advocated the preparation of a geological atlas of the Netherlands. His Overijssel Society had taken the lead and he wished the other provinces to follow. It took a number of years, conferences and ministerial committees to get the project started in 1852. In 1860 the complete maps were ready to be printed. They were shown at the 1862 World Exhibition in London and received an award there. At the tenth conference of agriculturalists in 1855, the leader of the project presented a so-called agronomic map of the Overijssel community of Vorden, in which the effects of human tilling and working of the grounds were included.

Political reform and economic stagnation were the key characteristics of the stage on which the first broad economic association in the Netherlands was founded, not just as a single-issue society or conference. The indefatigable De Bosch Kemper, who next to his many initiatives just mentioned was also the author of a handbook of penal law as well as a member of the Double Chamber which passed the new constitution in 1848, was again one of the founders. Political liberalism was carrying the tide, and most economic liberals were politically either liberals or moderate conservatives. To the progressive liberal Thorbecke, government intervention in the economic domain was not altogether anathema. For economists like Ackersdijk and Mees it was taboo. Confessional parties were yet to emerge, but evangelical considerations with regard to the situation of the poor can be noticed in the arguments of De Bosch Kemper, who nevertheless opposed regulation of the problem. The interventionism of Professor Tydeman from Leyden was, strangely enough, a relic of the Patriotic past.

2 The Statistical and Economic Association

In 1849 De Bosch Kemper published the first *Staatkundig en Staathuishoudkundig Jaarboekje* (Little Annual of the State and Economy), a 300 page compendium of the new constitution, the election results, and the budgetary and statistical data of the Netherlands and its colonies, plus a calendar of political events in the previous year. De Bosch Kemper's pedagogical aims were clear: in the turbulent times of 1848: 'all kinds of socialist ideas had been proposed, while losing sight of the real situation of the people'. Therefore his objective was 'to arouse public interest in the knowledge of the facts of society'.

At the Home Office, a Statistical Committee had existed between 1826 and 1830. Between 1825 and 1849, the mathematician and civil servant – later a professor of mathematics in Delft – Rehuel Lobatto had published the *Annual published by order of H.M. the King* (Stamhuis 1989: ch. 2). Its contents were population statistics and scientific essays. With the new political climate of 1848, a new Statistical Bureau was set up at the Home Office under one of Professor Ackersdijk's pupils. The bureau published the results of the census in 1849, 1859 and 1869. The first official *Statistical Annual of the Kingdom of the Netherlands* was published in 1851. Another organisation set up to collect statistical data was the newly founded Netherlands Society for the Advancement of Medicine. The improvement of the Population Register and of medical statistics went hand in hand, as the so-called hygienists among the doctors wanted to prove that health and social circumstances were closely connected.

In the province of Utrecht, the Provinciaal Utrechtsch Genootschap (Provincial Society of Arts and Sciences) (PUG) established a Committee for Dutch Statistics. In this society, we meet some familiar names: Sloet, De Bosch Kemper, Tydeman, Ackersdijk, Mees and Lobatto. One year after its foundation in 1846, the statistical committee discussed the founding of a statistical society with its colleagues of the Conference of Agriculturalists. The PUG also asked Thorbecke, in his capacity of Minister at the Home Office, to institute a statistical bureau and a statistical committee, the latter to be composed of civil servants and scientists. The Minister refused, arguing that first the municipal and provincial statistics should be reorganised.

The spark which finally ignited a fruitful cooperation between the Utrecht Society and De Bosch Kemper's 'Little Annual' came from a remark by Ackersdijk at a meeting of the Society in 1849. He drew the attention of the audience to De Bosch Kemper's booklet, and the author responded by soliciting for contributions to the next volume. This resulted in a 'meeting of contributors' in De Bosch Kemper's house in Amsterdam. Mooij has made it clear that Ackersdijk's initiative had been prompted by De Bosch Kemper himself through a suggestion to that effect in a letter (Mooij 1994: 46). From then on, De Bosch Kemper's *Jaarboekje* was published under the auspices of an editorial committee which included Ackersdijk, Mees and Thorbecke's successor in Leyden, Vissering.

At the contributors' meeting in 1856, Vissering proposed the founding of a Dutch Statistical Society, in order to publish the *General Statistics of the Netherlands*. The founding of societies had been considerably facilitated by the new law which regulated the freedom of association, a consequence of the new constitution. Thus in 1857 the Vereeniging voor de Statistiek was founded. De Bosch Kemper was the first president of the new society, which counted thirty-four members – the kernel being formed by contributors of the annual – and wished to unite all theoretical and practical users of statistics, whether medics, agriculturalists or economists. Indeed, a number of doctors soon joined the ranks.

In 1858 a State Committee for Statistics was instituted. De Bosch Kemper thought that the time had come to stop the publication of his 'Little Annual' (now on average numbering 400 pages) as the official Statistical Annual was a good alternative while the economic journal *De Economist*, founded in 1852 by J.L. de Bruyn Kops, offered an outlet for the more scientific contributions to De Bosch Kemper's periodical. Vissering however persuaded a majority of the editors to continue the publication and only four years later, in 1862, the Second Chamber voted against the budget of the State Committee. This gave the impetus for the Vereeniging to submit its regulations in order to obtain official recognition as a corporate body. Vissering produced three draft regulations, one of which was approved by the members.

From 1862 till 1892 the society existed under the name of Vereeniging voor de Statistiek in Nederland. De Bosch Kemper continued to be its president until his death in 1876. The 'Little Annual' was a tremendous success: in 1875 over 700 copies were sold. Ten years later, *De Economist* had only 472 subscribers. The membership of the Vereeniging slowly rose to almost 800 in 1890.

In practice the society was very critical of the statistical efforts of the Dutch government, which tried to minimise its data collecting work, limiting it strictly to the essential requirements of public administration. In 1862 the Home Office even tried in vain to transfer the publication of the official *Statistical Annual* to the Society. At the end of the decade, the ministry interrupted its publication after heavy criticism by the economist and MP, De Bruyn Kops. In the reshuffling of departments and founding of new ministries in 1878, the Statistical Bureau was abolished altogether.

At the general assembly of that year – where ironically the responsible minister, Kappeyne van de Copello, became a member – Vissering spoke of the consequences for the collecting of statistics, if this would be left to the lower clerks:

The government is not aware that statistics, the science of the facts of society, is a study which should be practised with great interest, for which one should be educated, and above all one should have a *heart* for.

[The abolition] brings us back into a situation which is worse than we have had for many years.

By the 1870s, a new generation of economists had come to the fore, the most prominent of whom was the self-taught N.G. Pierson, professor, banker and politician. Together with the politician Goeman Borgesius he proposed the founding of a (private) Statistical Institute by the Society in 1879. This opened its doors in 1884, with the young statistics professor Anthony Beaujon as its director. One year later he combined the director-ship with Pierson's chair of economics and statistics, after the latter's promotion to the presidency of The Netherlands Bank.

Thus the statistics of the Kingdom were collected and published by a private institute. This situation lasted for no less than eight years. Through-out these years the society and many politicians – the first socialist MP Domela Nieuwenhuis being one of them – continued to argue that the government should take back its proper responsibility in these matters. Finally, in 1892 the Central Statistical Committee was instituted as a public organisation. In 1899 a government headed by Pierson founded the Central Statistical Bureau (CBS) (Stamhuis 1989: ch. 4; Mooij 1994: ch. 3).

Between 1865 and 1883, the annual meetings of the society were also the scene of discussions following lectures by one to three members. In 1865, De Bosch Kemper gave his opinion on the following question: 'Will free education have an advantageous or disadvantageous effect on school attendance?' In 1872 the question was put forward whether the existing schools for the labouring classes would be able to solve the 'social question'. Pierson spoke on several occasions and continued to do so when the proposals were fully written (but not yet printed) and read to the meetings from 1884 till 1892. In 1890 his lecture on the effects of the actual poverty legislation led to lively discussion.

In 1892 the society changed its name to Vereeniging voor de Staathuishoudkunde en de Statistiek. The tradition was established that the annual proposals would concern one single subject and would be available in print. The same subject was covered by several authors, and the subject matter increasingly was purely economic. This tradition is carried on till the present day. In 1950 the society dropped the 'Statistics' from its name. It is now known as the Royal Netherlands Economic Society and can count more than 3,500 members. Since 1990 membership has included a subscription to *De Economist*. Thus one of the oldest economic societies in the world – only the British Royal Economic Society has a comparable early history in its cooperation between statisticians and economists – and one of the oldest economic journals are united.

3 Economics in a bourgeois journal: *De Gids*

In January 1837 a new literary journal came out. The subtitle of *De Gids* (The Guide) was 'Nieuwe Vaderlandsche Letteroefeningen' or 'New Patriotic Literary Exercises'. Its models were British and French literary and political journals such as the *Edinburgh Review* and the *Revue des Deux Mondes*. The adjective 'patriotic' in the subtitle did not refer to the late eighteenth century, for the editors abhorred the entire past century. The readers which the editors had in mind for the new periodical were the liberal intellectuals, and indeed within a few years the number of subscriptions exceeded 400, a sufficiently large number to generate even a small profit. In the preceding sections it has become clear that merely a few opinion leaders could have a strong influence in mid-nineteenth-century Dutch politics. In the first year, around 60 per cent of the contributions were of a literary character, compared to a meagre 4 per cent for issues of law, economy and society. Nonetheless, Tydeman and Ackersdijk were among the early contributors.

In the first ten years *De Gids* transformed itself from an organ of the liberal minority to the respected voice of an increasingly self-confident bourgeoisie. Its content became more and more politicised. Thorbecke himself was the author of an article in favour of an altogether different system of imposing a tax burden on the productive capacity of the nation (Aerts 1997: ch. 12).

In 1846 Vissering published his first article in *De Gids*, and a year later he became an editor. In 1849 he wrote an important article on the statistics of the Netherlands (Stamhuis 1989: ch. 3). In 1850 his inaugural lecture on 'Liberty, The Principle of Economics' was published in the May issue. In 1848 an anonymous author wrote on tax reform, in favour of direct taxes and against the many indirect taxes and excises. These ideas were in support of the new government's programme. De Bruyn Kops and other younger economists explained the liberal economic programme and wrote against French socialist ideas. The 'Poor Question' was discussed in much the same way as in the economic journals and the poverty conferences. But Aerts points out that the liberal economists were not in favour of robber capitalism and speculation: 'The economic liberalism in *De Gids*, however radical for the Netherlands, was always mitigated by a certain old-fashioned, pre-capitalist attachment to order, fondness of small scale, thoroughness and high moral ideas' (Aerts 1997: 215).

In the 1860s the younger economists like Pierson and the later MP and initiator of the first law to regulate child labour, Samuel van Houten, criticised the economism of the old liberals and wrote in favour of the German Historical School. But in the following decade 'chair socialism' went too far for Pierson. He pleaded for the integrity of science: economics should neither be in the service of the bourgeoisie, nor the labouring classes. For him this attitude had nothing to do with a fear of socialism; it simply reflected his scientific attitude.

The editor most attracted to socialist ideas was certainly the banker and professor H.P.G. Quack, whose magnum opus *De Socialisten* (subtitle: *Persons and Systems*) was an inventory of communitarian ideas from classical antiquity to his day. For thirty years he was an editor of *De Gids*. Aerts classifies him among the French Saint-Simonian capitalists who preferred a combination of a religious sense of community, hierarchical order and the fostering of economic growth to liberal individualism, egoism and intellectualism (Aerts 1997: ch. 19).

In this brief summary it is impossible to assess the real influence of *De Gids*, as compared to purely economic societies and their journals. But it is clear that the same debates which were held among the economists and statisticians were also communicated – and most often by the same authors – to a wider audience on the pages of this 'literary' journal.

4 Concluding remarks

It is remarkable that in the midst of various disciplines, societies and political movements, a few protagonists show up again and again at the various forums of societies and journals of all kinds. One meets the same professors, MPs, central bank directors and journal editors – sometimes uniting these capacities in one person – in very different environments. This chapter has argued that a number of continuous themes can be distinguished in their activities.

From the late eighteenth century, the issue of poverty was a rallying point for economists and reformers. This continued to be so in the first half of the nineteenth century, and was succeeded by the 'Social Question' in the second half. The improvement of the statistics of the Kingdom, applied to economic, agricultural and political data alike, was another unifying characteristic.

From the beginning of King William I's reign, economics was welcomed in academia as the science of modernity. Economics lectures were recommended if not made compulsory for future civil servants. Economists were expected to throw light on questions of the day. Thus it was only natural that in the aftermath of the constitutional reform of 1848, economic journals and societies would flourish. A privately felt responsibility for public affairs not only led to the production of the first geological atlas of the Netherlands, but even to the administration of the national statistics by a private association, the Economic and Statistical Society, for no less than eight years.

This society – since 1987 the Royal Netherlands Economic Society – claims to be the oldest economic society in the world. From its foundation the Society's contribution to the production of new economic knowledge bears the mark of what is now called the 'new production of knowledge' (Gibbons *et al.* 1994): heterogeneous and interdisciplinary knowledge production by teams of varying composition, in which academics and practical people produce temporary solutions for societal problems. If the Dutch economists before Pierson were not very innovative by the standards of their discipline, they certainly were modern in the application of their knowledge to solving the problems of the day, in interdisciplinary cooperation with statisticians, agriculturalists, geographers and medics. Of course in the nineteenth century the role of government in the composition of research teams and the setting of agenda's was much less pronounced than it is today. But this makes the achievement of the nineteenth-century Dutch economists all the more remarkable.

Note

* This chapter leans heavily upon four books: (1) Hans Boschloo's dissertation on Dutch nineteenth-century liberals and the Poor Question (1989); (2) Ida Stamhuis' dissertation on nineteenth-century Dutch statistics (1989); (3). Joke Mooij's history of the Royal Netherlands Economic Society (1994); and (4) Remieg Aerts' dissertation about nineteenth-century liberal culture as reflected in the literary journal *De Gids* (1997).

Bibliography

Aerts, R. (1997) *De Letterheren, Liberale cultuur in de negentiende eeuw: het tijdschrift De Gids*, Amsterdam: Meulenhoff.

Boschloo, T.J. (1989) *De Productiemaatschappij, Liberalisme, economische wetenschap en het vraagstuk der armoede in Nederland, 1800–1875*, Hilversum: Verloren.

Gibbons, M., Limoges, C., Nowotny, H., Schwartzman, S., Scott, P. and Trow, M. (1994) *The New Production of Knowledge, The Dynamics of Science and Research in Contemporary Societies*, London: Sage.

Hasenberg Butter, I. (1969) *Academic Economics in Holland, 1800–1870*, Den Haag: Martinus Nijhoff.

Knoester, A. (ed.) (1987) *Lessen uit het verleden, 125 jaar Vereniging voor de Staathuishoudkunde*; Leiden and Antwerpen: Stenfert Kroese.

Mooij, J. (1994) *Denken over Welvaart: Koninklijke Vereniging voor de Staathuishoudkunde, 1849–1999*; Utrecht: Lemma.

Schama, S. (1977) *Patriots and Liberators. Revolution in the Netherlands, 1780–1813*, London: Collins.

Stamhuis, I. (1989) *'Cijfers en Aequaties' en 'Kennis der Staatskrachten', Statistiek in Nederland in de negentiende eeuw*, Amsterdam: Rodopi.

Veldink, J.G. (1970) *W.C.H. Staring 1808–1877, geoloog en landbouwkundige*, Wageningen: Pudoc.

9 The Verein für Sozialpolitik from its foundation (1872) until World War I

Harald Hagemann

Along with the institutionalisation of economics at universities, the foundation of learned journals and the increasing publication of economic books, establishing associations of economists was an important stepping stone in the professionalisation process in Europe, North America and Japan in the second half of the nineteenth century. The Verein für Sozialpolitik (henceforth: Verein) was officially founded at a conference in Eisenach on 13th October 1873. However, after a preparatory meeting in Halle on 8th July, the first major conference on the 'soziale Frage' ('Social Question') had already taken place on 6th–7th October 1872 (in Eisenach where the Social Democratic Party had also been founded in 1869 on the initiative of August Bebel and Wilhelm Liebknecht), which explains why the foundation of the Verein is often dated to 1872. Thus the 1972 centennial conference, which took place in Bonn, had the title 'Macht oder ökonomisches Gesetz' (Power or Economic Law) – issues that were already at the forefront in the early years.

It should be emphasised that the Verein is the leading scientific association of *German-speaking* economists. Therefore, in addition to economists from Germany, members from Austria and Switzerland play an important role. In the first period of its existence until its dissolution in 1936 three meetings of the Verein took place in Vienna (1894, 1909 and 1926) and one meeting in Zurich (1928). After World War II it became a rule that annual meetings took place in Austria (Salzburg 1952, Innsbruck 1970, Graz 1981, Vienna 1989, Linz 1995, Innsbruck 2002) or Switzerland (Luzern 1962, Zurich 1974, Basel 1983, Lugano 1991, Bern 1997) from time to time.

The Verein was founded by a group of social reformers ('*Kathedersozialisten*') who were opposed both to the *laissez-faire* positions of the Manchester School, which in Germany was represented by the Congress, and to the revolutionary ideas of Marxism. Nevertheless, Manchester liberalism and the emerging socialism represented the two poles between which some of the major controversies about programmes and objectives (*Richtungskämpfe*) took place before World War I (see Lindenlaub 1967). The critical juxtaposition of capitalism and socialism was reflected in controversies between 'liberals' and 'conservatives' with regard to social policy.

1 Origins

The 1872 Eisenach meeting was attended by 159 participants, among them 22 university professors.[1] The professors had dominated the earlier Halle meeting, among whose 15 participants were a number of outstanding economists such as Lujo Brentano, Johannes Conrad, Bruno Hildebrand, Georg Friedrich Knapp, Wilhelm Roscher, Gustav Schmoller and Adolph Wagner. One of the non-professorial three participants was Ernst Engel, the famous Director of the Prussian Bureau of Statistics and name patron of Engel's law and Engel curves, who early on had contracted himself to improve the living standards of the working class, to investigate historically and statistically their living conditions and to study the situation of labour in Britain. On the initiative of the Hamburg journalist Julius von Eckhardt and the mediation of Wagner, who himself had delivered a much noted speech on the social question in the garrison church in Berlin on 12th October 1871, in May 1872 Schmoller sent out a number of invitations for the Halle meeting, which took place in the Hotel Stadt Hamburg and in his home.[2] Besides Albert Schäffle (who as the only important German economist never became a member of the Verein because of its dominance by Prussian conservatives) and Lorenz von Stein, Schmoller had been one of the first economists who directed the view of the larger public on the growing labour question and the necessary improvement of the living conditions of the working poor in a series of articles in the *Preußische Jahrbücher* (Schmoller 1864–5). In his subsequent history of small crafts in Germany during the nineteenth century, Schmoller (1870) emphasised the responsibility of the state for social policy.

After German political unification in 1871 the centre of state sciences shifted towards the capital, Berlin. Previously, the universities in the southwest, like Heidelberg and Tübingen, had been more important. In Heidelberg the central chair was held consecutively by Karl Rau (1822–65), Karl Knies (1865–97) and Max Weber (1897–1903). Rau, who was the author of the most influential German textbook in the nineteenth century, had introduced the tripartite division of economics into economic theory, economic policy and public finance, which became the established tradition in the teaching of economics at German universities, unchallenged until the 1970s. In 1835 he also founded the first scholarly journal in economics *Archiv der politischen Ökonomie und Polizeiwissenschaft*, which in 1853 was absorbed by the *Zeitschrift für die gesamte Staatswissenschaft*, founded in 1844 and published since 1986 under the title *Journal of Institutional and Theoretical Economics* and today the oldest economic journal in the German-language area. This journal was the creation of the members of the Staatswirtschaftliche Fakultät (Faculty of Public Economics) at the University of Tübingen, which itself had been founded by Friedrich List as the first special faculty for the Sciences of State in Germany in 1817.[3] The term *Staatswissenschaft* expresses the typical German symbiosis of state and economy as opposed to the more theoretical and abstract economics of classical British political economics. The founding editor, Robert von Mohl, was a professor of public law and a leading representative of southwest German liberalism who, like Rau and Bruno Hildebrand, the founding editor of the *Jahrbücher für Nationalökonomie und Statistik* (1863), became a member of the Frankfurt National Assembly in 1848–9.

The shift to the Friedrich-Wilhelms-Universität in Berlin, founded as a consequence of the early Prussian defeats in the Napoleonic wars and hitherto more renowned for philosophy and law than economics and the social sciences, can be exemplified by the three leading figures in the first decades of the Verein für Sozialpolitik: Gustav Schmoller, Adolph Wagner and Lujo Brentano (see Schmölders 1960; Waszek 1988). Wagner came from the University of Freiburg in the southwest of Germany to Berlin in 1870 and became the referee when Lujo Brentano submitted the first volume of his famous investigation *Arbeitergilden der Gegenwart* (Workers' Guilds of the Present) as his Habilitation in 1871 (see Brentano 1931: 43ff.). Brentano was born to a well-known Catholic patrician family with strong anti-Prussian sentiments, whose name had already become famous during the Romantic movement because of two poets, his aunt Bettina and his uncle Clemens.[4] The improvement of the conditions of the working classes and their position in the labour market that followed the establishment of trade unions became the central topic of Brentano's life. His ideas were shaped by the insights and the experiences during a visit to Britain in 1868–9 with Ernst Engel, whose strong interest in the labour question had a lasting influence on Brentano. However, in contrast to Engel's advocacy of profit-sharing schemes, Brentano favoured the organized coalition of workers as the decisive means to solve the social question. Finally Gustav Schmoller, who in 1872 had moved from Halle to the newly established German University in Straßburg, came to Berlin in 1882 – already the unchallenged leader of German economics and the Historical School – where he stayed until his death in 1917.

2 The Verein and the Congress of German Economists

Ironically, in the very same year, 1873, when the Verein was founded to focus on social policy, the influence of liberal ideas and economic policies was at its peak. With the elimination both of tariffs on the import of pig iron and the last export tariffs the free-trade movement celebrated its great triumph. The German free-trade movement had originated as a reaction against the introduction of protective duties on pig iron in 1844. After its beginnings as a movement strongly influenced by the ideas of Adam Smith and David Ricardo, the organisation took a more radical turn under the influence of Frédéric Bastiat, who had constituted an Association of Free Trade in Paris in 1846. John Prince-Smith, a naturalised Prussian citizen who had come from England, established a Deutsche Freihandelsverein (German Free Trade Union) in Berlin in March 1847. A decade later he was instrumental in the foundation of the Kongreß der deutschen Volkswirte (Congress of German Economists) in 1858. Soon afterwards the Congress, which did not restrict its themes to the area of international trade, was the mouthpiece of Manchester liberalism in Germany, covering all areas of economic and social life.[5] It had a strong influence in German universities and in government, in particular in Prussia (less so in the south of Germany). From the beginning the Congress attracted many practitioners and industrialists. However, many members of the Congress were ignorant of the poverty and problems brought about by the growing industrialisation process in Germany and the existing social relationships. This resulted in increasing opposition, first by Marx, Lassalle and the socialist movement, but more and more also among the ranks of academic economists. It was a leading Congressman, the journalist Heinrich Bernhard Oppenheim, who launched the attack on the social reformers in German universities and coined the term *Kathedersozialisten* (chair socialists) – a term most adequate for Wagner, whose views had been shaped by Rodbertus – to denounce them.[6] In the heavy controversies which followed, the Congress, despite the apparent success of liberal ideas in the realm of economic policy, went into an orientation crisis. Most members lost interest in changing the economic and social conditions, and extreme views of Manchester liberalism became more and more dominant. Hermann Schulze-Delitzsch, who belonged to the small minority who saw Manchester liberalism as in crisis and who, like Schmoller and Wagner, recognised the need for a more ethical science and for social reform, left the Congress in 1872. However, when the Verein was founded in the following year several Congressmen became members of the new Verein. Despite continuing animosities on both sides as expressed, for example, in a famous speech in the Reichstag in 1876 by Ludwig Bamberger, who heavily attacked the chair socialists, attempts to cooperate prevailed on both sides, and it was a Congressman, Rudolf von Gneist (Berlin), who was elected the first Chairman of the Verein.

During the controversies within the Verein Schmoller was the leading man in the 'centre', a grouping which also included his predecessor in the chairmanship Nasse[7]; Brentano and Karl Bücher, and later from among the young generation Max and Alfred Weber and Werner Sombart, were major representatives on the 'left'; Wagner was on the right, like most industrialists. It is a characteristic feature of the conservative bias of the recruitment policy in the Prussian university system during the period of Friedrich Althoff (1882–1907) that most leading representatives of the liberal current within the Verein had professorships outside Prussia, like Brentano in Vienna, Leipzig and Munich, Bücher in Basel, Karlsruhe and Leipzig, Max Weber in Freiburg and Heidelberg, and Alfred Weber in Prague and Heidelberg. By contrast, most of the leading conservatives were teaching at Prussian universities.

Although the Verein was widely regarded as a '*Professorengremium*', professors constituted only one-sixth of the members and one-fourth of conference participants. However, they had a two-thirds majority in the 'Standing Committee' in which most of the important work was done. Whereas industrialists participated from the very beginning it took until 1893 before the first social democrats attended meetings of the Verein. During the 1901 meeting in Munich the first woman participated as a listener. Two years later the number of women in the audience grew to 11 (see Kesten-Conrad 1911: 148). According to Prussian law women were not allowed to play an active role in 'political' associations. Only after a new German law for associations was passed in 1908 could Marie Bernays become the first woman to give an address at a conference in Nuremberg in 1911.

3 The Crisis Year 1879 and its long-term consequences

Although the Verein had been established as a forum for 'agitation' on social policy, it is less well known that, as early as 1881, the Verein had taken the decision to refrain from taking an 'official position' on policy issues, in order to avoid narrow majority decisions and a dominance of political influence. It was decided that the activities of the Verein should concentrate on scholarly issues only. This was the outcome of the events in 1879 which led to the first crisis of the Verein. The backdrop was the major decisions and reorientations in Bismarck's policy. Surprisingly, less upsetting for the Verein than the drastic change in the German trade and customs policy executed by Bismarck, was the launching of the *Sozialistengesetz* on 21st October 1878. The latter removed the 'Social Question' – the founding reason behind the Verein – from the agenda of its meetings for more than a decade; the former event endangered the survival of the young Association. Bismarck's reorientation towards protective tariffs not only led to turbulence in the political sphere and the general public but also caused major splits within the ranks of the Verein's members. The tariff question became the central topic of the 1879 conference, which was the first of a series of six conferences to take place in the 'neutral' and centrally located Frankfurt until 1890.[8]

The 1879 meeting which had been shifted from fall to spring to antici-pate the debate in the Reichstag was characterised by heavy controversy between free-traders and protectionists. This struggle was reflected in the differences of opinion between the Chairman Nasse, a committed liberal favouring free trade, and Schmoller, who followed the reorientation of Bismarck's trade policy.[9] It was Nasse who took the initiative for the meeting with the intention gaining a clear vote in favour of free trade using Congress support. Due to an agreement with the Congress some passages of the Verein's by-laws had been changed in 1876 to allow Congress members not only to participate in the Verein's meetings as guests but also to give them speaking and voting rights.[10]

Due to a carefully orchestrated administration of the conference by Nasse and Schmoller sympathisers and enemies of Bismarck's new protectionist policy alternated as speakers. There were changing majorities in the specialised sessions. For example, in a session in which the old Sombart, half farmer, half industrialist, brought in a resolution against protective tariffs the resolution passed with 52 against 50 votes, not least because of the support of Nasse who made a strong case against the new coalition of agricultural and industrial protectionists which characterised the situation. However, when it came to the vote in the general assembly only 63 members voted for free trade and 82 members against it. For the greater part this result was due to an unusually high number of industrialists attending this first of the Frankfurt conferences. Furthermore, Schmoller's behaviour and arguments during the meeting also played a decisive role. In winter 1862, after the new French-Prussian trade agreement, the young Schmoller had written an anonymous pamphlet *Der französische Handelsvertrag und seine Gegner* in which he strongly favoured a liberal trade policy and argued against high protective tariffs and too much respect for Austrian interests, positions which were quite common in the south of Germany at the time. Now at the 1879 Frankfurt conference in a synthesising historical speech Schmoller put the free-trade and protectionist policies of the large nations in comparative perspective, 'demonstrating' that the character of trade policy is not a matter of principle but a matter of practical value in the main political or economical upswings and downswings of nations, to conclude that in the current situation of the German economy (in which industry still suffered from the wake of the 1873 crisis, agriculture had to face strong competition from cheap corn imported from overseas since about 1876, and, as a result, the state suffered from insufficient tax income), protective tariffs are an adequate policy. Thus a rationale and legitimisation of Bismarck's drastic change in trade policy was given by the most influential member of the Verein who, for that purpose, had revised his earlier arguments.

Schmoller's view was strongly at odds with Brentano's analysis. The latter argued that Germany had developed into an industrial economy for which it was important to supply cheap food for the workers and the rapidly growing population and to generate export markets for industrial products. In analogy to the strong increase of wealth after the final abolition of the Corn Laws in Britain he came to the conclusion: 'The German economy requires free trade' (Brentano 1931: 172).

Brentano, however, could not attend the Frankfurt meeting because of typhus fever. It is an open question whether the appearance of this charismatic speaker would have changed the majority at the conference which left the Chairman of the Verein, Nasse, defeated. Nasse was also annoyed because he could not deliver his final address as Chairman due to a successful 'end of the debate' resolution. For some time Nasse, who was personally offended and left in a minority position, considered tendering his resignation as Chairman. However, the strong personal support by many members including Schmoller led to second thoughts and finally to a decision to stay. The turbulence at the conference had the above-mentioned result: the Verein was to abstain from final votes on sensitive policy issues in all future meetings. According to several observers and later commentators on the Verein's history, the first step towards its transformation into a *scientific society* had been made (see, for example, Albrecht 1961: 13).

The 1879 controversies had two further consequences. On the one hand the Verein retreated into more neutral topics. The 1880s were a decade in which agricultural problems, quite often rather bureaucratic and administrative ones, were the foci of the meetings. For many members this was so boring that they lost interest in attending the conferences. The decision to shy away from controversial issues also had the consequence that the Verein had little influence on Bismarck's great projects of social legislation, the introduction of accident, health and old-age insurance in 1884 and 1889, with which he tried to pacify the workers in the period of the anti-socialists laws. On the other hand, in March 1881 the Congress, whose Chairman Adolf Braun had already left the Verein immediately after the 1879 conference, cancelled the 1876 Bremen agreement which also had comprised an alternating rhythm of the biannual conferences of the two associations. However, the hegemony of protectionist policies in the 1880s which led many economists into opposition and the illiberal climate in the political sphere in general, as reflected in the anti-socialists laws, not only restricted the topics of the Verein's conferences but also in 1885 led to the dissolution of the Congress.

Within the Verein, the end of the 1879 conference marked the beginning of a long period of social conservative dominance. After the death of Nasse in January 1890 it found its natural expression in the election of Schmoller as the new Chairman. The conservative leadership of the Verein was predominantly a Prussian one, the liberal opposition predominantly a central and southern one.[11] This is best illustrated by the influential economists Schmoller, Wagner and Brentano. Although all three of them had been born in the south of Germany, it was only Brentano, the undisputed leader of the liberal left of the first generation of chair socialists, who retained the liberal Frankfurt tradition of his family and the democratic ideals of western Europe, and was alienated by any demonstration of power by the Prussian monarchy. Schmoller and Wagner, by contrast, are two famous cases of economists who deployed the strengths of the socialising power of the Prussian state in the period of German unification. Whereas Schmoller in a limited sense remained a liberal,[12] convinced that the civil service state (whose leading members got a greater part of their education from the chair socialists!) was best suited to overcome the class struggle, this cannot be said of Wagner. In a speech in the Prussian Upper House in 1913 Wagner stated: 'I have been occupied and owe it to Bismarck that I have become Prussian, and that I always have thought to be the greatest' (see Lindenlaub 1967: 156).

According to Brentano, Schmoller had accused him of representing, 'like Adam Smith, the economic doctrines of individualism and liberalism' (Brentano 1931:113). Brentano, on the other hand, believed that Schmoller saw in the sum of Bismarck's projects the work of a giant which could lead to great social reforms and that this was also the reason behind Schmoller's support of protective tariffs in 1879 (Brentano 1931: 112). Nevertheless, despite all differences of opinion on major subjects the relationship between Brentano and Schmoller was characterised by a lifelong friendship which may be regarded as the key stabilising axis of the Verein.[13] Schmoller instigated Brentano's appointment as editor of the *Jahrbuch für Gesetzgebung, Verwaltung und Volkswirtschaft im Deutschen Reich*, when the journal, founded in 1871, shifted its focus to economic and social issues and was renamed (*Volkswirtschaft* replacing *Rechtspflege*) in 1877; it soon became the leading journal of the younger Historical School. Schmoller also recommended Brentano as his successor for the Straßburg chair when he left for Berlin in 1882. Indirectly and five years later this led to a major conflict which disturbed the friendship between Brentano and Schmoller for the three years 1887–90 (see Brentano 1931: 125–34; Lindenlaub 1967: 162–8).

The reason for the disagreement was the dissertation on the working conditions in the cotton industry in Alsace by Brentano's student Heinrich Herkner (1887), the son of an industrialist from the German-speaking part of Bohemia who could view and judge the situation in the factories from both sides and also compare the situation in Alsace with that in other parts of Germany and Austria. Herkner's results were a confirmation of the suspicions Brentano had had from his first days in Straßburg, namely, that the non-transformation of the German *Gewerbeordnung* (Industrial Code) was an unjustified privilege for the industrialists in Alsace-Lorraine, targeted at raising sympathy for the German government at the expense of the workers who suffered lower wages and worse working conditions than in other regions of Germany. Herkner's study did not only cause an uproar among the patricians in Alsace but also deeply annoyed Schmoller who had developed close connections with them during his Straßburg decade, who 'approved the deeds of the ruling class like the Greek choir' (Brentano 1931: 134), and who now harshly criticised Herkner's study for which he made Brentano responsible.

It is not without a certain irony that it was Schmoller himself who, more than two decades later, made Herkner his successor: both for his chair at the University of Berlin in 1912 and as the Chairman of the Verein. Officially Herkner became Chairman only after the death of Schmoller in 1917, but in fact he had played a decisive role already, having been installed in 1911 Vice-chairman by Schmoller when the latter's health declined.[14] Meanwhile Herkner had become much more conservative than in his Straßburg days as a doctoral student, when he had entered Brentano's seminar (1885), or still in 1897 when he seriously considered candidacy for the regional parliament in Baden for the alliance of the liberal left including the social democrats.

During his ten years as a professor in Switzerland he changed his views. 'Zurich is the best place to give up any socialdemocratic sentiments' (see Lindenlaub 1967: 166), he wrote to Brentano in 1907. Shortly afterwards Herkner became Professor at the Technical University in Berlin-Charlottenburg. During his time there an intensive cooperation and friendship with Schmoller developed. As predicted earlier by Max Weber, Herkner gave up all radical-democratic ambitions and sentiments. Like Schmoller, Herkner came to praise the integrity and efficiency of the civil service and the ethical and moral values of the state. His ideas had been reshaped in a social conservative direction even before World War I. When finally after the War he gave up any intention of continuing to develop further social policy, like several other members of the second generation of chair socialists who had started on the liberal left,[15] he got into a deep conflict with his former teacher and mentor Brentano, who in the years of the young Weimar Republic was engaged in the struggle for the eight-hour working day.

4 The 1905 crisis and the generational conflict

With the end of the socialist laws and of Bismarck's long period as Chancellor, the Verein entered into a new phase which in many respects was a return to its roots, as symbolised by the new Chairman, Schmoller, who was elected at the Frankfurt conference in September 1890. The new Wilhelminian era saw the Verein engaged in a fight on two fronts: against the vested interests of reactionary industrialists and against revolutionary Marxist positions within German social democrats who rejected cooperation with 'bourgeois' social reformers and denounced the professors as '*Zuckerwassersozialisten*' ('sugar-water socialists') or, like Rosa Luxemburg, as 'knights of La Mancha swinging a sword of paper' (Lindenlaub 1967: 420). The war on two fronts was made most explicit in Schmoller's opening address at the 1899 Breslau meeting. However, whereas the social democrats, with very few exceptions, boycotted the meetings of the academic Verein, entrepreneurs did play a far more active role. This did not only influence votes, as at the important 1879 conference, but also led to several sharp confrontations, as at the 1890 meeting between Brentano and Henri Axel Bueck, the managing director of the organisation of German industrialists. Brentano made his usual plea for an organised coalition of workers, i.e. the establishment of trade unions, as the adequate means to improve the working conditions and to get a fair share for workers in the general increase of wealth. This caused Schmoller to criticise Brentano, at the end of the interruption of their friendship (who for that reason had not attended the 1888 meeting), for his idea that organised coalitions on both sides of the labour market were the best way to implement labour contracts. Bueck later had to leave the Verein after making inflammatory statements in the Prussian parliament in 1895 which caused Schmoller to intervene (see Boese 1939: 76–8).

Social questions were again very much at the centre of the meetings. It was against the background of the miners' strike in Westphalia that the right of workers to form coalitions had been put on the agenda of the last of the Frankfurt meetings. At the next conference in Berlin in 1893 (which replaced the 1892 Posen meeting cancelled because of a cholera epidemic), the young Max Weber gave his maiden speech based on his impressive study of 'The Situation of Rural Workers in East-Elbian Germany', in which he attacked the *Junkers*; he launched the same attack in his inaugural lecture at the University of Freiburg the following year where he succeeded Eugen von Philippovich, who had left for Vienna, to the Chair for Economics and Public Finance.[16] The housing question, which had been a key issue for the Verein since Engel, as the third main speaker besides Schmoller and Brentano, had focused on it at the initiating 1872 Eisenach meeting, once again was one of two central topics at the 1901 Munich meeting. The follow-up 1903 Hamburg meeting dealt with the situation of seamen as well as a general theoretical analysis of economic crises, with a remarkable keynote address given by Werner Sombart, a charismatic speaker.[17]

Issues of trade policy, for the first time since the 1879 controversies, became a central topic again at the 1901 Munich meeting. The reason was the danger of more and higher protective tariffs and a reversal of the new trade agreements policy followed in the 1890s by Chancellor Caprivi. This policy, for the greater part, had been shaped by a founding member of the Verein, Johannes Conrad, who was socially conservative and a member of the Verein's right but a committed free-trader. Most leading members participated in the Munich debate, which lasted for two full days, was marked by some differences of interest between the German and Austro-Hungarian positions and which, in contrast to the 1879 meeting, ended without any definite result.

A new crisis endangering the further existence of the Verein came four years later at the Mannheim meeting. The problem lay in the generational bias between the founding fathers of the Verein and some of the most outstanding representatives of the young generation, who were partly influenced by Marxian ideas, more restless and impatient, with less intention of making political compromises than members such as Schmoller. This younger generation had grown up with the experience that the central authorities, the monarchy, the parliament, the army and the civil service, were not able, if willing at all, to solve the 'Social Question' and to overcome the disintegration of society, but instead took refuge in the anti-socialists laws and other repressive measures. Their most brilliant minds were Max and his younger brother Alfred Weber, Werner Sombart and Friedrich Naumann, a trained pastor who became a professional politician of the liberal left. On the other hand, there was the growing minority of economists with pro-business sentiments who fought against any social policy and also publicly against the Verein. Some of these, such as Ludwig Pohle or

Ludwig Bernhard, were part-time members of the Verein, others such as Julius Wolf and Richard Ehrenberg always stood apart.

Thus the disintegrating tendencies within the Verein arose more due to the generational conflict with the radical democrats on the left. The controversy escalated at the end of the 1905 Mannheim conference, however, not in the context of 'The Labour Situation in Private Big Business' which was the focal point of the debates, with Brentano giving the opening address, surprising the audience this time with his proposal for the introduction of governmental coercion to solve labour disputes, against the changed historical background of a strengthened trade union movement confronted with economic concentration on the side of industry. The debates were characterised by the 'standard scenario': controversies between the two 'parties', with Brentano, many of his former students and the young radical democrats on the one side, and mainly members of the industrial organisations, very often non-members of the Verein, on the other side.

Afterwards Schmoller gave his address on 'The Relationship between Cartels and the State', thereby opening the final theme of the conference. In his usual way he was looking for a balanced compromise between the good economic results of cartels and the containing of possible dangers by public intervention; he concluded with the proposal to have state officials as members of cartels over a certain size. After a second specialised address by Robert Liefmann on cartels in the iron and steel industry the debate started, which was so heated that, for the first time in the Verein's history, another full day was required. In that debate Naumann gave a rhetorically brilliant contribution, heavily applauded by the audience, in which he denounced state intervention into cartels as nonsense, from a technical as well as an economical point of view. Naumann thereby indirectly accused Schmoller of having talked nonsense. Schmoller himself, in his concluding summary at the end of the meeting, reacted by accusing 'pastor Naumann' of using untenable Marxist arguments and of being a demagogue. Schmoller also criticised Max Weber, who had supported his friend Naumann in the debates and had attacked Schmoller's old-fashioned illusions on the role of the state. Weber was furious about what he regarded as a misuse of competence of the chairmanship by Schmoller, who as a speaker had the right to respond, even in a polemical way, against critique being raised, but as the Chairman had no right to censorship. Weber thus made a 'personal remark' after Schmoller's final word on behalf of Naumann, who had already left the conference. Naumann later attacked Schmoller in his weekly newspaper, to which Schmoller responded in an open letter to Naumann in another newspaper, and thus the conflict escalated.[18] Schmoller, who was personally hurt and, due to the great applause Naumann's charismatic speech had received, felt himself to be in a minority position, unacceptable for a Chairman,[19] saw the whole aims of the Verein being threatened. Consequently, Schmoller seriously contemplated resigning. It was to the great merit of Brentano, who actively engaged himself as a mediator, that he managed the crisis so successfully, keeping the Verein. Due to his personal friendship with Schmoller and his great authority among the 'Young Turks' of the liberal left, he was no doubt the only member able to do so. Brentano managed to convince Weber, who had already written a sharp private letter to Schmoller, not to react in the same way publicly in the *Frankfurter Zeitung*.

This was much appreciated by Schmoller, who followed Brentano's advice in explaining his intentions, especially the fact that he never wanted to act as a censor. In a long letter to Brentano of 29th October 1905, which was also addressed explicitly to Max Weber, and seemingly sent to most members of the Standing Committee of the Verein, Schmoller made his principal positions clear.[20] The text of the letter is most revealing concerning Schmoller's general understanding of the Verein's purposes. He emphasised the double nature of the Verein of being a scientific association as well as a forum attempting to influence practical social policy. Whereas, on the one hand, he always had tried bringing in controversial positions to make the debates more lively and to deepen an understanding of the problems, on the other hand he also made clear that, for reasons of internal coherence, but also the perception of the Verein among the general public, a certain centrist agreement and homogeneity was required. Schmoller went on:

> Through my performance I only avoided that all members who stand further right feel embarrassed and hurt. As much as the left wing of the Verein is necessary as the driving force, the right wing is equally necessary since it corrects overstatements and gives the Verein influence on the broad bourgeois classes whose social education is our main task. For social democrats we do not convert and influence anyway, the least by our general assembly, more likely by our studies.
>
> (Boese 1939: 119)

This statement is revealing in many respects. It makes perfectly clear that Schmoller was less engaged in sharp theoretical debates than in academic politics and in influencing the economic and social policies of his time. For that reason the Verein was a major medium to him which he therefore wanted to keep intact. Schmoller was also worried about the fact that several important conservative members, such as Conrad, Neumann, Sering and Wagner, had stopped attending regularly the meetings of the Verein. He found the active participation of these members necessary for not shifting the balance of the Verein too much to the left, which would endanger the effectiveness of the Verein in the Wilhelminian society. Compared to the young members on the left, Schmoller was a much greater realist, as was recognised, for example, by Max Weber when he gave up his attempts to found a new association further to the left. Schmoller also had a good sense of judgement concerning the scientific qualities of the two Webers and Sombart, or their and Naumann's rhetorical capabilities which, he confessed, were superior to his own. This comes out even in his more critical statements, of which two characteristic ones may be quoted. After the 1909 conference on value judgements he wrote in a letter to Arthur Spiethoff: 'If we would separate, the left wing will become a torso of radical officers without an army, the right a horde of corporals, both without any power and influence which we still have standing together' (Lindenlaub 1967: 417). Implicitly this statement gives a good picture about the differences in quality of the two parts of the Verein's 'troops' as well as their quantitative numbers. At the end of a 1908 meeting of the Committee on selection and adaptation of workers in big business, which had been initiated by Max Weber, Schmoller explained that for the next meeting a new rule should apply according to which the two Webers should not be allowed to talk for more than 55 minutes per hour (Lindenlaub 1967: 411). This 'lex Weber' is one of many indicators that at the beginning of the twentieth century Max Weber was the towering figure among the younger generation.

In the sequel to the turbulence of the 1905 meeting many proposals were made to reform the by-laws of the Verein. However, the only one which was approved was the one suggested by Brentano, that there should be no final resumé by the Chairman, a practice which had been in place since the 1907 Magdeburg meeting. In some sense the year 1905 marked a turning point which made it clear that the Verein had no clear centre now that the founding fathers had become old and there was a growing diversity in the young generation. A further result of this development was of a more structural nature. The period between 1890 and 1914 saw a strong growth in the number of students and faculty members, which went hand in hand with a growing specialisation, including the formation of business administration and the foundation of the first high schools of commerce.

5 Some famous controversies: the *Methodenstreit* and the *Werturteilsstreit*

As is well known, the dispute on method, the *Methodenstreit*, occupied German-speaking economists for several decades. Schmoller was hostile to the abstract axiomatic-deductive method of the classical economists and his neo-classical contemporaries. Instead he favoured the inductive method and emphasised the necessity of basing economic and social reasoning on sufficient knowledge of historical facts and statistical material. His dispute with Carl Menger, who had attacked the Historical School by asserting the necessity of abstract logical reasoning as well as the application of the exact methods of natural sciences to economics, launched a long battle about methods that Schumpeter judged to have been 'a history of wasted energies' (Schumpeter 1954: 814). However, although a major issue in the German literature since the beginning of the Menger–Schmoller controversy in 1883, the dispute on method played virtually no role in the Verein's meetings until 1905–9 .[21]

This is totally different to the other famous controversy, the *Werturteils-streit*, a fundamental debate about normative judgements, which for good reasons can also be called a 'second Methodenstreit' (see, for example, Winkel 1977: 155). Since the 1880s, the question whether economists or other social scientists should make normative judgements had been a hot issue in many debates within the Verein. This controversy escalated at the second meeting in Vienna in 1909, for which 'The Essence of Economic Productivity' had been chosen as one of two subjects. The organisation of the two Vienna conferences can be attributed to Philippovich, who as a committed chair socialist was a kind of outsider among Austrian economists, and who in 1911, together with Herkner and Otto Gierke, was elected as one of the Vice-chairmen of the Verein. The first conference in 1895 had basically established the Verein in Austria, raising the number of members from the Danube monarchy from 10–12 to 144, out of a total of 489 members (Boese 1939: 74–5). However, whereas the first Vienna conference took place without major controversy, this did not hold for the second, and it was Philippovich's opening keynote paper on 'The Essence of Economic Productivity and the Possibility of its Measurement' which became the target of heavy attacks by Werner Sombart and Max Weber, who managed to find value judgements even behind seemingly innocent concepts like 'productivity'. As is well known, to Weber scientific work had to be 'objective', i.e. free of personal values (see Weber 1904). The preferences and prejudices of researchers should not be allowed to interfere with theoretical analysis, the collection of empirical data and its 'objective' evaluation. However, this was not understood by Weber as a plea for theorising at the expense of engagement on practical policies, which was the central aim of the Verein from the very beginning. Instead he suggested several techniques of practical reasoning, such as tracing back value judgements to their ultimate premises, studying empirically the appropriate means for achieving social ends, and analysing the consistency and investigating for unintended side effects which would need to be balanced (see Verein 1910: 582).

At first sight it might seem strange that the controversy on value judgements, which had been virulent for many years, fully broke out only when the Verein, for the first time in its existence, had chosen a purely theoretical topic for its general meeting. Together with the style of some contributions, in particular Sombart's questioning whether economics had reached the state of a science, it led to the impression that a generational conflict was at the core of the controversies; Sombart's question received prominent feedback in the press where issues like the 'bankruptcy' of economics or the Verein were discussed, very much to the annoyance of Schmoller and most of the other older chair socialists. Thus, Knapp, in a letter to Schmoller of 3rd November, suggested restricting theoretical considerations which would only provoke the *Spektakelfreude der Jugend*[22] to an extra lecture instead of making them the core of the general debates. Fuchs in an earlier letter to Schmoller of 6th October 1909 went even further with his idea that it would be better both for the Verein and for theory when a new specialised association for theory would be founded (see Boese 1939: 135–7).

In fact, with the German Sociological Association, which held its first conference in 1910, a new organisation was established, mainly at the initiative of Max Weber, who was pushing for a clear separation of *social policy* and *social science proper* and was looking for a forum for value-free work and debate concerning the latter. However, after the second meeting in Berlin in 1912 he became so disappointed that he retreated from chairmanship. The reason was that, according to Weber's impression, with one exception all official speakers had offended the principle of strict exclusion of value judgements as stated in the by-laws. He concluded: 'I am absolutely fed up to appear as the Don Quijote of a seemingly untenable principle and to cause embarrassing scenes' (Marianne Weber 1950: 469).

The battle about norms and values in social sciences raged until the outbreak of World War I. It was neither settled in the German Sociological Association nor in the Verein für Sozialpolitik, whose 1911 Nuremberg conference was to be the last before the war,[23] after the meeting scheduled for Düsseldorf in September 1914 was cancelled because of the outbreak of war. With the new sociological association (of whose members at the time, more than one-half were institutionally recognised as economists), Weber only was looking for a place for scientific debate. He was neither questioning the Verein's mission nor giving up his own engagement for a more democratic society. In fact he joined forces with Brentano, Schmoller *et al.* against those anti-chair socialists, such as Pohle, Bernhard, Ehrenberg, Andreas Voigt and Adolf Weber, who used the controversy over value judgements for their own pro-business positions and for attacks against social policies which lacked any scientific foundation and were exclusively based on subjective value judgements (Lindenlaub 1967: 440–1).

Nonetheless, the selfconsciousness and security with which the old guard had pronounced their postulates for greater justice in the society were shaken. Schmoller, who seemingly was surprised at the Vienna meeting that now all judgements and policy claims were denounced as 'unscientific', did not participate in most debates and only weakly reacted to Weber's attacks, which can be explained only to a certain degree by his poor health. In his opening address to the Nuremberg meeting Schmoller defined the whole activities of the Verein as research functioning as preliminary work for public policy. His most elaborate reaction was the rewriting of his 1893 article on 'The Economy, Economics and its Method' for the third edition of the *Handwörterbuch der Staatswissenschaften* in 1911.[24] In the new version Schmoller distinguished between *objective* and *subjective* value judgements, pointing out that he never intended to make subjective ones based on class or party interests as necessary for scientific research, but that he wanted the success of objective ones on which great communities, nations, eras or the whole cultural world depend over and above the lopsided ethical and political ideals which prevail in economics. This is a clear reference to

Weber, who always had been decisive in separating the objective analysis of values in operation from the subjective projection of one's own values under the mantle of 'ethics', what he considered to be the main sin of Schmoller and his associates (see Weber in Verein 1910: 584).

In November 1912 Schmoller sent a letter to all members of the Verein stating that a further discussion of value judgements should be the focus of a meeting of the Committee, something which had already been suggested by Max Weber at the Nuremberg meeting. To aid preparations for debate an agenda consisting of four points was given: (1) the role of ethical value judgements in economics; (2) the relation of development tendencies to practical assessments; (3) the identification of the aims of economic and social policy; and (4) the relation of the general methodological principles to the special task of academic lecturing. All members of the Committee were asked to summarise their ideas in the form of short statements and theses until 1st April 1913 to allow the printing of them in the form of a booklet (Boese 1939: 145). Responses came from Epstein, Eulenburg, Goldscheid, Hartmann, Hesse, Neurath, Oldenberg, Oncken, Rohrbeck, Schumpeter, Spann, Spranger, M. Weber, von Wiese and Wilbrandt. The booklet of 134 pages was printed in a small amount and only distributed to the members of the Committee and a few discussants as a preparation for the meeting, which took place on 5th January 1914 in Berlin.[25] During that meeting the Austro-Marxist Carl Grünberg (Vienna) was the main opponent of Weber, who felt rather isolated and frustrated and prematurely left the conference. The debate on value judgements in German economics was without a final outcome at the outbreak of World War I.[26]

6 Publications of the Verein

It is a widely held opinion that it took decades for the Verein to mutate from a forum of agitation for social policies to a politically neutral scientific organisation. Although this interpretation contains an element of truth, it is also partly a myth, neglecting the fact that the Verein from its very beginning carried out important scholarly research. To see this we not only have to consider that 'the early history of the Verein für Sozialpolitik can indeed be described as a struggle between two different orientations in economics' (Backhaus 1994: 352), but also that the general meetings delivered more a forum for policy debates recognised by a wider public, whereas the scholarly work was primarily done and discussed in the Committee and published in the *Schriften des Vereins für Sozialpolitik*. Duncker & Humblot, then located in Leipzig (and Munich), later in Berlin, has been the publisher of the Verein's series from the beginning until the present day.

The scholarly output of the Verein was impressive in quantity, and by (but not exclusively by) the standards of the Historical School, also impressive in its quality. During its first period of existence the Verein published 256 volumes of expert opinions and 29 conference proceedings, of which almost 200 volumes, including the proceedings of the 21 meetings from Eisenach in 1872 to Nuremberg in 1911, were published up to 1914.[27] A speciality of the Verein were preparatory volumes for conferences, which clearly indicates that even the general meetings were not only a forum for policy debates but for a great part also for the presentation of the scholarly output to a larger audience within and outside the Verein.

Normally the *Jahrbuch für Gesetzgebung, Verwaltung und Volkswirtschaft im Deutschen Reich*, which in 1913 was renamed *Schmollers Jahrbuch* ... , is regarded as *the* scholarly journal of the Verein. This was never true in a formal sense.[28] However, with regard to content it clearly could be considered as the journal representing the Verein's centre, in particular after Schmoller had taken over the editorship from Brentano in 1881, and which he kept until his death in 1917. It was part of his policy normally not to publish articles which had the flavour of either Marxism or Manchester liberalism. In the few cases when it happened he mostly added a distancing editorial note. In the years between 1860 and 1874 Schmoller had published six articles in the *Zeitschrift für die gesamte Staatswissenschaft* but he stopped submitting papers when Schäffle became the main editor in 1875 (until 1903). Brentano, who published four papers in the journal from 1876–8, did not continue after his enemy Adolph Wagner became a co-editor in 1878. Together with his student Heinrich Dietzel, Wagner also used the journal for attacks against Schmoller in the latter's dispute over method with Menger. Although Johannes Conrad, who took over the editorship of the *Jahrbücher für Nationalökonomie und Statistik* from Hildebrand in 1878 (until 1915), had not the same liberal political impetus as his father-in-law, he followed an enlightened editorial policy which also gave room to important theoretical contributions, such as two long essays by Böhm-Bawerk (1886), who elaborated Menger's theory of value, allocation and exchange, and Knut Wicksell's 1892 article on 'Interest and Wages' on the development of the marginal theory of distribution. Whereas Brentano and Herkner published a few articles, Schmoller did not publish in the *Jahrbücher* during Conrad's editorship, probably because of the latter's favouring of free trade.

From 1904 onwards the young generation had their own journal, when Sombart and Max Weber, together with Edgar Jaffe, took over the editorship of the *Archiv für Sozialwissenschaft und Sozialpolitik*, founded in 1888 as the *Archiv für soziale Gesetzgebung und Statistik* by the social democrat Heinrich Braun to focus on the labour question. Although the journal from the very beginning followed a non-partisan approach and an international orientation, its quality got a further boost with the new editorship and the *Archiv* became the leading journal in the social sciences in the German-language area for the next three decades. The new title, in which *Sozialwissenschaft* (social science) comes first, clearly carries a Weberian message, and it is no accident that his groundbreaking methodological article on 'Objectivity' (Weber 1904) is included in the first issue under the new editorship. The journal continued with, and even further improved, the quality after 1922 when Emil Lederer became the new managing editor with Joseph Schumpeter and Alfred Weber as his two co-editors.

In the period of increasing specialisation several new journals were founded. The most important ones, still existing today, are the *Finanzarchiv*, focusing on all issues of public finance and founded by Georg von Schanz in 1884, and the *Weltwirtschaftliches Archiv*, focusing on international economics and founded by Bernhard Harms, a member of the young generation of the Verein, at the newly established Kiel Institute of World Economics in 1913. In Austria Böhm-Bawerk founded the *Zeitschrift für Volkswirtschaft, Sozialpolitik und Verwaltung* in 1886, which for a long period was edited by Philippovich. An important medium for economic discourse and a characteristic element of the professionalisation process in the German-language area in the late nineteenth century was the publication of major Handbooks, such as the *Handbuch der Politischen Ökonomie*, following Rau's tripartite scheme and edited by Schönberg in several editions in the 1880s and 1890s, or the *Handwörterbuch der Staatswissenschaften*, which first was published in six volumes between 1890 and 1894, and went into its third enlarged edition in 1909–11. Under the general editorship of Max Weber, the young generation started the innovative and ambitious project *Grundriss der Sozialökonomik* (Foundations of Social Economics). The first volume, containing Wieser's essay on social economics, Philippovich's article on the systems and ideas of economic and social policy and Schumpeter's famous contribution on the epochs of economic theory and methodology, came out just before the War.

7 Epilogue: some postwar developments

After the war, the Historical School, although still very influential in Germany, lost its once dominant position. In the early post-war years, practical policy issues such as socialisation, the reparation problem and great inflation played a decisive role.[29] In 1921 a major constitutional reform was made in which in addition to the *Haupt-Ausschuss* two subcommittees on Economic Theory (and Sociology) and Public Finance were founded. From the mid-1920s onwards, a new generation of theoretically oriented young economists entered the stage. Their influence became clearly visible with the 1928 Zurich meeting, which focused exclusively on business cycle theory. Major contributions were made by Adolph Lowe (born 1893), Friedrich August von Hayek (1899), Albert Hahn (1889), Wilhelm Röpke (1899) and Oskar Morgenstern (1902),[30] all of whom had to emigrate from Germany and Austria only a few years later.

The political events of the year 1933 marked an important turning-point for the economics profession in Germany. Most scholarly journals had to change editors if they were to survive – with the notable exception of Spiethoff, who remained the editor of *Schmollers Jahrbuch* (see Hagemann

1991). The intellectual emigration that was induced by the Nazis had long-term consequences from which German and Austrian universities never fully recovered. On 19th December 1936, the members decided to dissolve the Verein in order to avoid having to bow to the Nazis or being taken over by Nazi economists. The 1932 Dresden meeting, which turned out to be the last before World War II, was characterised by heavy controversy over the autarky question. It thus confirmed the fact that throughout six decades of the Verein's history, the problems of trade policy were much more at the centre of repeated struggles and permanent differences of opinion[31] than problems of social policy where the differences were relatively moderate among the academic members. This classic field of activity, in Imperial Germany, under heavy attack by industrialists from inside but even more from outside, was no longer a major concern for many members during the interwar period.

The Verein für Sozialpolitik was refounded in September 1948, when the first meeting in Marburg focused on the economic problems of German trade. The name Gesellschaft für Wirtschafts- und Sozialwissenschaften (Society for Economics and Social Sciences) was added in 1956.[32] In the year 2000 the Verein has 2,704 individual members, among them approximately 1,000 university professors from 20 countries, and 58 corporate members.

Notes

1 One participant was Vito Cusumano (Palermo) whose reports on the Eisenach conferences, together with Francesco Ferrara's critical response on 'Economic Germanism in Italy', initiated the debate on method in Italy.

2 Shortly afterwards Schmoller left for his new position in Straßburg. On 12th August Johannes Conrad was appointed his successor on the chair at the University of Halle, where together with the University in Frankfurt/Oder the first two chairs for Cameralism in Germany had been established in 1727. On the history of the Halle faculty between 1873 and 1914 see Hertner 2000.

3 For a detailed history of the German Sciences of State in the nineteenth century see the recent study by Lindenfeld 1997.

4 The founding member Brentano, who had abandoned Catholicism after the declaration of papal infallibility, later left the Verein für Sozialpolitik in May 1929 because he considered the association as having become reactionary. In particular he deplored the mutation of the Verein *für* Sozialpolitik into a Verein *gegen* Sozialpolitik by the younger generation, the silence of the Verein on the reintroduction and increase of tariffs on corn and the tacit agreement of most members to the deflationary wage policies thus supporting the danger of a social revolution. See Brentano 1931: 399–404.

5 For a detailed historical study of the German free-trade movement and the Congress see Hentschel 1975.

6 See his article 'Manchesterschule und Kathedersozialismus' on the front page of the *National-Zeitung*, 7th December 1871, vol. 24, no. 573. Note that the article was written eight weeks after Wagner's speech in the Berlin Garnisonkirche which had been followed shortly afterwards by another much noted lecture by Gustav Schönberg, then Professor in Freiburg, who argued for the foundation of special offices of labour throughout Germany. Schönberg's inaugural lecture at the University of Tübingen from 3rd July 1873 on 'The Ger-

man Free Trade Party and the Party of the Eisenach Meeting of October 1872'
(Schönberg 1873) gives a good impression of the two different schools of
thought in German economics. Interestingly, Wagner and Schönberg, who had
been the main targets of the attacks by liberal Congressmen (see Wittrock
1939), later felt more at the periphery of the Verein, which they could not
transform into a forum for social conservative agitation. Although Wagner in
particular was not successful in influencing the Verein with his state socialist
ideas, his presence in the Standing Committee helped to give the cooptation
procedure of new members a more conservative bias.

7 From the foundation in 1873 to the dissolution in 1936 the Verein had the
   following chairmen:

1873–1874	Rudolf von Gneist
1874–1890	Erwin Nasse
1890–1917	Gustav Schmoller
1917–1930	Heinrich Herkner
1930–1932	Christian Eckert
1932–1935	Werner Sombart
1935–1936	Constantin von Dietze.

8 Another reason for the move was the active participation of the mayor of
   Frankfurt Miquel. After the first four meetings in Eisenach, the 1877 Conference had taken place in Berlin where the members also gathered for their first
   post-Frankfurt meeting in 1893. From then onwards the place of the (normally
   biannual) conferences changed continuously.

9 See Boese 1939: 32–42. Boese's detailed chronology of events which was
   written after the dissolution of the Verein in 1936 is a reliable and indispensable source, in particular also because it is based on important archive material
   which was destroyed during World War II. However, with regard to judgements on issues of major controversies, readers should be aware that the author,
   a former assistant of Schmoller, has a strongly 'conservative-centrist' perspective. This, for example, is reflected in Boese's great understanding and sympathy for Schmoller's 'flexibility' in the protective tariff question following
   Bismarck's change of course. For a different perspective see, for example, Eisermann 1956. Boese also downplays the impact of Bismarck's anti-socialists laws
   on the Verein. For a more critical view see Brentano (1931: 122), who deplores
   the 'keeping the mouth shut' policy of the Verein during that period.

10 There was an element of reciprocity in the agreement which also gave members
   of the Verein a special status at the meetings of the Congress.

11 Interestingly, the leading representatives of the older Historical School,
   Roscher, Knies and Hildebrand, were teaching at universities in the centre and
   southwest of Germany: in Leipzig, Jena, Marburg, Heidelberg and Freiburg.
   Thus vom Bruch (1985: 135) comes to the conclusion that their economic
   doctrines were adapted to the ideals and purposes of the middle states.

12 In a different sense this also holds for Johannes Conrad, another leading
   conservative, who left the National-liberal party after they agreed to Bismarck's protectionist policy in 1879.

13 'Neither your socialism à la Friedrich Wilhelm I, nor my individualistic
   independence should ever separate us', Brentano wrote to Schmoller on 10th
   August 1877.

14 For a more detailed analysis of Herkner's role as the *Nachfolger* (successor) see
   the study by Backhaus and Hanel 1994.

15 Among others the list includes Walter Lotz, Brentano's long-time assistant,
   and Gerhard Schulze-Gävernitz. On the mutation of the latter from a radical
   social-liberal to a liberal imperialist see Krüger 1983.

16 For a thorough analysis of Weber's lectures at the universities of Freiburg and Heidelberg in the 1890s and an evaluation of his claim to be a member of the 'Younger Historical School' see Tribe 1995: ch. 4.

17 The debate on the general glut controversy and later on economic crises had been a main topic in nineteenth-century German economics. See Hagemann 1996: 90–5.

18 The intensity of the conflict and the different perceptions of it are still reflected in major works written more than three decades later. Contrast, for example, the Schmollerian viewpoint in the official history of the Verein by Boese (1939: 109–22), with the relevant passages in the Naumann biography by Theodor Heuss (1937: 316–19), the son-in-law of Knapp, and after World War II the undisputed leader of the Liberal Party and first President of the Federal Republic of Germany (1949–59).

19 In his open letter to Naumann of 18th October Schmoller emphasised the principle that theories which the Chairman finds problematic should not receive a majority within the Verein; a Chairman who has no majority in general and in the relevant questions should resign (see Lindenlaub 1967: 412). Interestingly, eleven days later in his letter to Brentano, Schmoller downgraded the importance of the controversies on the protective tariffs at the 1879 meeting, when the Chairman Nasse was left in a minority position, to an issue of minor importance for the Verein (see Boese 1939: 118). There is a clear contradiction in Schmoller's argument.

20 See Boese (1939: 116–20) for the full text of Schmoller's letter.

21 For that reason it is not covered in greater detail in this paper. In contrast to Menger, Böhm-Bawerk, Wieser and other members of the Austrian School were members of the Verein and played a more active role. Brentano (1931: 142) mentions in his autobiography that, as a member of the Historical School, he received a hostile reception from Menger when he came to Vienna in 1888 to succeed Lorenz von Stein (the Vienna ministry had first contacted Schmoller!). Brentano who before had criticised Menger because, in contrast to Jevons and Walras, he never gave proper credit to Gossen despite great similarities with his argumentation in the *Principles*, reacted in his inaugural lecture on classical economics by explaining why he had moved away from their abstract-axiomatic theorising in a more realistic-empirical direction.

22 With regard to 'youth' it should be emphasised that in 1909 Max Weber was already 45 and Sombart 46 years old, compared to Knapp (67) and Schmoller (71).

23 At that time the Verein had 671 members of whom 99 were members of the Committee (Boese 1939: 144).

24 See the 1949 Skalweit edition which makes explicit the differences between the two versions.

25 The contributions never did appear in the *Schriften* of the Verein and were only published in 1996 with an introduction by Nau.

26 See Boese 1939: 147–8. Unfortunately, the debates at the meeting were not documented.

27 For a full list see Boese 1939: 305–22, whose history of the Verein appeared as the final number 188 of the series. The proceedings of the 1872 Eisenach meeting are in fact the first volume but not numbered. The proceedings of the 1873 Eisenach meeting were published as no. 4. The higher number of volumes is explained by the fact that, beginning from no. 103 in 1902–3, up to 9 volumes constitute a number, as in the case of municipal firms, the second topic of the 1909 Vienna conference.

28 In fact it took until 1974 that *Schmollers Jahrbuch*, which had been renamed into *Schmollers Jahrbuch für Wirtschafts- und Sozialwissenschaften* in 1968 and into

Zeitschrift für Wirtschafts- und Sozialwissenschaften in 1972, became the official periodical of the Verein. From 1987 to 1999 it was sent to all members. Since 2000 the Verein has two new journals: the English-language *German Economic Review*, an international journal focusing on theoretical issues, and *Perspektiven der Wirtschaftspolitik*, a German-language journal focusing on economic policy issues. At the same time a new *Schmollers Jahrbuch*, published again by Duncker & Humblot, was revived which is *not* linked to the Verein. This journal story including the renaming implicitly tells a lot about the development of economics as a discipline.

29 For greater details see Boese 1939. Note that the name of the Verein was spelt 'Sozialpolitik' (with a 'z' instead of today's 'c') until its dissolution in 1936.
30 See vol. 173, II of the Verein's publication series, edited by Karl Diehl.
31 There is a strong parallel in Italy where the struggle between the free-traders and protectionists was also at the centre of the controversies among economists in the decades after political unification in 1861. See Augello 1989.
32 For more detailed information on the development of the Verein after World War II see Hagemann and Trautwein 1999, Schefold 1999 and the Verein's website: www.vwl.uni-muenchen.de/verein.

Bibliography

Albrecht, G. (1961) 'Verein für Sozialpolitik', in *Handwörterbuch der Sozialwissenschaften*, Stuttgart and Tübingen: Fischer and J. C. B. Mohr, vol. 11: 10–16.

Augello, M.M. (1989) 'The Societies of Political Economy in Italy and the Professionalization of Economists (1860–1900)', *HES Bulletin* 11: 99–112.

Backhaus, J.G. (1994) 'The German Economic Tradition: from Cameralism to the Verein für Sozialpolitik', in M. Albertone and A. Masoero (eds) *Political Economy and National Realities*, Torino: Fondazione Luigi Einaudi.

Backhaus, J.G. and Hanel, J. (1994) *Die Nachfolge – ein Versuch über Heinrich Herkner, den Volkswirt*, Marburg: Metropolis.

Boese, F. (1939) *Geschichte des Vereins für Sozialpolitik 1872–1932*, Berlin: Duncker & Humblot.

Brentano, L. (1931) *Mein Leben im Kampf um die soziale Entwicklung Deutschlands*, Jena: Eugen Diederichs Verlag.

Bruch, R. vom (1985) 'Zur Historisierung der Staatswissenschaften. Von der Kameralistik zur historischen Schule der Nationalökonomie', *Berichte zur Wissenschaftsgeschichte*, 8: 131–46.

Coats, A.W. (1960) 'The First Two Decades of the American Economic Association', *American Economic Review* 50: 555–74.

Eisermann, G. (1956) *Die Grundlagen des Historismus in der deutschen Nationalökonomie*, Stuttgart: Ferdinand Enke Verlag.

Hagemann, H. (1991) 'Learned Journals and the Professionalization of Economics: The German Language Area', *Economic Notes* 20: 33–57.

—— (1996) 'German Economic Journals and Economic Debates in the Nineteenth Century', *History of Economic Ideas* 4: 77–101.

Hagemann, H. and Trautwein, H.-M. (1999), 'Verein für Socialpolitik – the Association of German-speaking Economists', *Newsletter of the Royal Economic Society* 107, October: 7–9.

Hentschel, V. (1975) *Die deutschen Freihändler und der volkswirtschaftliche Kongreß 1858–1885*, Stuttgart: Klett.

Herkner, H. (1887) *Die oberelsässische Baumwollindustrie und Ihre Arbeiter, auf Grund der Tatsachen dargestellt*, Straßburg: K. J. Trübner.

Hertner, P. (2000) 'Vom Staatswissenschaftlichen Seminar zur Rechts- und Staatswissenschaftlichen Fakultät. Die Nationalökonomie in Forschung und Lehre an der Vereinigten Friedrichs-Universität Halle-Wittenberg, 1873 bis 1914', in A. Wenig (ed.) *Globalisierung und die Zukunft der Sozialen Marktwirtschaft*, Berlin: Duncker & Humblot.

Heuss, T. (1937) *Friedrich Naumann. Der Mann, das Werk, die Zeit*, Stuttgart: Deutsche Verlags-Anstalt.

Kesten-Conrad, E. (1911) 'Verein für Sozialpolitik', in *Handwörterbuch der Staatswissenschaften*, 3rd edition, Jena: G. Fischer and Duncker & Humblot, vol. 8: 144–52.

Krüger, D. (1983) *Nationalökonomen im wilhelminischen Deutschland*, Göttingen: Vandenhoeck & Ruprecht.

Lindenfeld, D.F. (1997) *The Practical Imagination. The German Sciences of State in the Nineteenth Century*, Chicago and London: The University of Chicago Press.

Lindenlaub, D. (1967) *Richtungskämpfe im Verein für Sozialpolitik. Wissenschaft und Politik im Kaiserreich vornehmlich vom Beginn des 'Neuen Kurses' bis zum Ausbruch des Ersten Weltkriegs (1890–1914)*, 2 vols, Wiesbaden: Franz Steiner Verlag.

Nau, H.H. (1996) *Der Werturteilsstreit. Die Äußerungen zur Werturteilsdiskussion im Ausschuß des Vereins für Sozialpolitik (1913)*, Marburg: Metropolis.

Schefold, B. (1999) 'Die Wirtschafts- und Sozialordnung der Bundesrepublik Deutschland im Spiegel der Jahrestagungen des Vereins für Socialpolitik 1948 bis 1989', *Zeitschrift für Wirtschafts- und Sozialwissenschaften* 119 (supplementary volume 8): 201–28.

Schmölders, G. (1960) 'Die wirtschaftlichen Staatswissenschaften an der Universität Berlin von der Reichsgründung bis 1945', in H. Leussink *et al.* (eds) *Studium Berolinese. Aufsätze und Beiträge zu Problemen der Wissenschaft und zur Geschichte der Friedrich-Wilhelms-Universität zu Berlin*, Berlin.

Schmoller, G. (1864–5) 'Die Arbeiterfrage', *Preußische Jahrbücher* 14: 393–424 and 523–47; 15: 32–63.

—— (1870) *Zur Geschichte der deutschen Kleingewerbe im 19. Jahrhundert: Statistische und nationalökonomische Untersuchungen*, Halle: Waisenhaus.

—— (1911) *Die Volkswirtschaft, die Volkswirtschaftslehre und ihre Methode*, Sozialökonomische Texte, ed. by A. Skalweit, Frankfurt am Main: V. Klostermann, 1949.

Schönberg, G. (1873) 'Die deutsche Freihandelsparthei und die Parthei der Eisenacher Versammlung vom Oktober 1872', *Zeitschrift für die gesamte Staatswissenschaft* 29: 493–532.

Schumpeter, J.A. (1954) *History of Economic Analysis*, London: Allen & Unwin.

Tribe, K. (1995), *Strategies of Economic Order. German Economic Discourse 1750–1950*, Cambridge: Cambridge University Press.

Verein für Sozialpolitik (1910) *Verhandlungen der Generalversammmlung in Wien vom 27. bis 29. September 1909*, Schriften, vol. 132, Leipzig: Duncker & Humblot.

Waszek, N. (1988) 'Die Staatswissenschaften an der Universität Berlin im 19. Jahrhundert', in N. Waszek (ed.) *Die Institutionalisierung der Nationalökonomie an deutschen Universitäten. Zur Erinnerung an Klaus Hinrich Hennings (1937–1986)*, St. Katharinen: Scripta Mercaturae.

Weber, Marianne (1950) *Max Weber. Ein Lebensbild*, 2nd ed., Heidelberg: Lambert Schneider.

Weber, Max (1904), 'Die 'Objektivität' sozialwissenschaftlicher und sozialpolitischer Erkenntnis', *Archiv für Sozialwissenschaft und Sozialpolitik* 19: 22–87.
Winkel, H. (1977) *Die deutsche Nationalökonomie im 19. Jahrhundert*, Darmstadt: Wissenschaftliche Buchgesellschaft.
Wittrock, G. (1939) *Die Kathedersozialisten bis zur Eisenacher Versammlung 1872*, Berlin: Emil Ebering.

10 The Swedish Economic Association from its foundation (1877) to the turn of the century

Rolf G.H. Henriksson

The observer from afar may be intrigued by the Swedish Economic Association[1] (henceforth: Association) as being possibly a significant component in the early institutionalisation of economics as a discipline in Sweden. Many may have been impressed by the renowned lecture Wicksell delivered at the meeting on 14th April 1898 (Wicksell 1898a). On that occasion Wicksell reported on his just completed seminal treatise, *Interest and Prices* (Wicksell 1898b). This work, which may be said to signal the rise of an independent Swedish line of economic thinking, has been described by a leading commentator as the start of modern macroeconomics (Leijonhufvud 1997: 1). However, the Association, which had been set up in 1877 'to promote the study of economics', contributed only marginally to building up the institutional base of professional economics at that time. The Association was quite active at the turn of the century but, as will be argued at the end of this chapter, it can only be said to have been of importance for the academic institutionalisation of economics in a very indirect sense.

The significance of the Association in the period under review is mainly of a different kind.[2] It played a central role in establishing the Swedish tradition of enlightened economic policy debate. In the Association, leading participants in economic policy making could publicly expound and defend their lines of action before a wider critical audience of concerned supporters and inform themselves of issues raised by their opponents.

This chapter offers some highlights of the founding process in 1877, seen against the background of antecedents that introduce a wider Nordic perspective (§§1 and 2). There follows an overview of the subsequent performance of the Association, illuminating the following aspects: the manning and logistical activities of the board (§3), the lectures and discussion themes considered within the setting of the economic policy involvement of its leading members (§4), and the connection with economics as an academic discipline (§5). The presentation concludes with some broader retrospective comments (§6).

1 Antecedents

The background to the start of the Association in 1877 is, according to the official chronicle, traceable to 1863 when, at the first Nordic Economic Meeting in Gothenburg, the main initiator, C.F. Waern, received a donation from P. Murén to be used as a start-up fund. The following section attempts to trace some of the preparatory steps behind the setting up of the Association.

1.1 *The initiators*

Murén was a prominent businessman, apparently of little formal schooling. He was an important member of the burgher estate in Sweden's four estate parliament prior to the representational reform of 1866, in which he played a central role. He remained very active for a while even after the start of the new parliament, where he belonged to the second chamber. However, he soon retired from the political scene after failing to create a broad liberal front in support of the government at the time (Thermaenius 1928). When the Association was set up in 1877, Murén was 72. Although he was regarded as an eminent figure at the founding meetings, this might have been more an honorary tribute than a sign of real influence.

Waern, another key founding member, was also a businessman, and like Murén, he too lacked a university degree.[3] He had received mainly commercial and engineering schooling related to the mining and ironworks sector, which over the centuries had been the mainstay of Sweden's export performance. From this educational base Waern seems to have continued his studies mainly on his own, expanding his cultural horizon perhaps even more than university studies could have done. He was later able to contribute even to historical scholarship. Important in Waern's education was apparently the time he spent abroad, most notably in France. But as a man involved in foreign trade, he must also have had considerable exposure to English influences. As evidence of his international status, one may note that in 1862 he was the Swedish representative at the international exhibition in London.

Waern's special quality in politics seems to have been his skills in achieving results by reaching consensus in a cautious business-like manner. He gained the reputation of being a man of compromise, although he apparently stood firm in defence of fundamental ends or values, to the point of appearing somewhat dogmatic. As a member of the Swedish parliament, Waern was already important before the representational reform of 1866, but his political capacity was not fully recognised until the new parliament, as underscored by his appointment as Minister of Finance in 1870. Although the economic policies of the cabinet in which he came to serve effectively acted more in defence of previously launched economic and political reforms than setting out on new adventures, Waern's period as

Minister of Finance, until his resignation in the middle of 1874, was still eventful and, as a test of his ability, successful.

According to Sweden's constitutional rules during that period, the government could legislate on many aspects of economic life without appealing to parliament as long as no major financial and fiscal dimension was involved. But as most important issues had such a dimension, they had first to achieve a majority in both chambers. Before the turn of the century, it was especially the second chamber that offered the main fiscal constraint on economic policy making, since its members represented the major tax base for government expenditure. As a Minister of Finance Waern inevitably had to contend with this fiscal constraint. The new representational system had given the majority in the second chamber to small landowners, who formed what was to be called the agrarian party. Of central concern to this party was the proposal that Sweden's old ground tax system should be replaced by a new system based on broader conceptions of taxable income and wealth. Naturally this issue presented a formidable blockage between the two chambers of parliament and was a burning issue in Swedish economic policy discussions.

Waern's attention to this contentious issue was only the opening move in a long-drawn-out game, but it decisively set the stage for the subsequent unfolding of events. In 1873 Waern expedited a parliament resolution known as the 'compromise'. This turned out to be a kind of 'no deal' decision. In this resolution the efforts of the circles around Oscar II (who had acceded to the throne in 1872) to reinvigorate Swedish military defence were blocked by the agrarian party in the second chamber, with the 'promise' that such a reform would only be accepted if the 'burdens on land' were lifted.

The subsequent unsuccessful attempts in parliament to settle the issue of a new tax base had consequences for a broad range of other issues. They had a bearing on the tariff issue, which was the most inflamed political contest in the period under review, but they also delayed advances on the social policy front.

Among other long lasting reforms introduced during Waern's period in government one should note in particular those in the sphere of monetary policy. After the Franco-German war of 1870–1, Waern was party to Sweden following Germany rather than France when settling for the gold standard. In 1873 Waern was also the signer, on the Swedish side, of the Scandinavian currency union, which included Denmark and (later) Norway. Important for the subsequent history of the Association was that Waern clashed with A.O. Wallenberg, the founder and powerful head of the Stockholms Enskilda Bank, Sweden's largest private commercial bank.[4] Wallenberg had been the main Swedish champion of making the French franc the hub of a reformed international currency system tied to gold rather than silver. He reacted very strongly to Waern's monetary policy stance. However, Wallenberg seems also to have harboured some personal resentment against Waern, for attaining in 1870 the post as Minister of Finance he himself aspired to (Nilsson 1994).

Throughout his years in the cabinet Waern remained a forceful proponent of the principles of *laissez-faire*. Although foreign trade treaties and tariffs had been removed from the economic policy agenda after the liberalisation measures of the 1860s (Montgomery 1921a and b), an important brainchild of Waern was the bilateral free-trade agreement between Norway and Sweden in 1873, which was eventually dismantled in the 1890s.

Due to his specific industrial background Waern was particularly knowledgeable in issues relating to the mining- and natural resource-based sectors. But on such issues some of his dogmatism came to the fore. After having failed to secure an outcome that safeguarded private property rights in a controversy concerning forestry legislation, Waern resigned from his government post as Minister of Finance.

1.2 The importance of the Danish precedent

Waern had participated not only in the 1863 Nordic Economic Meeting, but in the meetings in 1866 and 1872 as well. These meetings might be called 'unofficial' gatherings of 'officials' as part of the efforts of the Nordic countries to cooperate in various economic policy matters where agreements or a common solution seemed called for.

The 1872 Nordic Meeting in Copenhagen appears to have been particularly important. That was the year when Waern, as Minister of Finance, entered into collaboration with the Danes in establishing the Scandinavian currency union. The contacts Waern must have made with various Danish dignitaries and circles probably acquainted him with the discussions that led to the foundation in Denmark of the Nationaløkonomisk Forening (Economic Association) later in the year. This may have reawakened in his mind the idea of setting up a similar Association in Sweden. However, the design of the Danish association was not easy to emulate because it was geared to an institutional base of economics very different from Sweden's (Bergstrand 1877). Denmark, unlike Sweden, had a professional group of academically trained government bureaucrats whose university degrees were more oriented towards statistics than law and who could thus be called 'economists'. This enabled the Danish association to assume as one of its prime tasks the editorship of a journal (*Nationaløkonomisk Tidskrift*).

However, Waern may have been inspired also by the existence of economic associations in other countries. Except for the Cobden Club with its interest in policy making, Waern probably saw little in England to copy, since the English political economy network appears to have been institutionalised mainly informally. However, he may have been alerted to the existence of the Political Economy Club as it celebrated the Adam Smith centennial in 1876. Furthermore, on account of its economic policy stance, Waern was probably little disposed to follow the model of the German Verein für Sozialpolitik, which had been set up by the 'chair socialists' in 1873. Although there was also a more liberal economic association in the

German realm from which he could have drawn inspiration, Waern appears to have been little oriented towards the German scene. Instead, reviving his previous ties and contacts with French institutions, Waern perhaps looked more favourably on the Paris Société d'Economie Politique. This society may have seemed attractive because of its *laissez-faire* leanings, but also because it offered an organisational model for the Swedish association.

1.3 Preparatory steps

It was only after his resignation in 1874 from the post of Minister of Finance that Waern took a renewed interest in the old agreement he had with Murén. He returned to a seat in parliament while also assuming the position of head of Sweden's Board of Trade. Freed from his ministerial duties, he now had more time for the task of setting up the Association, but there were also new factors that prompted him to resume this project.

It is clear that he promoted the foundation of the Association in 1877 as an important ideological support for the *laissez-faire* cause. Given Waern's experience with the type of opposition internal to the liberal camp offered especially by A.O. Wallenberg, he perhaps felt the need for a forum where the *laissez-faire* view could be articulated for the benefit of the liberals themselves. But naturally he also sought to resist the rising new schools of economic thinking to the right and left, i.e. the Historical School and the socialists.

It is not known when Waern took the first steps, but he was reportedly engaged in efforts to institute the Association as early as 1876 (Palme 1927, Åmark 1927). But, while he apparently embarked on the task when the parliament was in session in the spring, he was too late to complete it before the sessions closed in the early summer. He therefore postponed further steps until the beginning of 1877.

This sequence of events suggests two interesting observations: not only does it provide evidence of the strong political anchoring of the Association, but it also suggests that in 1876 Waern attempted to launch the project somewhat suddenly. This points to some circumstantial events as possible activating factors. Just such an event may have been Waern's encounter with J.H. Palme in May 1876. When Waern approached Palme with the invitation to become the secretary of the planned association, Waern also mentioned that the idea was by no means new but that it had not been realised because a person fit for the task of secretary had previously not been found. Waern thought he had now found that man (Palme 1927).

2 The founding meetings

The foundation of the Association may be seen as a process that covered not only the constituting meeting on 29th January 1877, when the by-laws were adopted, but also a second meeting on 12th February, at which the membership was opened up, and a third meeting, on 12th March, when a board was elected.

The first of the founding meetings at the end of January was attended, in addition to Waern and the meeting Secretary J.H. Palme, by twelve persons, including Murén. At that meeting Waern presented a proposal for the Association, which, according to the minutes, was then discussed and adopted with minor changes.

The acceptance of Waern's proposal essentially meant setting up the by-laws of the Association. These were then to remain formally unchanged throughout the period under review. However, as will be discussed below, in the early years some rulings were amended informally in order to regulate a few organisational details. These amendments proved to be important in finally settling the objectives of the Association.

The stipulations for meetings, membership, membership fees, etc. were few and clear. It was decided that the Association should meet eight times a year with a summer vacation from June until September. The membership fee should be paid in the early months of the year. Anyone interested in political economy could join, but admission required endorsement by two prior members.

The Association was an immediate success. At the second meeting on 12th February the main issue on the agenda was the admission of the first round of new members presumably endorsed by the founders. From an initial membership of 60, in addition to the 14 founders, the number of members grew during the first year to reach the level of 160. The membership then continued to expand strongly and after five years it reached the range of 400–500, within which it then fluctuated up to the end of the century.

The first board was elected at the third meeting on 12th March. According to the by-laws, it was to be composed of five members including the Secretary. There should be a President and a Vice-president and also an editorial committee consisting of the Secretary and two members. In 1882 the size of this editorial committee was expanded to four members in addition to the Secretary. The board members were elected for one year. Re-election was allowed and became customary.

The wording in the by-laws concerning the goals of the Association require some comments. The central objectives were stated as follows:

§1 The goal of the Economic Association is to promote the study of political economy and contribute to the investigation of questions that belong to the domains of that science through lectures, discussions and publications.

In his reminiscences on the start of the Association, Palme recalled that the wordings of §1 were the result of rather lengthy discussions on the issue of whether the Association was to be set up as a free-trade society similar to the

Cobden Club or upon a 'non-confessional' basis. The latter position won. Palme wrote:

> Thus the Association had from the start decided to open its door not only to the friends of free trade and labour but also to those who held a different view concerning the means through which the common goal – the economic welfare of their beloved country – could be reached most securely.
>
> (Palme 1927: 78)

This political neutrality confined the purpose of the Association to serve as a forum for debates on economic policy and other economic topics. This point was never explicitly entered into the formal by-laws but became a key part of the 'constitution' of the Association.

Pertinent to the interpretation of the objectives, as stated in the first paragraph, is also the appeal to political economy. On this point one may note Palme's explanation of why the neutrality line was victorious. He argued that the crucial reason for the victory of the neutrality position was that within economics, as within any science, there must be no other norm than 'the search for truth regardless of confirmation or rejection of preconceived views' (Palme 1927: 78).

To this should be added that, while Palme's words underscored that the connection with economics was intrinsic to the Association, the appeal to economics in the by-laws leaves no doubt as to the subservient status of such scientific aims. On closer reading it seems clear that there were no ambitions to promote economic studies or contribute to investigations as scientific endeavours in their own right.

A point of great interest concerned the publication activity of the Association as stipulated in the by-laws. This was regulated in two paragraphs:

> §2 The association selects from its members [...] an editorial committee of two persons who together with the secretary are in charge of the publications issued in the name of the association.
>
> [...]
>
> §8 The association publishes a periodical containing accounts of the proceedings at the meetings in addition to original papers, reports and announcements.

One may note that these two paragraphs did not rule out the possibility that the Association might set up a journal akin to the Danish example and that it might also issue publications other than the mere proceedings.

3 The board and its secretaries

The meeting in 1898 at which Wicksell gave his renowned lecture (Wicksell 1898a) was the 123rd since its foundation in 1877. This figure reveals an impressive performance, not only cumulatively but also because it had been regularly sustained by five to six meetings a year over a twenty-year period. This logistical achievement is in itself a reason that calls for close attention to the activities of the board. But a more compelling reason is given by the deep involvement of the board members in the discussions for which the Association served as a forum, and by the fact that they themselves constituted its main connections with what they referred to as 'economic science'.

3.1 The development of the boards

Except for a number of transient chairpersons, one may record that throughout the period the posts on the board were generally kept solidly within a small inner circle gathering around Waern and Palme. Waern, who was elected President in the first board of 1877, was repeatedly to hold that post or that of Vice-president. When not serving in these chair capacities he was a member of the editorial committee. Waern appears to have been the main guiding light who ensured that the Association was maintained within the constraints of a discussion forum. He was himself a diligent participant in the debates at the meetings.

A most notable member of the first board was Professor F.F. Carlson, who was elected Vice-president. Carlson held a chair in history at Uppsala University, but was at the time government Minister of Ecclesiastical Affairs. He sat on the board only for one year, but there is good reason to note his presence, as he was at the time involved in reforming Sweden's educational system. The position to which Carlson was appointed in the Association may be seen as indicating a desire to be well anchored in clerical quarters at the highest possible government level, in order to obtain academic blessing for the enterprise. There is also the possibility that he was considered an agency through which the Association might possibly promote the standing of economics.

Another notable member of the first board was C.G. Hammarskjöld. Although he does not appear to have been central to the history of the Association, he deserves attention as evidence of the ambition to have on the board a formal academic representation of the field of political economy. He was at the time acting as Professor of Economics and Fiscal Law in the Faculty of Law at Uppsala University. Unlike Carlson, he served on the board for a more extended period. He belonged to the inside network of the Association for more than a decade, as can be inferred from the fact that he returned to a board position as late as 1890.

Among the members of the first board, attention must also be given to J.W. Arnberg as one of the members of the inner circle. He had previously made an academic career as a historian of Swedish eighteenth-century economic policy and thought (Arnberg 1855, 1864, 1868). At the time when the Association was set up, he had been appointed to one of the deputy positions with the Riksbank, Sweden's old parliament-ruled national bank. He was later (in 1883) to assume the position as First Deputy, i.e. Managing Director. Arnberg then retained that post through the crucial preparatory period of the grand reform of the Riksbank into a more modern central bank of 1897–1902. Arnberg should be particularly noted as perhaps the most prolific contributor to discussions in the Association.

One may be struck by the absence of Murén on the first board. However, as noted, his age may have made him unwilling to take on any responsibilities in the Association. Another name missing was Hans Forsell, whose absence is conspicuous as he was also a member of the inner circle and an important contributor to the meetings of the Association. Forsell had carried out pioneering work as an economic historian (Forsell 1866, 1875–88, 1884), for which he was later much appreciated by Heckscher (1927). But Heckscher also ranked him as the most brilliant name to have held public office in Sweden. Appointed Minister of Finance in 1875 when he was 32, Forsell must be counted as one of the most prominent among the founders. He may have been excused for failing to appear on the board in 1877 as his ministerial appointment was still fairly recent, but he was elected to the board as President the very next year and thereafter remained a permanent board member until 1893.

The above mentioned inner circle, consisting of Waern, Palme, Arnberg and Forsell, held the reins until the 1890s, when the various infirmities of ageing seem increasingly to have prompted them to retreat from public responsibilities. In that decade a new group was gradually taking over the leadership, marking a thorough break with the past. In 1898, the year of Wicksell's lecture, the transition was almost complete.

The transition appears to have been a fairly smooth process, despite the fact that none of the new members of the board had any strong apostolic tie with the origins of the Association. In 1893 Richard Åkerman, the new head of the Board of Trade after Waern, was elected President, probably with the blessing of the old regime as he had been a member of the Association since its starting year in 1877. However, he had not allied himself with the free-trade cause and was apparently in favour of extending tariff protection to industry after the 1888 victory of agrarian protectionism. The most important discontinuity pertained to the link with economics. Closer inspection of the composition of the Association's board in 1898 reveals that it no longer included any formal representative of academic economics.

3.2 The secretaries

Many of the key executive functions of the board rested with the Secretary; a few comments highlighting how the appointees to that position handled their tasks will illuminate some of the essential aspects of the development of the Association.

3.2.1 J.H. Palme (1877–81)

Palme had a low-level academic background in law and had, like Waern, spent a period of his youth abroad, particularly in France. Thus he had undoubtedly, through studies on his own, absorbed much the same type of *laissez-faire* economic policy message as Waern. However, their French connections may not have been the major uniting factor. Their links were undoubtedly strengthened by the circumstance that Palme, like Waern, also seems to have been an object of Wallenberg's aversion. Waern may, in addition, have been attracted by Palme's knowledge of the chair socialists, as Palme had studied their teachings deeply enough to voice trenchant criticism.

Palme had already at that time made a solid start in his career as the founder and director of Sweden's leading mortgage bank. In attaining expertise in the economics of town planning, Palme also displayed social policy interests as an urban land developer in the Stockholm area. In addition to serving as its first Secretary and then as a member of the board of the Association, Palme rivalled Arnberg as the most active participant in its meetings.

Among the statutory tasks of the Secretary, a potentially troublesome point concerned publication activity. On this aspect Palme and the Association almost immediately found a convenient solution through an agreement with the daily *Stockholms Dagblad*. This was the strongest press voice at the time in support of the *laissez-faire* views also held by the leading members of the Association. The initial agreement was that only summary reports would be published, but after the first year, the full texts of the lectures and discussions were printed. This arrangement with the *Stockholms Dagblad* lasted until the end of 1881.

3.2.2 Claes Westman (1882–90)

The Secretary after Palme was Claes Westman. He had been a member of the Association since its first year and had lectured at its meetings in 1880. As one of the early auditors of the Association he had taken an active part in its activities even before he was appointed. It should also be noted that prior to his appointment he was affiliated with *Stockholms Dagblad*.

Westman's credentials for the post of Secretary were as appropriate as Palme's. His formal background in political economy covered what at that time was required for the *jur kand*, the basic Swedish law degree. Like

Palme, he seems to have pursued further studies on his own, and had early on started to write on political economy themes. One of his chief merits was notably his official position as a Lecturer in Political Economy at the Tekniska Högskolan (Royal Institute of Technology), the university-level engineering school in Stockholm (Henriksson 1986), a position he had held since 1878. Westman was the first academic teacher in the field in Stockholm and, as an additional merit, could soon list an elementary textbook which was the outcome of his teaching (Westman 1885).

In the early phase of Westman's secretarial period, his formal duties were reduced and became more specific. Some of these changes had a bearing on the operational working tasks of the board but also had implications for the wider objectives of the Association.

The most important change was the ending of the arrangement with the *Stockholms Dagblad*. From 1882 onwards the Association took upon itself the task of publishing its proceedings, which naturally entailed increased work for the board. Thus it was informally decided to increase the editorial committee from two to four members, in addition to the Secretary. It was soon discovered that a group of five involved a greater amount of organisational work than a group of three, and perhaps the Secretary also felt that too much of the increased burden had now fallen on himself. The board attended to this matter in early 1884 and a regulation was set up stating that each member of the editorial committee should be responsible for arranging one meeting. This would ensure an annual round of five meetings in addition to easing the task of the Secretary, who could now concentrate on publication of the proceedings.

This regulation had important consequences for the Association's scope of activities. In the discussion regarding the assignment of work duties among the different members of the editorial committee, there was notably only a concern with the task of 'procurement' for the meetings. The other tasks of the committee fixed in the by-laws were apparently ignored. Thus the possibility that the Association might be in charge of publishing a journal akin to the Danish *Nationaløkonomisk Tidskrift* had been deleted from the programme. Consequently, any residual ambitions to promote the science of political economy as an end in itself had now been abandoned.

3.2.3 Hugo Hamilton (1891–6)

The next Secretary was Hugo Hamilton. Little need be said about how he performed his secretarial tasks except to note that the meetings and the proceedings during his period were well maintained. Hamilton was himself quite active as a speaker. As he had been a member of the Association since 1881 he should also be viewed as a link with the past.

Hamilton's credentials as an economist for the secretarial post were less strong than Westman's. His formal background in economics was limited to exposure to that field in the basic law degree and, unlike Westman, he was not in a position to cultivate more deeply any attachment he might have to economics as a theoretical pursuit. Therefore one surmises that Hamilton had earned the secretarial post by participating in the anti-tariff campaign in the late 1880s and through his free-trade stance as a secretary to the tariff commission at the time. He was presumably an ideologically reliable person in the eyes of the old inner circle as they prepared for the transfer of power to a new generation of leaders. This may have been of some importance since the key chairperson on the board, Richard Åkerman, as previously noted, was a protectionist.

3.2.4 Marcus Wallenberg (1897–8)

Marcus Wallenberg was still a fairly young man, yet he was very likely already the incumbent for the position he later held, together with his brother Knut Wallenberg, as the leader of the economic interests of the Wallenberg family and the family enterprise the Stockholms Enskilda Bank.

Wallenberg had once studied economics for D. Davidson at Uppsala University as part of the requirements for the *jur kand*. However, unlike most students, who took economics as one of the subjects in that degree, Wallenberg appears to have earned some additional credit points for Davidson. This probably laid the groundwork for a lasting relationship between them (Gårdlund 1976). In late February 1898 Davidson was invited to lecture on the central banking reform that had just been accepted by parliament (Davidson 1898). Among the discussants on that occasion was Wicksell. Wallenberg was not an admirer of Wicksell, but Wicksell's appearance may have aroused his desire to acquire greater knowledge of the study Wicksell had just completed (Wicksell 1898b). Thus Wicksell was invited to be the next lecturer and made the renowned delivery mentioned previously.

Wallenberg's resourceful personality is the key to understanding why his period as Secretary, although brief, was important as the final act in the Association's transition in the 1890s. The fact that he agreed to take on the duties of Secretary also proves how important he considered that post to be. While the 1890s was a preparation for the breakthrough in the academic institutionalisation of economics in Sweden, Wallenberg's secretarial period may also, at least in retrospect, be seen as marking the beginning of a new era in the history of the Association, during which its relationships with academic economists would undergo substantial modification.

4 Economic policy debates and involvement

The following sections offer some brief highlights of the major economic policy themes discussed at the meetings of the association.

4.1 *Trade and tariff policies*

The tariff debates naturally hold a special place of interest in the account of an Association that had been proposed as a free-trade society. As the crisis of 1878–9 again generated calls for tariff protection, the Association was very much the focus of protectionist aversions. To protectionists it represented the nerve centre for the free-trade cause, especially as Arnberg, as a leading member of its board, was appointed to head a parliament committee to investigate protectionist demands. Set up in 1880, this committee produced a rather dismissive report in 1881, which was discussed in the Association. This report and the discussion did little to quench protectionist attacks against the free-trade order. On the contrary, the foes of free trade received additional impetus through the establishment of an organisation named Svenska Arbetets Vänner (The Friends of Swedish Labour). In the summer of 1881 the protectionists staged a *coup d'état* at the Nordic Economic Meeting in Malmö, which seems to have been a blow directed specifically at the Association. The Association was not officially a sponsor of the meeting but its helmsmen served on the committee issuing the invitations; furthermore, its President Björnstjerna and Secretary-to-be Westman presided over the opening sessions during the first day of the meeting. However, the protectionists succeeded in ousting Björnstjerna from the presidency and replaced him with a man from their own camp (Westman 1882).

Having been taken by surprise at the Nordic Meeting, Waern, Westman and others on the board of the Association thereafter kept a more watchful eye on protectionist developments. However, an open battle did not fully break out until the spring of 1885, when the protectionists renewed their efforts and won public support due to the sustained depression. While not officially engaging the Association itself, in 1885 members of the inner circle on the board countered the protectionist advance by organising a society named Föreningen emot Livsmedelstullar (Society Against Food Tariffs), with the *Stockholms Dagblad* as a staff centre. Despite having stepped back as the publication agency for the proceedings of the Association, this daily still retained a strong tie with the society. Its editor C.O. Montan served for three years (1885–7) on the board of the Association as a member of the editorial committee.

The Föreningen emot Livsmedelstullar became the centre of a campaign that quickly emerged as a widely supported, almost populist, movement. The campaign was waged with a well-developed nationwide organisation to support free-trade candidates in the up-coming parliament elections. It was successful, but in the end it proved to have been of no avail.

There were two steps in the election. The first occurred in spring 1887. At this time the free-traders held the bastions. Their devotion to the cause of free trade was in some cases highly charged. A story has often been told about the heroism of F.F. Carlson, previously noted as a Vice-president of the first board of the Association in 1877. While fatally indisposed due to infirmities of old age, he had himself carried to his bench in the parliament on the day of the casting of the ballots to ensure victory for the free-trader side was his terminal political act before he died.

The free-traders also attained the sought-for majority in the next election in the fall of 1888, although by a narrow margin. But they failed in the last and most crucial battle. It was discovered that one member in the free-trader group, 'ångköks Olle' (Steam-kitchen Olle), on the Stockholm bench in the parliament, had not paid his taxes. As a consequence, the whole bench had to give up their seats and were replaced by protectionists. This shifted the majority vote in the parliament over to the protectionists, who were thus able to see their grain tariff bill accepted.

Once introduced, tariffs had come to stay. In the early 1890s further tariffs followed on industrial imports and were soon imposed on almost all products. Although the defeat on the tariff issue was a shattering blow for the leading members of the Association – and especially for the inner circle on the board – the Association itself was not affected to the same extent. There was, as previously noted, a change in the composition of the board in the 1890s as protectionists gained representation, but since the free-trade interest had a strong hold over the secretarial post, the liberal stance on the board was only slowly yielding to senescence. It would not be correct to say that the Association was captured by the protectionists and shifted from a liberal to a conservative regime. The important change in the Association – on the board as well as in its body of members – was rather that private businessmen now began to play a larger role. Corporate interest as opposed to bureaucratic interest was at this time beginning to make itself felt more strongly.

4.2 Issues of social policy and constitutional reform

As previously noted, taxation reform was a continuously vexing question in the parliament throughout the period under review and was therefore also a frequent topic at meetings of the Association. The blockage created by the so-called 'compromise' in the 1870s regarding the tax base and the defence reform was extended to issues of social policy. Social reform questions did not become prime issues until the 1890s, when the stalemate related to the 'compromise' began to ease.

Thus social policy was not a topic that prompted much debate before the end of the 1880s. There were several social policy lectures in the Association pertaining to reports of various government committees. However, these lectures were generally presented by outsiders to the Association. They were listened to with respect and attention but provoked no responses from the audience. Only in late 1888, when a work accident insurance proposal was presented, was there a thorough debate which continued into the next meeting in early 1889. This time sharp criticisms came above all from Arnberg, but also from Forsell and Palme, all members of the inner circle, against a proposal that was inspired by Bismarckian precepts.

Continued government social policy proposals were discussed in the Association in spring 1890. This time an old age insurance scheme was presented for review by C.G. Hammarskjöld. He had in 1890 once again become a member of the board, now as Vice-president, which may indicate that social insurance had now become one of the prime issues on the discussion agenda in the Association. Hammarskjöld advocated a decidedly *laissez-faire* solution. In the discussion, Arnberg, among others, was again a discussant, but his comments were this time offered with much less rancour than the criticism he had advanced two years earlier.

In the 1890s social policy issues were discussed in the Association with much more fervour and alertness than previously. It was on such a theme that Wicksell made his first appearance and attracted attention in the Association as a discussant. In December 1891 he was the sole commentator on a lecture presenting the German homestead law proposal (Wicksell 1891).

What seems to have sparked the turnaround in the nationwide debates on social policy was, more than anything else, the tariff controversy. Concerns about indebtedness, unemployment, emigration and other types of social evils related to the depression had, already by the early 1980s, alerted both free-traders and protectionists to issues of social policy reforms, but such issues did not receive centre-stage attention until after the tariff issue had been settled in 1888. The significance of the defeat of the free-traders was that it opened up new economic policy fronts, while questions of trade policy issues retreated from prominence.

This shift in the Swedish economic policy debate was also reflected in the discussions at the meetings of the Association. Here, as noted, economic liberalism generally remained strong on such broader fronts, but its defiant tones were moderated. The free-traders had in the tariff debate generally been forced to renounce their Manchesterian positions on social policy and had recognised the need for complementary private and social insurance programmes. Through this retreat they were successful in gaining the upper hand over those on the protectionist side who favoured Bismarckian centralised and comprehensive social welfare programmes financed by the state.

Furthermore, during the 1890s there was increasing pressure for suffrage reform, which in general tended to make economic policy issues secondary in importance to the demands for constitutional reform. In this respect the economic policy upheaval related to the introduction of tariffs took on dimensions that have made Swedish historians view it as the first serious stirrings of the later democratic movement (Sundberg 1961). Even these dimensions of the economic policy discourse received due attention in the discussions at the meetings of the association.

One should note, however, that social policy issues were not debated in the Association as frequently as, for example, capital market issues. It would appear that when called upon to act as speakers and discussants, members of the Association felt more comfortable with the latter type of topics. Since they belonged to the wealthy sector of the population, they were not only first hand experts but also, in such cases, involving themselves directly with issues that were more within their private domains of interest.

4.3 Banking and monetary reform

Persistent, and leading at times to quite heated debates, were the policy concerns in the Association referring to the changes in the money and banking sector. This chapter has already touched on how inflamed such issues could be in the period before the advent of the Association. As the previous accounts of Waern and Palme revealed, there was forceful opposition from Wallenberg. Even after the start of the Association, his voice remained influential in opposing the official economic policies on banking and money matters.

The central issue now concerned the aspirations and attempts of the Riksbank to perform the role of a modern central bank. After alignment with the gold standard and the setting up of the Scandinavian currency union in the 1870s, the Riksbank launched a policy of centralising the note issue in an effort to gain a more direct control over the money supply as a necessary prerequisite for more active policy involvement. Wallenberg, who had been brought up with the ideals of free banking along Scottish lines, was rather flatly overruled by his opponents who derived their reform ideas from the English Bank Charter Act of 1844.

Much of this debate with Wallenberg took place at meetings of the Association and involved not only Waern and Palme but also the two other members of the inner circle, Forsell and Arnberg.

Forsell was probably the man in the inner circle of the Association towards whom Wallenberg developed his strongest antipathies. Much of this should perhaps be attributed to Forsell's habit, when participating in political debate, to display a genuinely personal trait of rational probity, which made his incisive intellect somewhat sharp-tongued. In debates he therefore often antagonised his opponents. But there were also divergences due to real issues. Some of these went back quite far in time, while others were of more recent origin. Among the latter one may note the conflict that emerged in the 1878 crisis when Forsell, at the time Minister of Finance, refused to assist Wallenberg and the Stockholms Enskilda Bank after the collapse of the railroad boom (Nilsson 1994).

Forsell held the post as Minister of Finance until 1880. However this did not mean the end of his antagonism with Wallenberg. Forsell continued, in various contexts, but especially in the Association, to hold and preach views that were offensive to Wallenberg. This eventually resulted in somewhat of a personal showdown between them in 1885, shortly before the death of Wallenberg. Forsell, who in the Association defended the proposal to reform the Riksbank into a central bank, apparently retorted to criticism from

Wallenberg in a derogatory manner, which seems to have stirred even the audience (Åmark 1927).

Arnberg's involvement in the controversy with Wallenberg was not as defamatory as Forsell's, but the issues of substance were in fact more pointed. Arnberg emerged not only as the leader of the Riksbank, but also as having been the person who prior to his appointment had designed the policy line the bank endeavoured to follow. Arnberg had contributed the main ideas in the committee which, as early as 1881–3, prepared for the modernisation of the Riksbank. Arnberg's report had been a bitter blow for Wallenberg (Nilsson 1994).

After the demise of Wallenberg, monetary issues were for a while a lesser matter of concern in the Association. They returned with a vengeance in the 1890s as the preparatory committee for centralising the note issue eventually emerged with a proposal ready for a vote in parliament. This bill had just been passed at the time when, in 1898, Davidson and Wicksell offered their lectures (Davidson 1898; Wicksell 1898a).

5   The connection with economics as an academic discipline

As previously noted, the objectives of the Association entailed an appeal to political economy as a science, but it seems clear that there were no intentions to promote economics for its own sake. However, it is still of some interest to focus at least briefly on the development of relations with academic economists within the Association.

There was seemingly a promising beginning. At the first ordinary meeting on 12th March 1877, when the first board was elected, a lecture was given by the secretary Palme on the 'chair socialists'. However, lectures of this type were to be very scarce events in the coming years. No further lectures in this vein were given until 1883 when the death of Marx occasioned a lecture given by Johan Leffler (1883), who two years later would devote renewed attention to the chair socialists (Leffler 1885). But notably, as had been the case with Palme's lecture in 1877, none of Leffler's lectures provoked discussion.

The records suggest that lectures on broad intellectual themes did not awaken great interest at the meetings of the Association. Only a lecture, again given by Leffler (1892), dealing with 'Poverty and Progress' raised some discussion. But it should be noted that one reason why the audience was alert at that time was that Wicksell was present and, as was his habit, stood up as a discussant and declared his views on the matter (Wicksell 1892).

What is perhaps most striking as regards this paucity of theoretical topics is that so little attention was paid even to classical political economy. As this body of thought was increasingly being challenged, at least indirectly, in the economic policy controversies that sustained the Association, one might have expected some cursory exposition of the advances and revisions of classical economics, as presented, for example, in the works of J.S. Mill. However, only in the very first years, evidently thanks to Palme, were there occasional explanations of basic principles involving criticism of the theoretical arguments for tariff protection.

By virtue of its inner circle, the board of the Association included some of the best economic brains in Sweden, with much theoretical sense and balance in polemics. Although lacking professional academic credentials in the modern sense, Palme was a profound empirical synthesiser and Waern was a prudent economic policy scrutiniser. Arnberg and Forsell, who were both of proven academic excellence as economic historians, were also sharp analysts of current events. But none of these men explored economic theory in the formal systematic way that was the mark of academic teachers.

However, the Association sought from the start to maintain such an academic connection by enlisting professional representatives of economics on the board. C.G. Hammarskjöld was mentioned above as having provided that connection in the first five-year period, but thereafter until the 1890s the most prominent representative on this score was no doubt Leffler.

Johan Leffler had obtained a doctoral degree in economics at the University of Leipzig in 1876, where he had studied under Roscher. His dissertation dealt with the Swedish note issuing banks (Leffler 1876). Because of his German study background Leffler has generally been classified as a member of the Historical School. However, this label is somewhat problematic as he appears to have incorporated ideas from the Austrian School as well and should therefore best be characterised as an eclectic.

This eclecticism is what made Leffler particularly important in his day. As the present chapter has endeavoured to clarify, in Sweden before the turn of the century there were only a few scholars who tried to keep abreast of developments in economics abroad. Leffler, however, devoted considerable energy to the study of new approaches to economics and spread his knowledge through writings and teachings to a rather broad group of readers and students (Henriksson 1986). He had in 1878–81 made himself known in Gothenburg as a knowledgeable lecturer in political economy and at the conclusion of his Gothenburg lectures he published an elementary introductory survey text to the field (Leffler 1881).

However, Leffler's major contribution as a teacher was delivered in Stockholm, where he should be recognised as the first lecturer on the subject at Stockholm University. Here he taught, with some interruptions, for long periods from 1889 onwards until Cassel entered the scene in 1902. Although Westman, in view of his position as lecturer at the Royal Institute of Technology, is to be recorded as the first academic lecturer in Stockholm, it should be added that Leffler succeeded Westman at that college in the 1890s. Thus Leffler was in fact in charge of all academic teaching of economics in Stockholm during the 1890s.

But an assessment of Leffler should not be confined to the teaching side of his achievements. He must in addition be recognised as an empirical researcher (Leffler 1896). He also performed a significant role in what might be called the extramural antecedents to the academic institutionalisation of economics in Sweden. Leffler was throughout his life the secretary of the Lorén foundation. This was before the turn of the century the only Swedish agency that financed travel and study abroad, making it possible for, among others, Wicksell and Cassel to enter careers as professional economists (Wisselgren 1994).

Leffler also made important contributions on the applied or practical side of economics. Here his most notable achievement was as a member of a government committee exploring the needs and possibilities for setting up a postal savings bank. Less successful, but still interesting, was his attempt, after studying its precepts in France, to set up a workers' cooperative savings bank, for which he also served as Director until it went bankrupt. He was in addition, for a period of time, a member of parliament. As his crowning performance he was finally, from the beginning of the 1890s, Secretary of the Swedish Insurance Association and served as the editor of its periodical.

Leffler had appeared as a discussant in the Association as early as 1877. In addition to his frequent participation in the meetings as a speaker, which began in 1881 and continued until 1896, his most important contribution to the Association was his service on the board. He was a member of the editorial committee from 1882 until 1890. Although defying easy classification as a representative of the Historical School, Leffler made no attempt to hide his sympathies with this new line of economics. Thus the presence of Leffler on the board to some extent proves the strength of the neutrality line adopted by the Association. However, crucial to Leffler's good standing on the board was the fact that he supported a number of *laissez-faire* points on the economic policy agenda. Most important was that he stood on the side of the inner circle and participated actively in the campaign against tariffs both in parliament and in the Föreningen emot Livsmedelstullar.

Before he left the board of the Association in 1890 Leffler had even served as its Vice-president (1887). As a member of the board Leffler was very valuable to the Association on account not only of his intellectual versatility but also because of his multifarious exposure to economic life. He was particularly important as a member on the editorial committee, where he perhaps regarded the obligation to select a speaker of his own choice every year more as a right than a mere duty. It is possibly thanks to Leffler that so many of the meetings in the 1880s were devoted to social policy issues.

Leffler left the board in 1891 at a time when Westman also departed from the scene. As the Association did not fill the economics slots that now fell vacant, throughout the 1890s it lacked the direct tie with the discipline of economics that consisted of having an academically active economist on its board. This gap was only marginally compensated for at the meetings, where Leffler continued to lecture occasionally until 1896 and where Wicksell was also reported as a discussant. Thus the scientific authority of the Association had declined notably by the time Davidson and Wicksell held their lectures in 1898. Although Wicksell and Davidson even engaged in a mutual exchange of views, which may be recorded as the first discussion in the Association between two professionals, this was the harbinger of an era that was still to come. The old type of formal alignment with economics was not resumed until in 1906 when Davidson became a member of the board. Professional economists did not become regular participants at the meetings until World War I.

Thus the Association seems in no way to have been part of the process that led to the academic institutionalisation of economics in Sweden at the turn of the century. The central developments in this breakthrough occurred in the academic sphere. A key event was the setting up of *Ekonomisk Tidskrift* in 1899, Sweden's professional journal in economics. This was an undertaking by Davidson at the University of Uppsala. During those years Davidson was also important in helping Wicksell to be appointed to a teaching chair at the University of Lund in face of strong clerical opposition. Another important event was the establishment of the Socialvetenskapliga Institutet (Institute of Social Science) in Stockholm in 1903 by Gustav Cassel. Furthermore, during that same period the teaching of academic economics also began at the University of Gothenburg. In none of these developments did the Swedish Economic Association play a part.

How unrelated the Association was to developments within economics at the time is well illustrated by the reception it accorded the lecture delivered by Wicksell. That lecture was reportedly very well presented and Wicksell was entertaining, as usual. Yet this presentation to an audience usually prone to keen debate on banking and monetary issues was met with complete silence.

6 Conclusion

It seems clear that before the end of the nineteenth century the Association was quite successful in defending its prime objective of serving only as a forum for debates and information. This meant that, at least formally, it maintained a political neutrality stance and did not play a part in the official economic policy making of the country. As regards its subsidiary ambition to maintain a connection with academic economists, its formal achievement must be seen as somewhat less satisfactory and its real contact with scientific developments must be judged negligible. While in the early years the Association succeeded in retaining academic representatives of economics on the board, no such representation was attained in the 1990s.

The weak, and ultimately weakened, connection of the Association with academic economics may be seen to some extent as a consequence of its success as a forum for economic policy debate. However, it basically reflects the fact that economics in Sweden before the turn of the century lacked an independent institutional base from which the Association could draw. Economics was formally represented at Sweden's two universities, in Uppsala and Lund, only in the faculties of law, where it was taught in combination with fiscal and sundry cameral and administrative subjects. As economic ideas and teachings slowly emerged outside the faculties of law in subjects like political science, economics was still not formally recognised as a field in which examinations could be taken and grades could be obtained: one should note that students who attended Leffler's lectures were not pursuing academic degree work. There were early proposals for the establishment of more independent chairs in economics in Gothenburg and Stockholm but no steps were taken to carry out these plans until after the turn of the century (Henriksson 1986).

In this context one may note that the Association was strikingly passive in the period under review. It appears as if, in consequence of the neutrality stance in economic policy, the Association had also assumed a political non-involvement posture in what might be called science policy. Such a non-involvement stance precluded active attempts to promote the institutionalisation of economics. The universities of Lund and even Uppsala were probably beyond the reach of the association and perhaps also Gothenburg, but in the case of Stockholm an opportunity seems to have been lost. Here funds had become available for a chair in economics through a donation in 1877 and additional donations in support of academic teaching in Stockholm had been made later (Henriksson 1986). If the Association had so desired, the influential members of its board, among whom some were also members of the city board of Stockholm, could have exerted influence on the establishment of university teaching of economics in Stockholm leading to some kind of academic degree. But they failed to do so. The Association never took too seriously its own statutory task 'to promote the study of political economy'.

However, the Association should perhaps be credited rather than faulted for not promoting the setting up of a chair in economics in Stockholm. It is quite likely that the holder would have been some member of the Historical School and that such a solution would have pre-empted the opportunity of later appointing Cassel to the chair and would thus also have prevented the important establishment of the Social Science Institute.

In emphasising the main role of the Association as a forum of discussion it should finally be underscored that the very success in this endeavour, which formally deterred the Association from attempting to influence economic policy making directly, may in fact have been a more effective manner of exerting economic policy influence. The neutrality position meant that the Association exerted an indirect effect not only by opening up economic policy debate to public opinion and making it accessible to a wider group of concerned participants, but also by making it more enlightened by appealing to the authority of economics.

Notes

1 This is the name under which the Association presents itself in English today. Its name in Swedish is Nationalekonomiska Föreningen (literally: The Economic Society).

2 The literature on the history of the Association is scanty. The basic account is still the *festschrift* that appeared at the half-centennial (Nationalekonomiska Föreningen 1927), where the overview by Åmark is the central contribution. A later important anniversary survey was given by Heckscher (1953). The more recent contributions in Henriksson (1986, 1991a, 1991b) and Magnusson (1993) are mainly assessments and commentaries based on these early writings. Interesting highlights on some features of the early history of the Association are offered in Nilsson (1994). The present account, which should be viewed as a report on research in progress, builds mainly on the published proceedings of the Association (*Nationalekonomiska Föreningens Förhandlingar* 1878–1952). However, much information has been added from a large number of secondary sources as well as from research in the archival remains of the Association. A full documentation of sources as well as of the extensive list of secondary references will be provided in Henriksson (in progress).

3 Waern's life and contributions have not been the subject of extensive historical research. The information given here builds on research that started from the brief presentation provided in Fryxell (1927). A more detailed overview of his writings and economic policy views will be available in Henriksson (in progress).

4 Much of the many fascinating details of the story related in this chapter concerning the relationship between the Association and Wallenberg have been obtained from Nilsson (1994). Unfortunately he touches only marginally on the history of the Association, but nevertheless offers an excellent frame for further research on its early years.

References

Primary sources

Arnberg, W. (1855) *Om författningarna för svenska handelns upphjälpande under Gustaf II Adolphs regering*, Uppsala: C.A. Leffler.

—— (1864) *Om arbetets och bytets frihet*, Stockholm: P.A. Norstedt.

—— (1868) *Anteckningar om frihetstidens politiska ekonomi*, Uppsala: W. Schultz förlag.

Bergstrand, W. (1877) 'Politisk ekonomi', *Framtiden Ny följd* 1: 248–63.

Davidson, D. (1898) 'Bankreformen och näringslivet', *Nationalekonomiska Föreningens Förhandlingar* 21: 24–37, 43–6.

Forsell, H. (1866) *Bidrag till historien om Sveriges förvaltning under Gustaf den förste*, Stockholm: Josef Seligman.

—— (1875–88) *Studier och kritiker*, 2 vols, Stockholm: P.A. Norstedt & Söner.

—— (1884) *Anteckningar om Sveriges jordbruksnäring i 16e seklet*, Stockholm: P.A. Norstedt & Söner.

Leffler, J.A. (1876) *Die schwedishchen Zettelbanken*, Ph.D. dissertation, Leipzig: C.W. Vollrath.

—— (1881) *Grundlinjer till nationalekonomiken*, Stockholm: P.A. Norstedt & Söner.

—— (1883) 'Om Karl Marx', *Nationalekonomiska Föreningens Förhandlingar* 6: 67–79.

198 Henriksson

—— (1885) 'Katedersocialismen', *Nationalekonomiska Föreningens Förhandlingar* 8: 138–52.

—— (1892) 'Fattigdom och framåtskridande', *Nationalekonomiska Föreningens Förhandlingar* 15: 85–109.

—— (1896) 'De industriella arbeterskornas levnads– och löneförhållanden i Stockholm', *Nationalekonomiska Föreningens Förhandlingar* 19: 1–74.

Nationalekonomiska Föreningens Förhandlingar, 1878–1952.

Nationaløkonomisk Forening (1897) *Nationaløkonomisk Forenings festskrift 1897 I anledning av foreningens femogtyve–aarige bestaaen*, Kjøbenhavn: Det Nordiske Forlag Bogforlaget Ernst Bojesen.

Palme, J.H. (1895) *De hårda tiderna*, Stockholm: Iduns Tryckeriaktiebolag.

Westman, C. (ed.) (1882) *Förhandlingar vid det fjärde skandinaviska nationalekonomiska Mötet i Malmö 1881 utgivna av mötets sekreterare*, Stockholm: P.A. Norstedt & Söner.

—— (1885) *Nationalekonomins grunddrag*, Stockholm: Ivar Häggströms boktryckeri.

Wicksell, K. (1891) 'Anförande', *Nationalekonomiska Föreningens Förhandlingar* 14: 140–2.

—— (1892) 'Anförande', *Nationalekonomiska Föreningens Förhandlingar* 15: 99–100.

—— (1898a) 'Penningräntans inflytande på varuprisen', *Nationalekonomiska Föreningens Förhandlingar* 21: 47–70.

—— (1898b) *Geldzins und Güterpreise*, Jena: Gustav Fischers Verlag; English edition: *Interest and Prices*, London: Macmillan, 1936.

Secondary sources

Åmark, K. (1927) 'Nationalekonomiska föreningen 1877–1927', in Nationalekonomiska Föreningen 1927.

Fryxell, K.A. (1927) 'Carl Fredrik Waern d.y.', in Nationalekonomiska Föreningen 1927.

Gårdlund, T. (1976) *Marcus Wallenberg 1864–1943. Hans liv och gärning*, Stockholm: P.A. Norstedt & Söner.

Heckscher, E.F. (1927) 'Hans Forsell', in Nationalekonomiska Föreningen 1927.

—— (1953) 'A Survey of Economic Thought in Sweden 1875–1950', *Scandinavian Economic History Review* 1: 105–25.

Henriksson, R.G.H. (1986) *The Prehistory and History of the Institutional Breakthrough of Modern Economics in Sweden 1877–1917*, unpublished paper presented to the Kolloquium in Lüneburg 24–7 February 1986 on 'Die Institutionalisierung der Nationalökonomie and den Deutschen Universitäten'.

—— (1991a) 'Eli F. Heckscher: The Economic Historian as Economist', in B. Sandelin (ed.) *The History of Swedish Economic Thought*, London: Routledge.

—— (1991b) 'The Political Economy Club and the Stockholm School 1917–1951', in L. Jonung (ed.) *The Stockholm School of Economics Revisited*, Cambridge: Cambridge University Press.

—— (in progress) *Highlights on the History of the Swedish Economic Association*.

Leijonhufvud, A. (1997) 'The Wicksellian Heritage', *Economic Notes* 26, 1: 1–10.

Magnusson, L. (1993) 'The Economist as Popularizer: The Emergence of Swedish Economics 1900–1930', in L. Jonung (ed.) *Swedish Economic Thought Explorations and Advances*, London: Routledge.

Montgomery, A. (1921a) *Svensk Traktatpolitik 1816–1914*, Stockholm: Isaac Marcus Boktrykeriaktiebolag.

—— (1921b) *Svensk Tullpolitik 1816–1911*, Stockholm: Isaac Marcus Boktryckeriaktiebolag.

Nationalekonomiska Föreningen (1927) *Nationalekonomiska Föreningen 1877–1927 Minneskrift*, Stockholm: P.A. Norstedt & Söner.

Nilsson, G.B. (1994) *André Oscar Wallenberg III Ett namn att försvara 1866–1886*, Stockholm: Norstedts.

Palme, J.H. (1927) 'Minnen från Nationalekonomiska Föreningens tillkomst och tidigare verksamhetsår', in Nationalekonomiska Föreningen 1927.

Sundberg, P. (1961) *Ministärerna Bildt och Åkerhielm En studie i den svenska parlamentarismens förgårdar*, Stockholm: Christofers Bokförlag.

Thermaenius, E. (1928) *Lantmannapartiet Dess uppkomst, organisation och tidigare utveckling*, Uppsala: Almqvist & Wiksells Boktryckeri AB.

Wisselgren, P. (1994) *Lorénska stiftelsen och den sociala frågan*, umpublished discussion paper, Institutionen för idéhistoria, Umeå Universitet.

11 Orchestrating economic ideas: the formation and development of economic societies in modern Japan

Jiro Kumagai

At the beginning of the twentieth century, economic thought as epitomised by the German school seemed to occupy a predominant position in the teaching of political economy in Japan. This is clearly revealed in a significant comment made in 1901 by Ukichi Taguchi, a stern liberal and espouser of the *laissez-faire* of the Manchester School, who expressed his discontent that professors of almost all Japanese universities were teaching ideas from the German Historical and social policy schools (Taguchi 1927–8: 13, 402–6). Taguchi was the founder of the *Tokyo Keizai Zasshi* (Tokyo Economist) as well as the Tokyo Keizaigaku Kyokai (Tokyo Political Economy Club) (1887–1923). The former was an economic journal (first issued in January 1879, discontinued in 1923) that aspired to be a match for *The Economist* of London, while the latter was a sort of non-governmental academic society whose purpose was the diffusion and progress of political economy from the viewpoint of the British liberal school.[1] As this achievement of Taguchi's career highlighted, his displeasure with the contemporary economic education undoubtedly derived from his pro-British stance.

Yet just a decade prior to Taguchi's criticism of the German school, the situation of economic education in Japan appeared to be quite the opposite of his assessment. In fact, Noburu Kanai, a professor of Tokyo Imperial University and a strong authority within the Japanese social policy school, had in 1891 deplored the prevalence of British economic thought in Japanese academic circles. According to Kanai, quite a few Japanese economic scholars still worshipped the old schools of J.S. Mill, Henry Fawcett and Henry Dunning Macleod as if their principles were golden rules. Even some scholars who advocated German political economy were satisfied with their dependence on the English translations of Wilhelm Roscher's writings. But the old school had been uprooted in Germany half a century before, and a wide range of pioneering social studies had been making remarkable progress there. Even in conservative Britain, contended Kanai, the old school was undoubtedly at a low ebb. Kanai thus concluded that British liberal political economy was behind the times and that its admirers were like country girls who boasted hairstyles that were in vogue a few years ago in Tokyo but long since out of fashion there now.

Kanai further surveyed the current situation of political economy in Britain, the United States, France, Germany and Austria, and declared that Japan should adopt the latest political economy of Germany, i.e. 'chair socialism', which stood between the *laissez-faire* school of German free-traders and the radicalism of the German Social Democrat Party (Kawai 1939: 424–37).

The contrasting assessments of Taguchi and Kanai, albeit extreme in their stances, regarding the prevailing political economy in Japan towards the turn of the century was symbolic of the transformation of ideas Japan would undergo, from pro-British to pro-German. Behind this transformation, needless to say, lay a momentous constitutional and political choice, in which Japan decided to adopt the Prussian model for modernisation instead of the British type. On this score some mention of the constitutional and political problems constitutes a pre-requisite for subsequent discussion of the formation and development of economic societies in late nineteenth-century Japan.

1 Political crisis of Meiji 14

By the time Taguchi launched the Tokyo Keizaigaku Koshukai (Tokyo Political Economy Lecture Society),[2] a publishing project consisting of the translation of British texts on political economy,[3] pro-German ideas had begun to penetrate various spheres with what was called the political crisis of Meiji 14 (viz. 1881). This crisis was sparked by political conflict regarding the Japanese constitution, and involved a clash between pro-German statesmen as represented by Hirobumi Ito, and pro-British statesmen represented by Shigenobu Okuma. In the wake of this conflict, Japan's model of modernisation shifted from a British and French perspective to a German orientation.

It was Kowashi Inoue who assumed a pivotal role behind the scenes of this political struggle. Inoue was an acute and vigorous government councillor with the belief that only Prussia among the European nations was close to Japan by virtue of its social and political conditions. Inoue believed that the Emperor should hold the reins of government outright, as seen in the Prussian constitution. Writing to Ito in July 1881, Inoue insisted that petitioners who were calling for the opening of the Diet drew their inspiration from the pro-British constitutional draft prepared by Yukichi Fukuzawa and the Kojunsha (literally: Mutual Friendship Club, est. 1880 by Fukuzawa). In the background of this popular movement, argued Inoue, lay a revolutionary spirit that had begun to take shape in Japan as a result of the reception of British and French ideas. To cope with this torrent of ideas and movements, continued Inoue, we must ardently introduce two different studies, viz. Chinese classics to encourage loyalty and allegiance and German studies to foster conservative ideals in the minds of the people. Inoue further added that children from the ex-*samurai* stratum should not enter Fukuzawa's Keio Gijuku School (est. 1868, from which the Keio Gijuku University developed) (Okubo 1957: 82–3).

Inoue's criticism was levelled not only at Fukuzawa and the Kojunsha but also at Okuma, who was one of the central figures of the government at the time as well as a close political friend of Fukuzawa. Okuma had already submitted his constitutional draft to Tomomi Iwakura, the Chief Councillor of the government. Okuma's draft was more conservative than the Kojunsha's, but from the pro-German statesmen's point of view they were in essence the same.

The political conflict surrounding the constitution took a sudden turn with the exposure of what was referred to as 'the problem of the disposal of the government-owned property in Hokkaido' in the summer of 1881. This disposal problem marked an overture to the political upheaval known as the political crisis of 1881.

Since 1869 the Hokkaido Bureau of Development had invested massive financial resources in Hokkaido, constructing government-owned facilities to help promote and develop industries there. Harbours, shipyards and facilities for the encouragement of industries, amongst others, were constructed under the project. However in 1881 the Hokkaido Bureau of Development decided to sell off these facilities at an unbelievably low price to a business magnate who had close relations with the government. The disclosure of this decision provoked a nationwide outcry against the government and eventually gave momentum to the movement for freedom and peoples' rights that clamoured for the opening of the Diet.

The government councillors, who smelled the threat of the political alignment between Okuma and Fukuzawa behind this odious movement, unanimously decided at a crucial meeting to oust Okuma from the government. They also passed the proclamation of cancellation of the disposal of governmental property in Hokkaido. Okuma, a member of the government councillors, was absent from this decisive meeting as he was on his way to the Tohoku district in order to attend the Emperor's visit there. Thus Okuma was expelled from office, so to speak, by a default judgement. Bureaucrats of the Okuma faction were thereupon obliged to submit resignation letters and key figures of Fukuzawa's faction, such as Fumio Yano, a chief drafter of the Kojunsha's constitution and one of Okuma's most intellectual supporters, Tsuyoshi Inukai (referred to below), and others were purged.

Ito, who emerged victorious from this political strife, wisely contended that there would be no other way to calm the political upheaval than by proclaiming the governmental principle of the constitution and the opening schedule of the Diet. Following a heated discussion the councillors' meeting accepted Ito's proposition and, subsequently, the imperial edict was proclaimed on 12th October 1881 announcing that the Diet would open in 1890.

Ito undertook a study tour from 1882 to 1883 in preparation for drawing up the draft of the constitution. Whilst on his tour Ito met Rudolph Gneist, A. Mosse and Lorenz von Stein in Berlin and Vienna. Ito and his colleagues believed that Stein would be ideal as their legal advisor, but Stein declined their offer on the grounds of his age. On Stein's recommendation, the government invited Hermann Roesler to serve as legal advisor on constitutional and commercial laws. Roesler cooperated with Inoue in working out the draft of the imperial constitution, and the Great Japanese Imperial Constitution was promulgated in 1889.

2 The emergence of German studies: the Society for German Studies

Inoue naturally thought that it was crucial for a firm establishment of the Meiji constitutional order to disseminate German ideas among the people. For this purpose in 1881, just before the above-mentioned imperial edict was proclaimed, with the support of influential statesmen and bureaucrats, he established the Doitsugaku Kyokai (Society for German Studies).

As the Doitsugaku Kyokai was set up against this background of political conflict, it served as a kind of test of allegiance and of political position. In fact, prominent intellectuals who had links with the Kojunsha, such as Amane Nishi, a distinguished proponent of Japanese enlightenment, Kei Hara, later Prime Minister, and other distinguished persons, changed ranks and joined the Society for German Studies (Yamamuro 1984: 293–4). The Society was crowned with honorary members comparable to a galaxy of dignitaries: Hirobumi Ito, Aritomo Yamagata, a powerful figure in the army and later Prime Minister, Masayoshi Matsukata, a prominent financier and later Prime Minister, Koki Watanabe, President of Tokyo Imperial University, Hermann Roesler, Paul Mayet and Karl Rathgen, who later assumed the lectureship of state law and statistics at Tokyo Imperial University. The latter three were foreigners employed by the government for the modernisation of Japan.

The Society vigorously translated and published books of German *Staatswissenschaft* and founded the Doitsugaku Kyokai Gakko (School of the Society for German Studies) (later Dokkyo University) in October 1883 as a rival to Fukuzawa's Keio Gijuku school and Okuma's Tokyo Senmon Gakko (Tokyo School of Special Studies) (est. 1882, from which the Waseda University developed). In October 1883 the Society published the first issue of the monthly journal, *Doitsugaku Kyokai Zasshi* (Bulletin of the Society for German Studies), which continued for 65 issues until February 1889.

The fundamental ideas of the Doitsugaku Kyokai seemed to be expressed in the speeches and articles of H. Roesler. Roesler endeavoured to demonstrate the superiority of German studies over British and French social sciences by stressing the significant writings that embodied political sciences in Germany.[4] In the 1885 spring general meeting of the Society,

Roesler argued that the characteristic of the British spirit lay in 'common sense', which meant nothing but 'common knowledge', and common knowledge was only partial and superficial knowledge devoid of any true insight into the profound and essential order of phenomena. German studies, by contrast, aimed to reach the inherent truth, and thereby remain immune from the influence of immediate and apparent aims and feelings to which common knowledge was susceptible. The purpose of the Society, Roesler contended, was to promote German studies in Japan and to save the Japanese people from being dazzled with ideas based on British superficial common knowledge (*Doitsugaku Kyokai Zasshi*, 21, 15th June 1885: 22–34).

As for political economy, Roesler maintained in a series of five articles entitled 'Keizai Enkakushi' (History of Political Economy) that Adam Smith's free-trade doctrine was full of contradictions and that his demand–supply theory primarily rested on self-interest, which was nothing but a merchant's viewpoint, and as such it was a false argument for explaining economic phenomena (*Doitsugaku Kyokai Zasshi*, 32, 15th May 1886: 48).

The criticism of Adam Smith and British economic thought, and the positive appraisal of the German Historical School by the Doitsugaku Kyokai were derived from a recognition of the historical peculiarities in the economic development of different countries. The particularity of each country was emphasised specifically by Paul Mayet. Primarily referring to F. List's *Das nationale System der politischen Ökonomie*, Mayet argued in a lecture entitled 'Keizairon' (On Economy) at the autumn general meeting of the Society in 1885 that just as German economists learnt that the principles of the Smithian school had no universal applicability, so the Japanese would realise from their own experience that British free-trade theory was limited. Free trade certainly brought about the prosperity of Britain, which received enormous benefits from the implementation of this policy. Germany, by contrast, adopted the protective policy of the Historical School and obtained a great many benefits from it. With these arguments, Mayet encouraged Japanese people to study the writings of Roscher, K.G.A. Knies, L. von Stein, B. Hildebrand, A. Wagner, G. Schmoller and L. Brentano (*Doitsugaku Kyokai Zasshi*, 25, 15th October 1885: 44–9).

As seen in these arguments, the Doitsugaku Kyokai certainly advocated that a protective trade policy be adopted in Japan as was the case in Germany and the United States in that period, and rejected the universal benefit of free trade, of which Britain was virtually the sole beneficiary. However, what we must bear in mind is that as the heart of the Society for German Studies lay in founding and propagating *Staatswissenschaft* for political aspirations, the advocacy of a protective trade policy did not occupy the nucleus of the activities of the Society.

3 The Society for Japanese Economy and the Society for National Economy

Apart from the activities of the Doitsugaku Kyokai that was fundamentally *Staatswissenschaft*-oriented, those who favoured the ideas of a national economy and protective trade policy organised the Nihon Keizaikai (Society for Japanese Economy) (est. 1885) and the Kokka Keizaikai (Society for National Economy) (est. 1890). Both Societies numbered about 120–30 members as of 1893 (Soyeda 1893: 335–7).

The Society for Japanese Economy was steered mainly by Tsuyoshi Inukai (later Prime Minister but assassinated by militant rightists), Yoshikazu Wakayama and Shiro Shiba. They were all strongly influenced by Henry Charles Carey, the American protectionist economist. Inukai translated an English version of Carey's *Principles of Social Science* in 1884–8 and used Carey's writings as his authority during a controversy with Taguchi over free trade and protectionism in 1880–1. Wakayama was one of the earliest proponents of protectionism in Japan and his work, *Hogo Zeisetsu* (On Protective Tariff) (1871), was said to be the first introduction of Carey to Japan. Shiba went to the United States to study in 1879, majoring in political economy at both Harvard and Pennsylvania, where he studied the works of Carey.

As these developments indicate, one might expect that the ideas of the Society for Japanese Economy would be very strongly influenced by H.C. Carey. However, it should be remarked that Tsunetaro Nakagawa, presumably the first proponent of the ideas of the German Historical School in Japan, was also a member of the Nihon Keizaikai. His work, *Keizai Jitsugaku Koza* (Lecture on Practical Political Economy) (2 vols, 1886–7), was written chiefly by using the writings of Roscher and aimed to 'remove a preconception of traditional British school of political economy and teach the kernel of practical economic studies' (Sugihara 1972: 19–20). So one could say that the Nihon Keizaikai comprised not only Carey's ideas but also the thought of the German Historical School, albeit to a lesser degree.

Inukai and other members of the Society criticised British political economy as cosmopolitan and emphasised the national peculiarities of each economy. The manifesto circulated upon the establishment of the Society asserted that a nation's economy ought to be determined by its unique history and statistics which reflected the situation and circumstances of the nation (Mishima 1998: 214).

This protectionist society, however, gradually dissolved into a mere salon for intellectuals and politicians. In consequence a new protectionist organisation was needed and the Kokka Keizaikai came into being. Leading promoters of the new Society were Tetsunosuke Tomita, then Vice-president of the Bank of Japan, and Sadamasu Oshima. Tomita in particular seemed to be the driving force in setting up this society. He had studied political economy in the United States, where he had an opportunity to meet H.C. Carey. However, being aware of the importance of List, at the end of 1889 he offered Oshima an opportunity to translate List's *Das nationale System der politischen Ökonomie* from the English translation and published it through the Society for Japanese Economy Press. Therefore F. List, together with Carey, and Roscher to a lesser extent, were the theoretical props of this society.

The manifesto of the Kokka Keizaikai expressed the basis of their protectionism as follows.

> Power derives from wealth. The problem of independence is ultimately attributed to the problem of wealth, and productivity is the sinew of national wealth. Therefore, it is of the utmost importance for the independence of Japan to strengthen the nation's productivity. Our national wealth will be ensured in the present world by changing the balance of foreign trade in our favour. Favourable balance of trade is a symbol of the nation's productivity. To increase our productivity in competition with advanced countries, we must adopt a protective policy. But regrettably we cannot pursue such a policy at present because of the existence of unequal treaties among western countries.
>
> (Mishima 1998: 146)[5]

In accordance with the manifesto, the Society was engaged not only in academic research but also in activities for the abolishment of the enforced low tariff of 5 per cent and the revision of the unequal treaties. From this viewpoint, the Society exerted a leading role in setting up the Society for Encouragement of Raw Cotton by holding a special meeting in December 1893. It also argued against the freedom of residence of foreigners among the Japanese. The record of the Society can be traced in its monthly bulletin, *Kokka Keizaikai Hokoku* (Bulletin of the Society for National Economy), first published in December 1890 and lasting until its 50th issue in September 1896 (Mishima 1998: 205–13).

4 The ascendancy of German studies: the establishment of the Society for State Sciences

Although the Doitsugaku Kyokai advocated a protective trade policy based on the German Historical School, its essential purpose, as remarked above, lay in the propagation of *Staatswissenschaft*. In this regard, it might be said that the direct succession of the ideas of the Society of German Studies was the Kokka Gakkai (Society for State Sciences). The Kokka Gakkai was set up as an academic society of the Department of Political Science of (Tokyo) Imperial University in 1887. With the establishment of this Society, the predominance of German studies in Japanese academia was established.

Tokyo University was founded in 1877 with four faculties: law, science, letters, and medicine. The teaching of political science and political economy was included in the faculty of letters. But when Tokyo University was renamed in 1886 as Imperial University (further renamed as Tokyo Imperial University in 1897 when Kyoto Imperial University was founded), political science and political economy were transferred to the faculty of law.

This change in the educational system and the enrichment of the law school reflected the policy of Hirobumi Ito and Kowashi Inoue, who gave priority to *Staatswissenschaft*. The establishment of the Society for State Sciences came into being within this context. In matter of fact, it was designed in compliance with Ito's request. With a rough draft of the imperial constitution completed in 1887, Ito felt the need to teach people the principles and practice of the constitution. As he believed that the best way to achieve this purpose would be to form a Society devoted to this cause, he expressed these thoughts to Koki Watanabe, President of Imperial University. Watanabe approved of Ito's proposition and established the Kokka Gakkai in 1887 with the purpose of 'studying various subjects that belong to *Staatswissenschaft*, such as administration, public finance, diplomacy, political economy, political science, statistics and others' ('Honkai Enkaku no Gaiyo' [An Outline of the History of the Society], *Kokka Gakkai Zasshi*, 9, 100, June 1895: 383).

The Society published a number of books and a journal as well as holding lectures and meetings in order to achieve its purpose. Among these activities, the most important was the publication of the *Kokka Gakkai Zasshi* (Journal of the Society for State Sciences), which has continued to this day as the journal of the law faculty of Tokyo University.

The first meeting of the Society was held in March 1887 with the presence of over one hundred people, composed – amongst others – of governmental bureaucrats, graduates of Tokyo University, journalists and a number of academics. At the opening address, Watanabe delivered an oration entitled 'Honkai Kaisetsu no Shushi' (The Purpose of the Establishment of the Society) in which he stressed the urgent necessity for scholars to devote their energy to the study of *Staatswissenschaft* that would underpin 'the newly born state with a solid footing' (*Kokka Gakkai Zasshi*, 1, 1, March 1887: 5).

As the aims of the Society declared, political economy was classified as part of the study of *Staatswissenschaft*. In this respect the Society journal contained a fair number of essays related to political economy, and the leading writers for the journal represented the mainstream of studies on political economy until the early twentieth century, when the activities of the Japanese Association for the Study of Social Policy came into predominance.

As far as political economy was concerned, noticeable were Kenzo Wadagaki's articles in the Society journal. Wadagaki was one of the graduates of the Faculty of Letters of Tokyo University in its first stage and in 1884, immediately following his return from study in Germany and Britain, he succeeded Ernest Francisco Fenollosa in the chair of political economy. Fenollosa, a young graduate of Harvard, was the first teacher of political economy at Tokyo University. His lectures were mainly based on the writings of J.S. Mill, J.E. Cairnes, W.G. Sumner and F.A. Walker. He attached particular importance to Mill's *Principles of Political Economy* during his teaching period from 1878 to 1884. Wadagaki, in contrast to Fenollosa, taught first and foremost German economic thought, in accord with the government's intention. The tradition of Mill's political economy on which Fenollosa had laid emphasis was to some extent taken over by Tameyuki Amano (a former student of Fenollosa's) of the Tokyo School of Special Studies (Sugihara 1972: 10).[6]

In an article entitled 'Zaiseigaku Taii' (Outline of Public Finance) in the first issue of the Society journal, Wadagaki emphasised the necessity for a transition in public finance from the British liberal school to the German interventionist approach as represented by Stein, Wagner and others. Largely relying on the explanation of public finance by the Italian economist Luigi Cossa, and referring to the writings of Stein, Wagner, Roscher and Johann Caspar Bluntschli, Wadagaki traced the history of public finance and contended that the recent theory of German chair socialism was superior to Smith's doctrine. Whereas Smith confined the role of state to the safeguard of the rights of individuals, chair socialism laid stress on the state's role in the encouragement of business and the enactment of social legislation. Based on this view, Wadagaki insisted that government must fulfil its duties by means of public finance (*Kokka Gakkai Zasshi*, 1, 1, March 1887: 5–20).

In another article entitled 'Kodam Shakaito' (Chair Socialism), Wadagaki also brought in a full-scale review of the German social policy school with the intention of criticising both British non-interventionist thought and revolutionary socialism (*Kokka Gakkai Zasshi*, 2, 13, March 1888: 133–9).

As shown in these articles, one might say that Wadagaki almost ignored the historical methodology of the German Historical School (although he was a member of the Society for Japanese Economy) and practically identified the Historical School as the social policy school in which professorial socialism was highly esteemed. Public finance was regarded as part of *Staatswissenschaft* and the government was expected to administrate social legislation. Therefore, when Kanai, a former student and later colleague of Wadagaki, praised Wadagaki by saying that he 'almost alone advocated historical study of political economy by depending on the German school, and ushered in a drastic change in economic study against the trend many professors were inclined to adopt in order to explain the doctrine of British school', the German school in Kanai's terms virtually meant the social policy school (Yasaku 1914: Jogen [introduction]).

Kanai among others developed Wadagaki's idea and played a leading role in the formation and development of the Nihon Shakai Seisaku Gakkai (Japanese Association for the Study of Social Policy) (1896–1924), the first authentic academic society of economic studies in Japan.

5 The formation and development of the Japanese Association for the Study of Social Policy

Political economy was, as mentioned above, considered part of state sciences under the supremacy of *Staatswissenschaft*. But against the background of the advent of social problems that were brought about as a result of the rapid development of Japanese capitalism, the economic thought of the German social policy school was ranked the dominant political economy.

In April 1891 young and spirited students and progressive bureaucrats who learnt political economy and political science at Imperial University gathered to set up a society for the study of social policy. This was the origin of the Japanese Association for the Study of Social Policy, founded in the wake of the German Verein für Sozialpolitik. At first it had only a few members, but its supporters increased along with the growing seriousness of social and labour problems caused by the development of industrial revolution in Japan after the Sino-Japanese War. Eventually it came to include almost all economic thinkers in academic and bureaucratic positions.

In organising and developing the Association, the central figure was Noburu Kanai. He entered Tokyo University in 1881 and spent a period of study abroad from July 1886 to November 1890. He studied chiefly under Gustav Schmoller and Adolf Wagner, and on his way back to Japan he visited England and observed the slums in London. After returning to Japan, he was appointed Professor at Imperial University, where he played a path-breaking role in disseminating the ideas of the German social policy school through lectures and papers, although he was not regarded as an original thinker in the history of Japanese economic thought.

Kanai, Kumazo Kuwata, another leader of the Association, and other central members drew up the manifesto of the Association in 1899. It declared that the Association was founded to achieve social harmony between capital and labour by dint of social policy under the authority of the state, and criticised both *laissez-faire* and socialism as a means to solve social and labour problems (*Shakai Seisaku Gakkai Shiryo Shusei*, 1977–8, 1: 1–2).

The Association held its first annual meeting at the end of 1907 at Tokyo Imperial University for the presentation and discussion of papers devoted to the common theme of the Factory Law. A succession of labour disputes following the Russo-Japanese War was the reason why the Factory Law was dominant in the proceedings. Being open to the public, it attracted a large audience of as many as seven or eight hundred. The second day of the meeting was assigned to presentations of various free subjects, such as 'On the Nature of Labour in relation to Labourers and Capitalists', 'Power of Money and Power of Men', and 'Agriculture and Social Problems'. From the time of this very first annual meeting, the Association consistently retained this style of meeting, viz. the presentation and discussion of a common theme on the first day and an open forum on the second. The Association published the reports of its annual meetings under the designation *Shakai*

Seisaku Gakkai Ronso (Treatises of the Association for the Study of Social Policy) until its dissolution in 1924.

In his opening speech, Kanai, the first President of the Association, told the audience that he was against both *laissez-faire* and socialism and that the main aim of social policy was not only to protect the labourers, but also to achieve harmony in the country by the protection of labourers. For this purpose, argued Kanai, what was needed in the first place was for the Factory Law to be enacted.[7]

Kanai's thought came to represent the leading viewpoint of the Japanese social policy school and owing to his strenuous activity, the social policy school became dominant in Japanese political economy, with its headquarters at Tokyo Imperial University. But even at the first meeting of the Society, there appeared two views opposing the position of Kanai and his followers. One was the paternalistic opinion represented by Juichi Soeda on the right, and the other was the liberal and progressive approach embodied by Tokuzo Fukuda on the left, as it were.

Soeda studied at Cambridge for a time, and was subsequently Minister of Finance and then President of the Japan Industrial Bank. He maintained at the first meeting that the Japanese should take pride in their traditionally good relationship between capital and labour, i.e. the master–servant relationship inherited from feudalism. He stressed that favourable re-appraisal of the master–servant relationship would enable the factory legislation to function more easily and effectively.

This view was severely criticised by some members, from among whom the most acute rejoinder came from Fukuda, who had studied under Lujo Brentano and was a professor at Tokyo Higher Commercial School. Fukuda pointed out that the feudalistic but compassionate harmony in the master–servant relationship that Soeda evaluated as an appropriate means to solve the labour problem was really the very obstacle to the improvement of labourers' conditions. The problem of the Factory Law was neither that of the master–servant relationship nor of charity and benevolence, but one of economic rationality. In contrast to the goals of the Association, which declared itself against both *laissez-faire* and socialism, Fukuda was more inclined to favour *laissez-faire*, for it meant self-help. Thus Fukuda argued that the state, society and other organisations should refrain from intervention in people's social and economic affairs unless they had difficulty helping themselves. From this viewpoint Fukuda backed the need for the Factory Law (*Shakai Seisaku Gakkai Shiryo Shusei*, 1977, 1: 96–102).

The significance of Fukuda's thought was that it was directed towards the independence of political economy from *Staatswissenschaft* in the sense that the state was not positioned in the centre of social policy, but treated as a means to achieve the improvement of a society that ought to be structured upon self-help principles.

At around the time of the first meeting in 1907, the members of the Association numbered about 100. But with the first meeting, the Association was accepted as the one and only nationwide society of economic studies. At this time, some of the professors in the commercial schools of Tokyo, Kobe and Osaka were not satisfied with mere practical business education. They aimed to enhance the importance assigned to political economy within the academic curriculum and thereby wished to promote their school to the status of a commercial university.[8] Well-known private schools also wished to acquire the formal status of a university.[9] As a step towards achieving the aim of enriching their academic reputation, higher commercial schools and private universities sent their professors to foreign countries for study. Annual meetings of the Association offered those professors who were increasing in numbers and acquiring good academic backgrounds the opportunity to be recognised as fully fledged scholars. Against such a backdrop the number of members of the Association increased markedly; in 1919 it reached 231 and by November 1922 it had risen to 282. Membership was not solely confined to professors of universities; it included bureaucrats, businessmen and even social movement activists. Thus the Association developed into 'the forum of Japanese economists' and demonstrated 'the authoritativeness of economic studies in Japan' (Ouchi 1978: 226).

In its heyday, before the end of World War I, the Association assumed the task of orchestrating various scholars with diverse economic ideas. Economists, ideologically spanning a spectrum from pro-socialism at one extreme to neo-classical economics at the other, were encouraged and supported by the Association, and they were to render remarkable services to the development of economics in Japan. Fukuda, for example, a distinguished contributor to the introduction of the neo-classical school to Japan, became an outstanding tutor of non-Marxian economics. On the other hand, Hajime Kawakami (1879–1946, Kyoto Imperial University), one of the leading members of the Association as well as a distinguished Marxian economist, exerted a significant influence on Japanese economics. Thus economic studies in Japan undisputedly owed a great deal to the Nihon Shakai Seisaku Gakkai.

6 The disintegration of the Japanese Association for the Study of Social Policy

However, diversity of ideology inherent in the Association inevitably resulted in its eventual downfall in 1924. Particularly with the Russian revolution, the ideological cleavage within the Association deepened as pro-Marxist economists expanded their force in the Association and harshly criticised the traditional reformism of the Association, which espoused harmonious relationships between capital and labour.

A considerable number of members, appalled at the increasing ideological conflict, began to lose enthusiasm and interest in the Association. Presenters and attendants at the annual meetings gradually declined, although the number of members did not necessarily decrease, due to the fact that there was no other alternative nationwide economic association. In spite of the pressing common theme of 'labour union' of the thirteenth meeting in 1919, our research indicates there was only one presenter of the common theme, Shinzo Koizumi (Keio Gijuku University), and still worse, his paper was read by another because of his absence due to illness. In the case of Fukuda, he refused to allow the Association to print his presentation in its journal, a protest with the purpose of demonstrating that he stood aloof from the ideological strife in the Association (*Shakai Seisaku Gakkai Shiryo Shusei*, 1978, 13: 6). In such ways ideological differences undoubtedly led to an immediate breakdown of the Association, although the disastrous effect of the Kanto earthquake of 1924 may have had some influence.

The fundamental cause of dissolution of the Association seemed to lie in its character *per se*, that is, its overemphasis on policy recommendations and a disregard for theoretical research. Members became not only sickened by ideological strife but also bored and dissatisfied with mere policy proposals that were not necessarily based on economic theory. Thus the Association eventually lost its *raison d'être*. Following the disintegration of the Association, nationwide economic societies that specialised in their own particular fields started to appear.[10]

Notes

1 The Tokyo Political Economy Club had many branch associations in localities and held regular monthly meetings with speeches and discussions in Tokyo. It numbered over 130 as of 1893 (Matsunoo 1996: 106; Soyeda 1893: 335). It appointed committees for the investigation of economic problems and for policy proposals. Its first investigation and report in 1888 concerning the fall of the value of silver was noteworthy for it dealt with the monetary disturbance that launched not only Japan but most of the world into a heated debate on the *fin de siècle* depression.

2 The Society would in time develop into the Tokyo Political Economy Club.

3 The Tokyo Political Economy Lecture Society issued the following translations during 1882–3. Most ended in partial translation, yet Taguchi's publishing house later published complete translations of these works along with other British liberal and free trade economic writings. Walter Bagehot, *Lombard Street*; Leone Levi, *The History of British Commerce and of the Economic Progress of the British Nation*; Herbert Spencer, *Principles of Sociology*; James Gilbart, *Lectures on the History and Principles of Ancient Commerce*; Adam Smith, *The Wealth of Nations*; Henry D. Macleod, *The Theory and Practice of Banking*; John E. Cairnes, *The Character and Logical Method of Political Economy*; Kate McKean, *Manual of Social Science, being a Condensation of the 'Principles of Social Science' of H.C. Carey*.

   The translations of Jevon's *Money and Mechanism of Exchange*, Henry Fawcett's *Manual of Political Economy*, and F.A. Walker's *Science of Wealth* were planned, but not issued by the Society in spite of the announcement of publication (Matsunoo 1996: 86–7; Sugihara 1984: 279–80).

4 Significant writings on *Staatswissenschaft* and political economy referred to by Roesler were as follows: Rudolph Gneist, *Der Rechtsstaat*; J.C. Bluntschli, *Lehre vom modernen Staat*; J.C. Bluntschli, *Deutsche Staatslehre und die heutige Staatswelt*; Adam H. Müller, *Die Elemente der Staatskunst*; Friedrich List, *Das nationale System*

der politischen Ökonomie; Lorenz von Stein, *Lehrbuch der Volkswirtshaft*; H. Roesler, *Vorlesungen über Volkswirtschaft*; Adolf Wagner, *Finanzwissenschaft* (*Doitsugaku Kyokai Zasshi*, 6, 15th March 1884: 9).

5 Treaties of amity and trade between Japan and five Western countries (the USA, Great Britain, Russia, France and Holland) in 1868 were unequal treaties to Japan in terms of tariff autonomy and extraterritorial jurisdiction of foreigners. The extraterritorial jurisdiction of foreigners was abolished in 1899 and tariff autonomy was recovered in 1911.

6 The thought of British liberalism, including J.S. Mill, which was introduced quite passionately in the early Meiji period, retained its influence among scholars of private schools, critics, intellectuals, and journalists. We should bear in mind the existence of this undercurrent of pro-British liberalism in modern Japan. The Tokyo Political Economy Club of Taguchi may be cited as one of the major contributors to this aspect of thought in modern Japan, although Taguchi's idea of *laissez-faire* went too far beyond J.S. Mill's moderate liberalism.

7 The Factory Act was promulgated in 1911 and enforced in 1916. The Association for the Study of Social Policy undoubtedly made a great contribution to its enactment.

8 The Higher Commercial School was founded in 1887 and renamed Tokyo Higher Commercial School in 1902 when Kobe Higher Commercial School was established. The former was promoted to Tokyo University of Commerce in 1920. The Higher Commercial School of Kobe and Osaka was promoted to Kobe and Osaka University of Commerce respectively in the later 1920s.

9 For several years after the Specialised School Decree (Senmon Gakkorei) was promulgated in 1903, renowned specialised schools were then renamed as universities. But it was not until 1920 that well-known private universities, such as Keio, Waseda, Meiji, Hosei, Chuo, Nihon, Kokugakuin and Doshisha were legally approved as universities with the promulgation of the University Decree (Daigakurei) of 1918.

10 The following nationwide societies were founded in the 1920s and 1930s: Japanese Society for Agricultural Economics 1924; Japanese Society for Business Management 1926; Socio-Economic History Society 1930; Japanese Statistics Society 1931; Japanese Economic Society 1934. The reconstruction of the Association for the Study of Social Policy was carried out in 1950 when the Society for the History of Economic Thought was also founded (Ikeo 1999: 32).

Bibliography

Journals of the societies concerned

Doitsugaku Kyokai Zasshi (Bulletin of the Society for German Studies), no. 1, 15th October 1883 – no. 70, 15th July 1889.

Kokka Gakkai Zasshi (Journal of the Society for State Sciences), no.1, 15th March 1887 – still continues as the Journal of the Law Faculty of Tokyo University.

Kokka Keizaikai Hokoku (Bulletin of the Society for National Economy), no. 1, December 1890 – no. 50, September 1896.

Shakai Seisaku Gakkai Shiryo Shusei (Collection of Historical Materials of the Japanese Association for the Study of Social Policy), ed. Shakai Seisaku Gakkai Shiryo Shusei Hensan Iinkai Kanshu, 13 vols and one suppl. vol. 1977–8, Tokyo: Ochanomizu-shobo. Orig. *Shakai Seisaku Gakkai Ronso* (Treatises of the Association for the Study of Social Policy), 15 vols, 1908–22, Tokyo: Dobun-kan.

Tokyo Keizai Zasshi (Tokyo Economist), no. 1, 29th January 1879 – no. 2138, 1st September 1923; repr. 1981, Tokyo: Nihon Keizai Hyoron-sha.

Articles and books

Fujii, T. (1998) 'The Japanese Social Policy School: Its Formation and Breakup', in S. Sugihara and T. Tanaka (eds), *Economic Thought and Modernization in Japan*, Cheltenham and Northampton: Edward Elgar.

Garon, S. (1987) *The State and Labour in Modern Japan*, Berkeley: University of California Press.

Iida, K. (1984) 'Nihon Shakai Seisaku Gakkai to Keizaigaku Kenkyu' (The Japanese Association for the Study of Social Policy and Economic Studies), in Society for the History of Economic Thought, Japan, *Nihon no Keizaigaku* (The History of Economic Studies in Japan), Tokyo: Toyo Keizai Shinpo-sha.

Ikeo, I. (1999) 'Gakujutsu Kenkyu to Kokusaika' (Academic Researches and Internationalisation), in I. Ikeo (ed.) *Nihon no Keizaigaku to Keizaigakusha: Sengo no Kenkyu Kankyo to Seisaku Keisei* (Japanese Economists and Economics: Research Circumstances and Policy Formation in the Post-War Era), Tokyo: Nihon Keizai Hyoron-sha.

Ishida, T. (1984) *Nihon no Shakai Kagaku* (Social Sciences in Japan), Tokyo: Tokyo Daigaku Shuppan-kai.

Ishii, R. (1967) 'Kokka Gakkai no Seiritsu' (The Establishment of the Society for Study of State Sciences), *Kokka Gakkai Zasshi* 88, 9 and 10: 519–36.

Kawai, E. (ed.) (1939) *Kanai Noburu no Shogai to Gakuseki* (The Life and Academic Achievements of Kanai Noburu), Tokyo: Nihon Hyoron-sha.

Kumagai, J. (1998) 'Enlightenment and Economic Thought in Meiji Japan: Yukichi Fukuzawa and Ukichi Taguchi', in S. Sugihara and T. Tanaka (eds) *Economic Thought and Modernization in Japan*, Cheltenham and Northampton: Edward Elgar.

Matsunoo, H. (1996) *Taguchi Ukichi to Keizaigaku Kyokai* (A Study of Taguchi Ukichi's Economic Thought and the Political Economy Club), Tokyo: Nihon Keizai Hyoron-sha.

Mishima, N. (1998) 'Shiryo: Kokka Keizaikai, Nihon Keizaikai ni kansuru Kisoteki Kosatsu' (Materials: Basic Investigation regarding Society for National Economy and Society of Japanese Economy), in Keio Gijuku Fukuzawa Kenkyu Senta, *Kindai Nihon Kenkyu* (Modern Japan Study) 15: 131–229.

Morris-Suzuki, T. (1989) *A History of Japanese Economic Thought*, London: Routledge.

Okubo, T. (1957) 'Meiji 14 nen no Seihen' (Political Crisis of Meiji 14, viz. 1881), in *Meiji Seiken no Kakuritsu Katei* (The Process of Establishment of the Meiji Government), Tokyo: Ochanomizu-shobo.

Ouchi, H. (1978) 'Nihon Shakai Seisaku Gakkai no Unmei to Gendai Nihon Keizaigaku no Shimei' (The Destiny of Japanese Society for the Study of Social Policy and Mission of Current Japanese Economics), in *Shakai Seisaku Gakkai Shiryo Shusei*, suppl. vol.1, Tokyo: Ochanomizu-shobo. Orig. *Shakai Kagaku Koza* (Lectures on Social Sciences), 6 (1957), Tokyo: Kobundo.

Pyle, K.B. (1974) 'Advantages of Fellowship: German Economics and Japanese Bureaucrats, 1890–1925', *Journal of Japanese Studies* 1, 1: 127–64.

Society for the History of Economic Thought, Japan (1984) *Nihon no Keizaigaku* (The History of Economic Studies in Japan), Tokyo: Toyo Keizai Shinpo-sha.

Soyeda (Soeda), J. (1893) 'The Study of Political Economy in Japan', *Economic Journal* 3, June: 334–9.

Sugihara, S. (1972) *Seio Keizaigaku to Kindai Nihon* (Western Political Economy and Modern Japan), Tokyo: Mirai-sha.

—— (1984), 'Meiji iko Shusenji madeno Keizaigakushi Kenkyu' (Study of History of Economic Thought from Meiji to the End of the World War), in Society for the History of Economic Thought, Japan *Nihon no Keizaigaku* (The History of Economic Studies in Japan), Tokyo: Toyo Keizai Shinpo-sha.

Sugihara, S. and Okada, K. (eds) (1995) *Taguchi Ukichi to Tokyo Keizai Zasshi* (Ukichi Taguchi and the Tokyo Economist), Tokyo: Nihon Keizai Hyoron-sha.

Sugihara, S. and Tanaka, T. (eds) (1998) *Economic Thought and Modernization in Japan*, Cheltenham and Northampton: Edward Elgar.

Sugiyama, C. (1994) *Origins of Economic Thought in Modern Japan*, London and New York: Routledge.

Sugiyama, C. and Mizuta, H. (eds) (1988) *Enlightenment and Beyond: Political Economy Comes to Japan*, Tokyo: University of Tokyo Press.

Sumiya, E. (1958) *Nihon Keizai Gakushi* (A History of Japanese Economic Thought), Kyoto: Mineruva Shobo.

Taguchi, U. (1927–8) *Teiken Taguchi Ukichi Zenshu* (Complete Works of Ukichi Taguchi), 8 vols, Tokyo: Teiken Taguchi Ukichi Zenshu Kanko-kai; repr. 1990, Tokyo: Yoshikawa Kobun-kan.

Tokyo Daigaku Hyakunenshi Henshuu Iinkai (ed.) (1986) *Tokyo Daigaku Hyakunenshi: Bukyokushi 1* (History of Tokyo University: History of Departments, vol. 1), Tokyo: Tokyo Daigaku Shuppan-kai.

Yamamuro, S. (1984) *Hosei Kanryo no Jidai: Kokka no Sekkei to Chi no Rekitei* (The Age of Law Bureaucrats: Design of State and History of Intellectuals), Tokyo: Bokutaku-sha.

Yasaku, E. (ed.) (1914) *Wadagaki Kyoju Zaishoku 25nen Keizai Ronso* (Economic Essays Dedicated to Kenzo Wadagaki in Commemoration of the Twenty-fifth Anniversary as Professor in the Imperial University Tokyo by his Colleagues, Friends and Disciples), Tokyo: Yuhikaku.

12 Economists and professional organisations in pre-World War I America

William J. Barber

The formation of professional societies necessarily presupposes the existence of some sense of professional identity. In America, the emergence of a clear sense of an identity among economists involved considerable struggle and the outcome was by no means foreordained. In the light of properties of the American polity, this circumstance is perhaps not altogether surprising. The populist dimension of American democracy – never too far below the surface – harbours an innate suspicion about the claims of alleged 'experts' on matters of economic and social policies. The authority of expertise in the natural sciences, in most matters, is recognised (the recent attitudes of various state educational authorities with regard to the teaching of 'evolution' vs. 'creationism' are notable exceptions). The findings of social scientists enjoy at best a problematic status in the eyes of the general public. In this domain, there are always more laymen than experts and each has but one vote to cast. These considerations are essential to an understanding of the way economists (and social scientists more generally) have defined themselves at different moments in time and of the particulars of the organisations they have elected to construct.

1 Pre-professional stirrings: the American Social Science Association

In the United States, an organisation proclaiming the study of economic problems as part of its mission pre-dated the emergence of a body of economists with a defined identity. The creation of the American Social Science Association (ASSA) in 1865 was the case in point. This Boston-based organisation was inspired in the post-Civil War flush of enthusiasm for social reforms.[1] Its organisers charted an ambitious programme. As they set out the Association's overall purpose in the Constitution:

> Its objects are, to aid the development of Social Science, and to guide the public mind to the best practical means of promoting the Amendment of Laws, the Advancement of Education, the Prevention or Repression of Crime, the Reformation of Criminals, and the Progress of Public

Morality, the Adoption of Sanitary Regulations, and the diffusion of sound principles on questions of Economy, Trade, and Finance.[2]

It was presupposed here that the collection and dissemination of facts on social and economic conditions would be sufficient to mobilise the public behind remedies for perceived ills. In the vernacular of the time, investigation should be accompanied by agitation and then by action.

Following the lead of the British Association for the Promotion of Social Science (founded in 1857), the ASSA's founders subdivided the work into four 'departments': Public Health, Jurisprudence, Education, and Economy, Trade, and Finance. Within their ranks there were enough doctors, lawyers and college professors to staff the first three departments respectively. The work of the Department of Economy, Trade, and Finance – which was expected to cover a wide array of topics, including pauperism, the 'relation of employers and employed', hours of labour, the national debt, tariffs and taxation, the control of markets, the value of gold and 'all questions connected with the currency'[3] – presented something of a problem. The ASSA – and the country – lacked a cadre of trained personnel equipped to deal dispassionately with these issues (the first Ph.D. in political economy to be produced by an American institution had to wait another decade until 1875, when Harvard awarded a doctorate in this field). As an expedient, the organisers first called upon the President of Yale, Theodore Dwight Woolsey, to chair the Department of Economy, Trade, and Finance. A Congregational clergyman by training, he had lectured on political economy in the tradition of moral philosophy to Yale seniors (throughout much of the nineteenth century, such an arrangement had been a standard part of presidential duties in the denominationally-affiliated institutions of higher learning). In his ASSA role, Woolsey was shortly to be relieved by David A. Wells, the Commissioner of the Revenue in the Federal government. Wells was a figure of stature: his practical experience in government had led him to renounce his pre-Civil War support of protective tariffs and he had now become one of the nation's most outspoken advocates of free trade.[4] Meanwhile, the ASSA looked to the business community to supply the bulk of the members of its Department of Economy, Trade, and Finance.

In 1874, the ASSA's conception of its approach to economic matters underwent a sea change, foreshadowing a fissure in the character of American economic discourse that would come into high prominence in the next decade. The departmental structure was reorganised, with two departments emerging from what had been the Department of Economy, Trade, and Finance. David A. Wells stayed on as a leader in the new and free-standing Department of Finance. He was joined by two men with professorial titles: in view of the fact that academic appointments for specialists in political economy were then a rarity, this was noteworthy.[5] Both men were affiliated with Yale and both had arrived there via unconventional routes.

Educated to be a clergyman, William Graham Sumner had been called to Yale from his parish in New Jersey when a newly installed President of the University chose to break with precedent. Because the usual presidential lectures on political economy/moral philosophy were not to his taste, he recruited Sumner and deputised him to fill this curricular space (Sumner subsequently became an intensely conservative spokesman for Social Darwinism). The second member of the professoriate – Francis Amasa Walker – was affiliated with Yale's Scientific School and brought a wealth of practical experience to the classroom. A Civil War hero, Walker had reached general officer rank in the Army at the prodigiously young age of twenty-five; he had also served as the superintendent of the 1870 census.

The ASSA's newly created Department of Social Economy presented a quite different face toward the world. In the first decade of its existence, evidence of relevant expertise in its membership was lacking. Its chair – William B. Rogers, founding President of the Massachusetts Institute of Technology – brought a background in geology to this assignment. The rank and file membership included a number of women and several clergymen. Substantively, the Department took the 'plight of the poor' as its jurisdiction and it tended to approach its investigations with a reformer's zeal.

2 Early initiatives in mounting professional groupings among economists

By the mid-1880s, the number of Americans holding advanced degrees in political economy had expanded to a point approaching a critical mass susceptible to professional mobilisation. There was still a scarcity of home-grown PhDs in this subject matter, however. In the 1870s, three American institutions awarded a total of three doctorates in political economy; the decade of the 1880s saw the award of eleven such degrees by five institutions.[6] The major suppliers of advanced work in political economy to young Americans were the universities in Germany, to which they migrated in considerable numbers.

The 'Germanisation' of a significant body of recruits to political economy was to have formidable consequences. In the first instance, it sharpened a divide that was already latent among those engaged in serious work on economic issues. The 'Young Turks' with a German exposure tended to identify themselves as members of a 'new school'. As the more militant among them saw matters, the methods and the conclusions of an 'old school' that had looked to English political economy for inspiration should be denounced. Deductive reasoning in economics was held to be suspect: proper procedure called instead for direct empirical investigation of economic reality. Similarly, the notion that economic 'laws' could be identified – ones with universal validity throughout time and space – needed to be purged. No less important in the 'new school' programme was rejection of the 'old school's' veneration of *laissez-faire*. The message that instead should be conveyed was that state intervention could make a constructive contribution to economic improvement.

The mid-1880s witnessed escalation in the rhetorical warfare between members of these rival camps. This meant, in turn, that possession of an advanced degree in political economy was not itself an adequate badge of professional identification. One needed to inquire further into the particular 'school' to which an aspiring professional belonged. After all – in the bitterest moments of the *Methodenstreit* of the 1880s – members of the competing schools were not reluctant to brand rivals as charlatans and quacks. There was a further implication here: the ASSA could not become the vehicle for the professional mobilisation of economists. 'Old schoolers' such as Sumner were disenchanted with the 'do-goodism' aspect of the ASSA's activities. At the same time, 'new schoolers' – sympathetic though they might be with the reformist dimension of the ASSA's style (as exhibited, for example, in the posture of its Department of Social Economy) – were put off by the amateurism of this group.

Two organisational initiatives in this period merit comment. The first – known as the Political Economy Club – bore some resemblance to a society of the same name in London, then more than a half-century old. Its members – which included businessmen, journalists and academicians – gathered from time to time to dine and to discuss papers presented on current economic topics. In its beginnings (the inaugural meeting was held on 30th November 1883), there was a distinct 'old school' cast to the membership. A doctrinal slant was unmistakable in the selection of officers. The presidency was filled by Simon Newcomb, an astronomer-economist whose writings on economic topics displayed an enthusiasm for abstract model building.[7] J. Laurence Laughlin, then an instructor at Harvard, served as Secretary (Laughlin's conservative perspective was shortly to be in evidence in an edition of John Stuart Mill's *Principles* that he adapted for an American audience: the pro-market aspect of Mill's thinking was emphasised, whereas Mill's attention to the ameliorative potentialities of state intervention was suppressed). A number of members were veterans of the ASSA: among them, Sumner, Walker (by then President of the Massachusetts Institute of Technology) and Wells. An ideological purity test, however, was not a precondition for election. In 1884, three alumni of the German experience with 'new school' sympathies were elected – Richard T. Ely, Edmund J. James and Henry Carter Adams – but they appear to have taken little part in the proceedings. Despite this concession to diversity, the Political Economy Club remained a select group which lacked what was needed in an organisation that could represent the profession at large.[8]

A second initiative was launched in 1884 by Edmund J. James and Simon Patten of the University of Pennsylvania. Both were German-educated 'new schoolers' who sought to enlist support for a Society for the Study of National Economy that would replicate the German Verein für Sozialpolitik.

This enterprise, though obviously calculated to attract 'new schoolers', went nowhere. Two factors contributed to its failure. The degree of statism in the German model was more than most Americans were prepared to stomach.[9] In addition, the Pennsylvania roots of the proposers – which then were very much linked with high protectionist absolutism – compromised their ability to reach a national audience.[10]

3   The academic environment of the Johns Hopkins University as a catalyst

The organisational drive that ultimately succeeded in producing a professional association of economists was a by-product of some in-house turmoil at the Johns Hopkins University, an institution created in 1874 with a charge to compete with German universities (and all other comers) in the production of graduate students with doctoral degrees in the liberal arts and sciences. Two strong personalities with interests in political economy were on the scene there. Simon Newcomb, President of the Political Economy Club, occupied a professorial chair in mathematics; Richard T. Ely, with a doctorate from the University of Heidelberg, held the title of 'Associate' in Political Economy, an untenured position.[11]

In their approaches to political economy, the two men were at opposite poles. Ely, writing from the German Historical perspective, challenged *laissez-faire* and called for the scholar to be engaged actively in setting the world to rights. In his vision, economics should be purged of doctrines linked to natural laws that were beyond human manipulation and of conclusions arrived at by deductive procedures. Newcomb, on the other hand, drew inspiration from Britain's William Stanley Jevons and championed the value of mathematical procedures in economic inquiry. Though a staunch advocate of the benevolence of the invisible hand, Newcomb maintained that economics should aspire to become a positive science, free of contamination by normative judgements. The two men operated from different departmental bases at Johns Hopkins. Nevertheless, the terms of their coexistence within the same institution became a matter of contention in the mid-1880s.

Warfare broke out between them in 1884. Ely fired the opening salvo in an essay attacking the sterility of the methods of the 'English' school. He asserted that 'mathematico-economic works' represented 'a not very successful attempt to develop further the older abstract political economy' and that 'works which have advocated the application of mathematics to economics form no essential part of the development of economic literature' (Ely 1884: 60). Newcomb's ire was aroused and he asked Daniel Coit Gilman, President of Johns Hopkins, for 'an opportunity to say a few words about your department of political economy before the impulse which has been given me by Dr. Ely's pamphlet entirely dies out. It looks a little incongruous to see so sweeping and wholesale an attack upon the introduction of any rational or scientific method in economics come from a university whose other specialties have tended in the opposite direction'.[12] Newcomb went public with his indictment of Ely's position in November 1884, characterising Ely's work as an example of fundamental intellectual confusion and as an 'irrational' proceeding (Newcomb 1884).

For Ely, more was at stake in these exchanges than the outcome of a methodological battle. He feared for his survival as a member of the Johns Hopkins faculty. Newcomb had status within the university's power structure and was clearly the more distinguished in the eyes of the wider academic world. However, in his efforts to bolster his position on the local scene, Ely could draw on resources that Newcomb could not match. He had influence over an able and articulate group of graduate students who could defend his position – and they did so, depicting Newcomb as an amateur who lacked competence to comment on economic affairs.[13]

Ely's decision to launch the American Economic Association (AEA) in 1885 contained an element of opportunism. When Edmund J. James and Simon Patten of the University of Pennsylvania failed in their attempt to organise economists of the 'new school' in a Society for the Study of National Economy, Ely moved quickly. He was well aware of President Gilman's propensity to look favourably on members of the Johns Hopkins faculty who promoted the name of the young institution before the national scholarly community (Johns Hopkins, in fact, played a pioneering role in the founding of scholarly journals and societies in the 1870s and 1880s). Ely later wrote that the organisation of professional associations was the 'sort of thing [...] in the air at the Johns Hopkins and was encouraged by the authorities' (Ely 1938: 135). For his part, he took pains to keep 'the authorities' apprised of his activity. Writing to Gilman in July 1885, he observed that proposals had been 'submitted to a large number of the younger economists of the country and favorable replies have been received in every case with no exceptions'. Ely foresaw the makings of 'an influential movement' and one which he trusted would 'benefit the Johns Hopkins University'.[14] This bit of academic entrepreneurship did him no harm in his bid for reappointment at Johns Hopkins.

Although Newcomb was isolated from the newly formed national organisation of economists, he was still not silenced. The two men re-aired their differences publicly in 1886 in *Science* (the journal of the American Association for the Advancement of Science).[15] Both then re-stated familiar positions. Ely maintained that concern with what ought to be was inherent in the work of the political economist; that economists should seek to understand the 'laws of Progress' and to show how they could be directed to promote the economic and social growth of mankind; and that the ethical ideal was 'simply the Christian doctrine of talents committed to men, all to be improved' (Ely 1886: 531). Newcomb, on the other hand, maintained that it was a 'contradiction in terms' to regard discussion of what ought to be as 'science'; that the principle of 'non-interference' in economic affairs also favoured progress, but sought its achievement by giving individuals the widest possible latitude for choice; and that public intervention was suspect because governments were incapable of acting on 'sound business principles' (Newcomb 1886a). In an unsigned review of Ely's book, *The Labor Movement in America* (1886), Newcomb was even more outspoken in his denunciation of Ely's work, saying it displayed a 'lack of logical acumen' and an 'intensity of bias'. Newcomb concluded with the following comment: 'Dr. Ely seems to us to be seriously out of place in a university chair' (Newcomb 1886b: 294). Newcomb also informed Gilman privately of his negative appraisal of Ely's competence, advising him that 'very little attention [was] paid to the analytic process' in Ely's teaching at Johns Hopkins.[16] After observing the performance of Ely's graduate students (whom he had been asked to examine in May 1886), Newcomb reported that 'the main teaching seems to have been directed toward the administrative and economic policies of the leading countries of the world, especially Germany'. In Newcomb's judgement, 'the candidates showed an almost deplorable want of training in the power of logical analysis of the economic theories that move men and determine the course of our industry at the present time. [...] [T]hey were amply able to grapple with the subject, had it only been presented to them, but that was quite new to their minds'.[17]

On the local scene, Ely nevertheless won the skirmish of the mid-1880s and was appointed to an associate professorship for a three-year term in 1887. He was not successful, however, in his push for appointment to a permanent professorship five years later. Ely felt slighted by Gilman's refusal to advance his status and left for the University of Wisconsin.[18]

No doubt some type of national organisation of economists would have emerged in late nineteenth-century America. But both the timing and the early shape of the AEA owed something to the ethos of Johns Hopkins in the mid-1880s and to the tensions between Newcomb and Ely over the correct approach to economic inquiry. Ely's initiative in organisation building served a public interest, but it also served a private one.

4 The establishment of the AEA

Ely, as an organisational activist, moved into high gear in the late spring and summer of 1885. And he made no attempt to disguise that his intention was to mobilise a force to counter the influence of 'the Sumner–Newcomb crowd'.[19] He invited the like-minded to join him in September at Saratoga, New York. The date and place were selected to coincide with the annual meetings of the ASSA and the American Historical Association, founded a year earlier by Herbert Baxter Adams, an Ely colleague at Johns Hopkins.

In preparation for this gathering, Ely circulated a statement of the proposed Association's objectives and a draft platform. These documents deserve detailed inspection. The 'Objects of This Association' were set out as follows:

I   The encouragement of economic research.

II   The publication of economic monographs.

III The encouragement of perfect freedom in all economic discussion.

IV   The establishment of a bureau of information designed to aid all members with friendly counsels in their economic studies.

(Ely 1887: 6)

Ely's draft platform was noteworthy for its inclusion of language some might hold to be incompatible with the scholarly objectivity expected in a learned society. Ely distributed it, however, without noting a potential conflict between the objective of 'encourag[ing] perfect freedom in all economic discussion' and the 'party line' projected in his Platform. It read as follows:

Platform.

1   We regard the state as an educational and ethical agency whose positive aid is an indispensable condition of human progress. While we recognise the necessity of individual initiative in industrial life, we hold that the doctrine of *laissez-faire* is unsafe in politics and unsound in morals; and that it suggests an inadequate explanation of the relations between the state and the citizens.

2   We do not accept the final statements which characterised the political economy of a past generation; for we believe that political economy is still in the first stages of its scientific development, and we look not so much to speculation as to an impartial study of actual conditions of economic life for the satisfactory accomplishment of that development. We seek the aid of statistics in the present, and of history in the past.

3   We hold that the conflict of labor and capital has brought to the front a vast number of social problems whose solution is impossible without the united efforts of Church, state and science.

4   In the study of the policy of government, especially with respect to restrictions on trade and to protection of domestic manufactures, we take no partisan attitude. We are convinced that one of the chief reasons why greater harmony has not been attained, is because economists have been too ready to assert themselves as advocates. We believe in a progressive development of economic conditions which must be met by corresponding changes of policy.

(Ely 1887: 6–7)

These documents sparked a lively discussion among the fifty or so persons assembled at Saratoga to chart a course for an American Economic Association. Ely opened the debate by elaborating on the purposes he had in mind. With regard to the 'Objects' of the Association, he added that 'one aim [...] should be the education of public opinion in regard to economic questions and economic literature'. This was essential because 'in no other science is there so much quackery and it must be our province to expose it and bring it into merited contempt' (Ely 1887: 15).[20] In addition, he felt called upon to address the question 'Why have any platform at all?'. His answer was twofold. In the first instance, it was 'not easy to arouse interest in an association which professes nothing'. A second consideration was no less important. He regarded it as imperative to alert the public to 'the fundamental differences between economists'. 'It [was] essential', he maintained, 'that intelligent men and women should distinguish between us and certain economists in whom there is little faith' (Ely 1887: 18–19).

At a number of points, the language approved by those assembled in the charter meetings departed from what Ely had submitted. The term 'Platform' disappeared and was replaced by a 'Statement of Principles' and the general tone was amended to be less provocative. Reference to the 'immorality' of *laissez-faire* was deleted, although a commitment that the state had a positive role to play remained. Proposition II in the Ely draft of a Platform was revised to acknowledge value in the work of earlier economists, while still contending that future progress in the discipline would come from the 'historical and statistical study of actual problems', rather than from 'speculation'. The importance of the church to the solution of social problems was reaffirmed (in view of the fact that some twenty clergymen – most of whom were active in the Social Gospel movement – participated in the decision making, this outcome was not surprising) (Furner 1975: 75). Those present at the creation did insist on an escape clause as an addendum to the Statement of Principles. This took the form of a 'note' observing that this Statement provided 'a general indication of the views and purposes of those who founded the AEA, but is not to be regarded as binding upon individual members'.[21]

Selection of officers further signalled the direction of the AEA in its early years. Though not present at the Saratoga meeting, Francis Amasa Walker – who had indicated his willingness to accept – was designated as President. This augured well for the fledgling organisation's survival prospects. Walker was widely revered as a man of accomplishment and judgement. All of the other officers – Ely as Secretary (and Chief Operating Officer); Edwin R.A. Seligman (Columbia) as Treasurer; Henry Carter Adams (University of Michigan and Cornell) as First Vice-president; Edmund J. James (University of Pennsylvania) as Second Vice-president; and John Bates Clark (Smith College) as Third Vice-president– had been inoculated by the German experience and might easily have been written off as rebellious youth by their disciplinary rivals. Walker, a generation older, brought a dignity and *gravitas*; he was genuinely interested in being a party to a regular forum in which new ideas could be explored. He was also ready to distance himself from Sumner, with whom he had had more than one altercation when they overlapped as members of the Yale faculty in the 1870s.

A further feature of the AEA's initial structure calls for comment. The by-laws stipulated that seven standing committees should be organised dealing, respectively, with Labour, Transportation, Trade, Public Finance, Exchange, General Questions of Economic Theory, and Statistics. There were overtones here of the 'departments' into which the ASSA had been divided. Although the standing committees were duly formed, they did not – as might have been anticipated – produce team reports to enlighten the public.[22] The AEA instead supported a series of monographs written by individual authors.

When the dust settled on the AEA's first year of operations, the organisation could list the enrolment of 182 members. Academic economists accounted for only a very minor fraction of the membership (although they supplied all of the officers). The lists included some twenty-three clergymen (past and present), a substantial cadre from the business community and/or the world of economic journalism and six women. Andrew Carnegie had subscribed to a life membership. A future President of the United States – Woodrow Wilson, then on the faculty of Bryn Mawr College – was among the charter members. No doubt Wilson's experience as a graduate student with Ely at Johns Hopkins had something to do with this connection.[23] Ely must, however, have been disappointed with the response from the ASSA whose members had certainly been specifically courted: only thirteen of them had elected to join (Furner 1975: 75).

5 Teething troubles in the AEA's infancy

Ely did not come away from the inaugural meeting with everything he had hoped for, but he could still draw satisfaction from a respectable showing. Issues regarding the Platform – now softened as a 'Statement of Principles' – continued to be bothersome. As President of the organisation, Francis Amasa Walker took exception to the language on the grounds that it effectively excluded some conservative economists – importantly, those based at Harvard and Yale – from membership. In correspondence in April 1887, he expressed strong feelings on this matter, noting that the Platform was 'the real stumbling block'. 'It should never have been adopted', he wrote; 'it should be repealed at our next meeting. [...] If my stepping down from the presidency would promote harmony and extend the usefulness of the Association, I shall cheerfully yield to any one who may be named – even Sumner'.[24] At the third annual meeting, held in Philadelphia in December 1888, Article III of the Constitution – i.e., the 'Statement of Principles' – was deleted. In his presidential address, Walker hailed this action, proclaiming that the mistakes at Saratoga – when 'certain declarations and statements which were not needful, and proved embarrassing' were endorsed

– had been corrected. The Association could now embrace nearly all 'active economic workers' (Walker 1889). This olive branch brought Charles F. Dunbar, Harvard's senior economist, and Arthur T. Hadley, a younger member of Yale's faculty, into the ranks.[25]

This was not to be the last setback for Ely's agenda. At the fourth annual meeting in Washington in December 1890, his wings were clipped again. The AEA, on the recommendation of its executive committee, voted to create a committee on publications with powers to determine which manuscripts should receive the AEA's imprimatur. To that point, Ely had regarded this function as his prerogative as AEA's Secretary. Negative reaction to the manner in which Ely had discharged that part of official business could be backed with some substance. Under his management, there had been a decided tilt toward monographs written by acolytes at Johns Hopkins and by sympathetic 'new schoolers' based elsewhere. He had also provided a substantial platform for Sidney Webb, who contributed a seventy-three-page monograph on 'Socialism in England'.

For Ely, worse was to come. In the late summer of 1892, he was manoeuvred into resigning as Secretary of the organisation he had been instrumental in creating. Momentum for change had been building for a while. Ely's unilateral decision to hold the annual meeting of 1892 at Chautauqua, New York (a Methodist summer camp where he supplemented his income as a lecturer) tipped the balance. Change in the AEA's management structure soon followed. In Ely's final report as Secretary of the AEA, one can detect a tinge of bitterness. The action to strip the Secretary of control of publications, he indicated, had been in error because the publications committee was inclined to approve projects without regard to budgetary constraints. That was something that a secretary with a general overview should contain and he recommended that 'unity of administration' be restored. But he conceded that, henceforth, the site of the annual meeting should be decided after extensive consultation and announced a year in advance (Ely 1893).

Ely stood down from this post unhappily. He did so with achievements that deserved to be recognised. When he left the secretaryship, the AEA's numbers had grown to 732 members (Ely 1893: 127). He also took pride in having something to do with inspiring economists in Britain, Australia and Japan to organise themselves along the lines of the AEA model (Ely 1891).

6 Changing of the guard in 1892

In 1892, Harvard's Charles F. Dunbar assumed the presidency of the AEA and Edward A. Ross – then of Cornell and an Ely protégé since graduate student days at Johns Hopkins – became Secretary.[26] Throughout the land, the shift in the AEA's management was understood as marking a significant reorientation. Henry W. Farnam of Yale – who attended his first AEA meeting at Chautauqua in 1892 – probably reflected the sentiments of many. Writing to Sumner about this experience, he observed: 'This is the first time that Yale has been represented at one of these meetings by one of its professors and I think that it created a good impression to have one of them there'. Farnam added that he had been made a vice-president of the organisation. 'In view of these changes', he inquired, 'do you not think that you would like to join? I know that there is a strong desire to have you and that you would find yourself quite in sympathy with the present spirit of the society'.[27] Sumner declined this and all subsequent invitations. By 1894, even Simon Newcomb had joined the Association. J. Laurence Laughlin – who had become Head Professor of Economics at the University of Chicago when it opened in 1892 – was (apart from Sumner) the only prominent 'old-schooler' to remain a non-member.

By the early 1890s, there were ample reasons why economists on both sides of the barricades in the struggles of the preceding decade should decide that it was opportune to mute their differences.[28] Further bloodletting – at least in public – would be unseemly and counterproductive. Economists of all persuasions were then eager to claim standing as 'professionals', not least because they wished to solidify a secure position for the discipline in the expanding university system.

The success of some colourful amateurs in capturing the popular imagination added urgency to this regrouping. To the aspiring professionals, it was humiliating when the untutored could arouse the public. Two examples are worthy of attention. Henry George, a journalist with only an elementary education, was particularly effective in mobilising opinion. His *Progress and Poverty*, first issued in 1879, became a best seller. George had been inspired to write it by his experience in California where he observed overnight fortunes created from the appreciation of land values as its territory was being rapidly settled. The 'monopoly power' conveyed by the private ownership of land, he concluded, was the root of all evil: unearned rents distorted the income distribution and land speculation idled productive resources. The remedy he proposed was a 'single tax' through which the state would appropriate these ill-gotten gains. Less significant, but still embarrassing, was the work of William Harvey, a lawyer, sometime silver miner and ultimately a publisher in Chicago. His *Coin's Financial School*, published at the time of the highly charged national debate over bimetallism in the 1890s, insisted that permanent prosperity would be assured through free coinage of silver at a silver–gold ratio of 16 to 1. Harvey added liveliness to his argument by depicting an imaginary debate involving a small child who confounded a learned economist named Laughlin with the cogency of his case for a crude quantity theory of money (the real-life Professor Laughlin was not amused!) Altogether, it behooved the professionals to bury their differences and to present a joint front against amateurism and quackery.

In the climate of the 1890s, a closing of ranks had a further recommendation. By this time, economists with advanced degrees had become a substantial presence in American higher education. Expansion in the number of academic jobs was not necessarily accompanied by an enlargement of employment security among job-holders. There was no lack of potentially explosive issues – among them, the legitimacy (or otherwise) of labour unions in a world which had experienced some violent strikes; the populist calls for the relief of farm distress through elevated prices for agricultural commodities (the backdrop for much of the campaign for 'free silver'); the merits (or otherwise) of public ownership and/or regulation of public utilities and railroads. Academic economists were frequently pressed to take positions on these matters. It became increasingly clear, however, that it could be hazardous should their positions offend important donors (in the case of private colleges and universities) or politically strategic trustees and regents (in the case of state universities). The decade of the 1890s witnessed a number of high-profile cases in which academic appointments were placed in jeopardy and – more often than not – were lost. Ely (who had moved to the University of Wisconsin in 1892) managed to survive his 'trial'. Edward W. Bemis (at the University of Chicago), E. Benjamin Andrews (at Brown) and Edward A. Ross (earlier at Cornell, but then at Stanford) were less fortunate.[29] Such cases helped to spur a sense of professional consciousness in which economists of quite divergent persuasions rallied to support fellows targeted for victimisation.

Although the AEA had put the divisive battles between the 'schools' behind it, two friction points within the organisation remained. One turned on a regional issue – in particular, the resentment of mid-western members towards what they took to be the dominance of the eastern seaboard in the AEA's management. The Association's officers pondered seriously the prospect of dealing with a secession when an organisation styled as the Political Science Association of the Central States was formed. This threat evaporated in 1895, however, when Henry Carter Adams of Michigan was elected to the AEA's presidency and Indianapolis, Indiana, was chosen as the host city for the annual meeting.[30] More problematic were the hard feelings generated by the rivalry between ambitious Ph.D.-granting institutions. A number of them established in-house journals and came to regard them as central to their institutional identity. Thus, Harvard launched the *Quarterly Journal of Economics* in 1886. In the same year, Columbia created the *Political Science Quarterly* which, its title notwithstanding, had considerable economic content. In 1889, the *Annals of the American Academy of Political and Social Science* – a project affiliated with the University of Pennsylvania – began to make its regular quarterly appearance. The University of Chicago began publishing the *Journal of Political Economy* in 1892, the year that the University opened. Simultaneously, Yale began producing *The Yale Review*, a quarterly devoted to economic, political and historical topics. These journals were in direct competition with the AEA's search for quality materials for its own publishing programme. But this was only a part of the problem. For a considerable time the journal-publishing universities, acting on their perceived self-interest, effectively blocked the creation of a quarterly journal sponsored by the AEA: *The American Economic Review* did not come into existence until the organisation was more than a quarter-century old.

7 Professionalisation as understood at the AEA's 25th birthday party

When the AEA gathered to celebrate its landmark 25th birthday, Ely spoke of the mellowing that had transpired over the preceding quarter-century. The doctrinaire enthusiasms of the German-inspired 'Young Turks' who were present at the christening had long since passed. He emphasised the constructive work of the organisation in promoting economic understanding for the public good. The standing committee structure in the architecture of the original constitution, he acknowledged, had not been as productive as had been hoped. However, various AEA special committees had rendered outstanding service to the nation (Ely 1910). Two were noted for particular commendation: the special committee with responsibility to recommend on the design of the decennial Federal censuses and the Special Committee that reported in 1900 on colonial finance.[31]

It was appropriate to celebrate professionalism on this anniversary. But it should be pointed out that the prevailing conception of professionalism had undergone a subtle, but profound, metamorphosis during the AEA's lifetime. In the first instance, the hallmark of the professional was identified with a posture towards a specific body of doctrine and towards a particular method of studying economics. As the AEA matured, professional behaviour was instead associated with a readiness to entertain competing arguments and with a willingness to evaluate them on their merits. It was altogether fitting that Chicago's J. Laurence Laughlin – who had stood aloof from the organisation until 1904 – should speak with regard to that point at the anniversary celebration. As Laughlin then remarked: 'The narrow and special tenets contained in [the AEA's] initial constitution inevitably gave way to a more liberal charter; and this widening of its point of view in economics, is of that character out of which only true progress in intellectual development is possible. It is not out of agreements, but out of differences that we receive the greatest gain [...] ' (Laughlin 1910: 100).

Notes

1 In correspondence with officers of the ASSA (who had invited him to be their guest in the United States), John Stuart Mill commented as follows on this phenomenon: 'What you say about the new start which the mind of America has been led to make by her long and arduous struggle, is exactly what I foresaw from almost the very beginning. I wrote in January, 1862, and often said in the years following, that if the war lasted long enough, it would very likely regenerate the American people, and I have been seeing more and more clearly since it closed, that to a considerable extent it has really done so, and in particular, that reason and right feeling on any public subject has a better chance of being favorably listened to, and of finding the national mind open to comprehend it, than at any previous time in American history' (Mill 1874: 138).

2 As quoted in Haskell 1977: 161.
3 See Haskell 1977: 105.
4 Wells was to acquire a considerable international reputation. His various honours included election by the French Academy to the seat vacated by the death of John Stuart Mill.
5 Harvard was the first American university to venture into this terrain with the appointment of Charles F. Dunbar to a chair in political economy that he occupied in 1871. Dunbar appears not to have participated in the ASSA's activities.
6 See Parrish 1967: 1–16. In the 1890s, twelve institutions awarded 95 doctorates.
7 Newcomb's textbook – to be published in 1885 – developed a version of the quantity theory of money, including proposals for stabilising the general price level, that anticipated Irving Fisher's approach to the equation of exchange.
8 This account relies heavily on A.W. Coats, 'The Political Economy Club: A Neglected Episode in American Economic Thought', in Coats 1993. Though most members were ardent free-traders, membership was also offered to two protectionists from the Philadelphia area.
9 A number of features of the James–Patten proposals for a Constitution of the Society for the Study of the National Economy were not well calculated to win broad-based support in the United States: among them, the assertion that 'the state is a positive factor in material production and has legitimate claims to a share of the product'; and 'the true method of obtaining purity and economy in our administration is through the assumption of its proper functions by the state, since the consequent importance and dignity of government service would force public attention, attract the best class of citizens to the consideration of public affairs, and necessitate the greatest economy in administration'. The full text of this document is reproduced as Appendix III in Ely's autobiography. See Ely 1938: 296–99.
10 On these points, see Coats, 'The American Economic Association, 1885–1904', in Coats 1993.
11 This section draws heavily on Barber 1987.
12 Simon Newcomb to President Gilman, May 14th 1884, Gilman Collection, Special Collections, Milton S. Eisenhower Library, Johns Hopkins University.
13 One of them characterised Newcomb's approach to political economy as that of an 'astronomer who *has* seen the stars, and nothing else, all his life'. (Shaw 1885).
14 Ely to Gilman, July 11th 1885, Gilman Collection.
15 It should be noted that the American Association for the Advancement of Science – following the lead of its British counterpart – created a section on Economic Science and Statistics which became operational in 1882. Thus, it was not aberrational that the methodological debates of the mid-1880s should appear in the Association's journal. Subsequently, however, the work of this section attracted little attention from economists. The section did provide an outlet, however, for scientists who wished to express themselves on economic matters.
16 Newcomb to Gilman, May 28th 1886, Gilman Collection.
17 Newcomb to Gilman, May 14th 1886, Gilman Collection.
18 When Ely informed Gilman that he had an offer in hand to go elsewhere, and requested advancement in his position at Johns Hopkins, Gilman advised him to make his decision about another position 'on its merits' (Gilman to Ely, January 4th 1892, Gilman Collection).
19 Ely to Albert Shaw, May 7th 1885, as quoted in Hawkins 1960: 81.
20 Statement of Dr Richard T. Ely.

21 Statement of Principles, in Furner 1975: 36.
22 In the first decade or so, reports on the proceedings of the AEA's annual meetings acknowledged the continuing existence of standing committees. Frequently these took the form of a statement by the chairman to the effect that difficulty in arranging meetings of committee members had precluded preparation of a report. See *Publications of the American Economic Association, 1887–1895, passim.*
23 'List of Members of the American Economic Association', *Publications of the American Economic Association, 1887–1895*: 43–6.
24 Walker to Edwin R.A. Seligman, April 25th 1887, as quoted in Furner 1975: 116.
25 Both Dunbar and Hadley were to become presidents of the AEA.
26 When commenting on these events when the AEA celebrated its fiftieth anniversary, Ely insisted that the change in command should not be construed as a 'swing to the right'. As he then put it: 'While we did elect as our second President, Professor Dunbar of Harvard and while he was a progressive of the old school, but still of the Old School, not fully understanding, we felt, the significance of the American Economic Association, we elected him without opposition and with my hearty endorsement. His election signified neither a swing to the left nor to the right, but catholicity. I nominated my successor, Professor E.A. Ross' (Ely 1936: 141–50).
27 Henry W. Farnam to Sumner, September 5th 1892, Sumner Papers, Yale University Manuscripts and Archives.
28 The paragraphs immediately following draw on Barber 1994.
29 For details on these cases, see Barber 1993.
30 For the details on the infighting surrounding this episode, see Furner 1975, especially ch. 11.
31 The special committee on Colonial Finance, chaired by Jeremiah Jenks, characterised the stimulus behind this project as follows: 'It seemed wise to the committee to secure information regarding the fiscal methods and economic conditions of typical modern colonies and to endeavor, on the basis of that information, to suggest tentatively some general principles which might be applicable to the government of the new dependencies of the United States' (Jenks *et al.* 1900).

References

Barber, W.J. (1987) 'Should the American Economic Association Have Toasted Simon Newcomb at Its 100th Birthday Party?', *Journal of Economic Perspectives* 1: 179–83.
—— (ed.) (1993) *Economists and Higher Learning in the Nineteenth Century*, New Brunswick, NJ: Transaction Publishers.
—— (1994) 'The Position of the United States in the International Market Place for Economic Ideas, 1776–1900', in M. Albertone and A. Masoero (eds) *Political Economy and National Realities*, Torino: Fondazione L. Einaudi.
Coats, A.W. (1993) *The Sociology and Professionalization of Economics*, London: Routledge.
Ely, R.T. (1884) 'The Past and Present of Political Economy', *Johns Hopkins University Studies in Historical and Political Science* 2: 5–64.
—— (1886) 'Ethics and Economics', *Science* 7, 175: 529–33.
—— (1887) 'Report of the Organization of the American Economic Association', *Publications of the American Economic Association* 1: 5–20.

—— (1891) 'Secretary's Report on the Progress of the American Economic Association', *Publications of the American Economic Association* 6: 177–81.

—— (1893) 'Report of the Secretary', *Publications of the American Economic Association* 8: 127–9.

—— (1905) *The Labor Movement in America*, New York and London: Macmillan; originally published, 1886.

—— (1910) 'Remarks at the Anniversary Meeting', *Publications of the American Economic Association*, 3rd series, 11: 47–93.

—— (1936) 'The Founding and Early History of the American Economic Association', *American Economic Review/Supplement* 26: 141–50.

—— (1938) *Ground Under Our Feet: An Autobiography*, New York: Macmillan.

Furner, M.O. (1975) *Advocacy and Objectivity: A Crisis in the Professionalization of American Social Science*, Lexington: University Press of Kentucky.

Haskell, Th.L. (1977) *The Emergence of Professional Social Science: The American Social Science Association and the Nineteenth Century Crisis of Authority*, Urbana: University of Illinois Press.

Hawkins, H. (1960) *Pioneer: A History of the Johns Hopkins University, 1874–1889*, Ithaca, NY: Cornell University Press.

Jenks, J., Hamlin, C.S., Seligman, E.R.A. and Shaw, A. (1900) 'Essays in Colonial Finance by Members of the American Economic Association', *Publications of the American Economic Association*, 3rd series, I.

Laughlin, J.L. (1910) 'Remarks at the Anniversary Meeting', *Publications of the American Economic Association*, 3rd series, 11: 99–104.

Mill, J.S. (1874) 'Letter' (dated 1870), *The Journal of Social Science* 5: 138.

Newcomb, S. (1884) 'The Two Schools of Political Economy', *The Princeton Review* 14: 291–301.

—— (1886a) 'Aspects of the Economic Discussion', *Science* 7, 176: 538–42.

—— (1886b) 'Dr. Ely on the Labor Movement', *The Nation* 43: 293–4.

Parrish, J.B. (1967) 'Rise of Economics as an Academic Discipline: The Formative Years to 1900', *Southern Economic Journal* 34: 1–16.

Shaw, A. (1885) 'Recent Economics Works', *The Dial* 6: 210–13.

Walker, F.A. (1889) 'Recent Progress of Political Economy in the United States', *Publications of the American Economic Association* 4: 246–68.

Index

Printed in the United States
by Baker & Taylor Publisher Services